D1555353

IN SERVICE
OF THE
REPUBLIC

IN SERVICE OF THE REPUBLIC

THE ART AND SCIENCE OF ECONOMIC POLICY

VIJAY KELKAR

AND

AJAY SHAH

PENGUIN
ALLEN
LANE

An imprint of Penguin Random House

ALLEN LANE

USA | Canada | UK | Ireland | Australia
New Zealand | India | South Africa | China

Allen Lane is part of the Penguin Random House group of companies
whose addresses can be found at global.penguinrandomhouse.com

Published by Penguin Random House India Pvt. Ltd
7th Floor, Infinity Tower C, DLF Cyber City,
Gurgaon 122 002, Haryana, India

Penguin
Random House
India

First published in Allen Lane by Penguin Random House India 2019

Copyright © Vijay Kelkar and Ajay Shah 2019

All rights reserved

10 9 8 7 6 5 4 3 2 1

The views and opinions expressed in this book are the authors' own and the
facts are as reported by them which have been verified to the extent possible,
and the publishers are not in any way liable for the same.

ISBN 9780670093328

Typeset in Bembo Std by Manipal Technologies Limited, Manipal
Printed at Thomson Press India Ltd, New Delhi

www.penguin.co.in

To our parents,
who set us out on this path.

Contents

Preface

India has come into middle income, with a $3 trillion economy. We had a great surge of growth from 1991 to 2011, drawing on a new intellectual framework of policy that was built from 1977 onwards. For the first time in India's history, there was a substantial decline in the number and the share of those in poverty.

The period after 2011 has seen a retreat from the optimism of 1991–2011. This is a cause for great concern. We have a finite window of opportunity with a young workforce. We must get rich before we get old.

We need to change course and obtain the sustained economic growth through which we will utilize our workforce, which will get us to the edges of the advanced economies in thirty years. We must do this in order to transform the lives of hundreds of millions of people, to meet our tryst with destiny. We must do this to stave off the social stress that will come from a large mass of people who are not working. For these reasons, the great question of the age is: *Why did the reforms introduced from 1977 onwards deliver success during 1991–2011, but falter thereafter?*

What is to be done? In this book, we try to tell a story about why we underperformed, and how to get back on the growth turnpike. Intensification of the 1977–2011 strategies will not suffice: what is required is rethinking the foundations. While we have got to a $3 trillion economy, we are lagging on creating the institutional frameworks of an ambitious middle-income emerging economy.

Economic policy operates at the intersection of economics and politics. The ideal policy pathways must be worked out on blackboards, but then the conflicts of democratic politics are played out and determine the policy choices in the real world. Hence, our analysis draws as much on the timeless themes of building the republic as it does on public economics. In India, the modernization of the political system and the economy is taking place at the same time—and feeding into each other. In this process, economic policy strategy must serve the larger objective of building the republic. The foundations of liberal democracy—the principles of debate, dispersion of power, the rule of law and curtailing executive discretion—are integral to solving the difficulties of economic policy that afflict India today.

There is science in a core of economics and politics. These are the areas where the analytical foundations and empirical evidence are strong. And then, beyond that, there is a large class of questions where we have opinions and insights, but the scientific foundations are lacking. This is where the policy thinkers and practitioners have to form judgements in each situation that may diverge from each other, and feel their way into the world through intuition and experience. This is the art of public policy. We take on the left-brain and the right-brain aspects.

We care about the ideas and we care about translating them into action. Some parts of the book are more analytical and conceptual, while others are more practical and directly link to action.

When the rubber hits the road, there are tangible policy questions in each area, such as oil exploration or inflation targeting. There are many fascinating areas of work in progress, all across the Indian landscape, where there is the 'slow boring of hard boards' of policy reform. While we draw on examples from many domains, this is not a handbook of policy papers. We offer general insights that are valuable across diverse fields.

We live in an age of social media. The degradation of norms of discourse and the lowering of technical bars in the policy discourse have harmed the ability of liberal democracies to find politically stable compromises. Our attempt in this book is to help recover common ground, to find a shared intellectual framework and vocabulary that a lot of us may be able to agree upon. Towards this objective, we have stuck to what we hope is the relatively non-controversial terrain. This has involved downplaying issues of ethical preferences and income redistribution.

Put together, we are sixty years in this field, and have been talking about the grand questions for the last twenty years. The genesis of this book lies in Shekhar Shah's invitation to Vijay Kelkar to deliver the C.D. Deshmukh memorial lecture, at the National Council for Applied Economic Research (NCAER), on 27 January 2017. The enthusiastic feedback from that lecture led to the idea that an extended version of this would be an interesting book. We hope it will be thought-provoking and trigger many exciting conversations.

Part I

Foundations

1

The purpose of government

Everyone has felt the irritation of having multiple different chargers for different devices. There is a chaos of chargers with USB-B, USB-C, Apple lightning, etc., interfaces, all of which are incompatible with each other. This is operationally inconvenient as sharing of chargers is not feasible. It also leads to a greater extent of electronic waste in the form of unused chargers.

An exasperated person may say, 'Can't we have a government that standardizes this?' Could a government add value by coercing all electronics companies to make only one kind of charger? At first blush, this may seem like an appealing idea. This is the sort of thing a muscular Indian government might come up with—a law that forces all technology companies to only sell consumer products in India that use (say) the USB-C charger.

While this might be plausible at first blush, when we go deeper into the problem, there are all kinds of difficulties.

If we had to have a government choose the one charger to rule them all, how would this be done? Who would choose? How would we be sure that these persons would think for the best interests of society, and command vast intellectual capacity?

How do we know that the right decision will be made, despite intense lobbying by all technology companies? What if there are certain devices made in Taiwan, which are extremely capable and cost effective, but use a prohibited charger? Will we ban Indian consumers from using them?

Suppose the USB-C charger is made a standard via government imposition. What if there are small devices, such as wristwatches, where the USB-C charger is too bulky?

How will charger standardization be enforced? Who will watch for violations? Will we have customs officials to watch goods shipments to prevent equipment from coming in, which uses any of the forbidden chargers? Will we have the police raid factories looking for violators who produce equipment with the wrong charger? What about individuals who travel abroad and are carrying their own personal equipment, which they promise will not be used in India? What penalties will we impose in all these cases? Will a black market develop for chargers that violate the rule? Will we enforce laws to prevent such developments?

Or is all this too difficult, and we turn to taxation and subsidies? Perhaps we can tax equipment which has the wrong charger and subsidize equipment that has the right charger. That will have its own complex consequences. And, we have to ask, will the gains exceed the (large) welfare cost associated with the use of public funds?

Standardizing chargers for electronic devices is not a particularly important problem! It is a tiny, inconsequential problem. But in this small illustration, we see how government intervention, even in such small problems, rapidly turns into a mess.

What objectives should the state pursue?

As we have seen with a simple problem like USB chargers, it is not easy to choose the problems where we want intervention by the state. The first question in the field of public policy is: *What objectives of public policy are appropriate?* Should the government own or operate an airline? Courts? Restaurants? Watchmaking factories? Parks? Should a government gift money to poor people? Feed poor people? Run hospitals? Outpatient clinics? Factories that make medicines? Factories that make medical instruments? Trucks? Tanks? Standardize chargers?

The state is the most powerful actor in society. The state has the capacity to coerce, the capacity to inflict violence upon private persons. Many people get giddy at the prospect of wielding state power, and come up with woolly ideas for state intervention. Each of us has a few pet peeves, and we are quick to propose the use of state power to pursue our own value judgements.

In India, we have a government that runs temples, restaurants, airlines and banks. Our government until recently enforced criminal sanctions against gay sex, has criminal sanctions against marijuana and plans to criminalize the use of crypto-currencies like bitcoin.[1]

We may think it is obvious that the government should not run restaurants, but the Tamil Nadu government runs Amma kitchens, and seems to do this rather well. We may think it is obvious that the government should not run a factory that makes wristwatches, but the public sector company, Hindustan Machine Tools (HMT), long had a monopoly making wristwatches in India.

There is a vast array of objectives that a state can potentially pursue through government action. But there is a big gap between dilettantism in public policy and the professional capability of actually making it work. We need the intellectual capacity to envision how a plausible-sounding intervention will actually work out. The first milestone in this journey is asking: Should the government be doing this? Can we go beyond gut feeling, to an analytical toolkit through which we can think about the appropriate objectives of government?

Freedom works well

To understand what the state should do, we should first appreciate what free men and women do all by themselves. Most of the great achievements of mankind can be traced to the creativity and drive of free persons.

The normal rhythm of the market process is one where firms compete to obtain greater profit. Firms energetically look for actions that will yield higher profit. This drives a ceaseless process of improving the product and reducing the cost of production. This is done by understanding the consumer better and through technological change.

Firms are given no guarantee of profit or survival. The market system demands ceaseless innovation. Every now and then, some firms that fail to cater to the needs of customers go out of business. And, when the profit rates of incumbents become attractive, new firms are created to compete in this business.

Therefore, firms must endlessly run on a treadmill, trying harder to please consumers with better and cheaper products. The productivity gains of a firm (through greater capital investment or through better technology) generate higher wages for workers as their contribution to output goes up.

All these good things happen out of the mere self-interest of firms and consumers. This free-market process induces prosperity, creativity, innovation and individual freedom. No central planning or control is required, to get to an endless process of economic growth and prosperity.

Societies where the freedom of individuals is prized are those that harness the energy of their people. The most prosperous countries of the world are liberal democracies. Every now and then, there is envy of the growth rates that an authoritarian regime in China has been able to produce, but few would want to live there. *Immigration is the sincerest form of flattery*, and this is where liberal democracies stand out.

We in India are very used to state domination of society. It comes as a surprise to recall remarkable achievements in history that are mostly born of individual initiative.

We tend to assume that the exploration of (say) Antarctica is the work of some government agency. But it was a private person—Vasco da Gama—who found the first sea route from Europe to India. A private person—J.R.D. Tata—first purchased planes and set up an airline in India. These achievements were not planned and run by the Portuguese or British governments; they took place at the initiative of *private* persons.

Similarly, in India, we tend to think that space exploration is the work of Indian Space Research Organisation (ISRO) which is a government organization. But the frontiers of space exploration today are increasingly going back from government organizations like NASA or ISRO into private hands, with firms such as Blue Origin or SpaceX. The reuse of rockets yields an 80 per cent cost saving, and this frontier is being pushed by private space exploration firms.

Engineers can often visualize simple designs, and are too quick to thrust their schemes upon society. As we have seen with USB chargers, there is a big gap between engineering and public policy. A recurring theme of this book is an appreciation of 'self-organizing systems', of the uncoordinated decisions of individuals left to themselves, that discover order by themselves. The organic development of the economic system, with freedom in the hands of each individual, works better than instructions from the top.

Even in the history of engineering, we see the weakness of state-led projects. There was once a rivalry between two standards in computer networking. A global club of governments developed and pushed a standard called X.25. An inchoate collection of academics and hobbyists developed an alternative standard called TCP/IP. The self-organizing system won, despite being backed by no state. The organic evolution of TCP/IP gave us the Internet, and X.25 died out.[2]

At the heart of the state is coercion

> *A state is a human community that (successfully) claims the monopoly*
> *of the legitimate use of physical force within a given territory.*

Max Weber, The Vocation Lectures, 1919

While the state is often seen as benign or benevolent, almost like an uncle or a parent, we have to remember that at the heart of the state, there is violence. The state acquires a monopoly upon violence. States establish conditions where nobody is permitted to engage in violence, but the state is able to inflict violence. States use the threat of violence in order to obtain obedience on taxation and behaviour.

> *The individual has a soul but the state is a soulless machine. The state*
> *can never be weaned away from violence to which it owes its existence.*

Mahatma Gandhi

All state activities fall into two categories. In the first case, the state can use force to modify behaviour. A law can be enacted, that forbids a certain activity (e.g., killing, defamation or sedition) and threatens violators with punishment ranging from monetary penalties to imprisonment to death. In the second case, the state obtains tax revenues and spends this money in certain ways. But obtaining tax revenues is itself done through the threat of violence. The state demands that residents must pay certain taxes, and threatens us with monetary penalties or even prison time if these demands are not complied with.

The big idea of liberal democracy is to limit state violence into a controlled, predictable and just form. In an ideal democracy, we consent to an ethical regime of coercion. When the checks and balances surrounding the state are imperfect, state violence can be applied in unjust ways.

Every state action come at the cost of coercing private persons. These restrictions limit individual freedom, which reduces human welfare in and of itself. When we impose a tax of Re 1 upon a person, we take away that person's freedom to spend that Re 1.

Addressing market failure is the legitimate ground for coercion

> *The important thing for government is not to do things which individuals are doing already, and to do them a little better or a little worse; but to do those things which at present are not done at all.*

> John Maynard Keynes

The role for the state is born of a class of problems where freedom does not work so well, where the free market yields poor outcomes. This is the zone of 'market failures', where free men and women, all by themselves, obtain results that disappoint. Where the free market fails to deliver efficient economic outcomes, this is termed 'market failure'. Market failures come in four kinds: Externalities, Asymmetric information, Market power and Public goods.

Externalities are the situations where persons impact upon each other in ways that are not intermediated through voluntary agreements between these persons, where people impact upon each other in ways that were not negotiated. Consider a factory that emits pollution upon residents without their consent. This pollution is an example of a 'negative externality'. We can think of an alternative arrangement, where the factory and the residents of the neighbourhood negotiate an agreement, and the residents are paid a fee in return for the privilege of polluting the air. If this were done, the pollution would be intermediated through a market transaction that is voluntarily entered into by all parties, and there is no externality.

Pollution comes in many kinds, from the burning of crop residues in fields, to loudspeakers, to electric lights, to sneezing. All these can induce negative externalities upon other persons without their consent.

There are also *positive* externalities. A university that triggers off a hotbed of entrepreneurship in its neighbourhood is inducing a 'positive externality'. It imposes beneficial impacts upon nearby households, without their consent. Research and development expenses, that produce new knowledge, impose positive externalities upon society at large. Similarly, a forest that protects biodiversity and captures carbon induces a positive externality.

Whether positive or negative, externalities involve gains or harms that are imposed upon bystanders, which do not directly feed back upon decision makers through the normal market process. When externalities are present, in general, freedom does not give the best outcomes. The free market tends to overproduce things which induce negative externalities and underproduce things that induce positive externalities. When externalities are present, there may be a role for the state to step in, exercise its monopoly of coercive power, and induce better outcomes.

As an example, the criminal justice system exists in order to prevent the externality imposed by one person who inflicts personal harm upon another person. The state runs the criminal justice system, through which the externality of crime is blocked. We empower individuals through state action, when the criminal justice system generates deterrence. When the fear of crime is removed, individuals are free to pursue life, liberty and happiness.

Asymmetric information is found in situations like a customer buying medicines at a shop. The customer has no way of knowing if the medicines are adulterated. This fear changes the behaviour of customers and (ultimately) producers.

A high degree of asymmetric information can create conditions under which voluntary or market-based transactions become infeasible. As an example, these situations are seen with credit or insurance markets, where the market can even cease to exist owing to the inability of private persons to solve the problem of asymmetric information. These missing markets fall under the problem of market failure associated with asymmetric information.

Market power is found when a few firms achieve a dominant position in a market. Monopolies tend to reduce the output and raise the price. Left to itself, the free market system delivers poor outcomes in the areas where one side of the market wields disproportionate power. For example, the Italian firm Luxottica controls 80 per cent of the global market for eyeglasses.[3] This gives them the ability to earn supernormal profits.

Finally, *public goods* such as clean air are underproduced by the free market. In technical jargon, public goods are things that are 'non-rival' and 'non-excludable'. Clean air is 'non-rival', as my breathing clean air does not diminish the amount of clean air available to you. Clean air is 'non-excludable', as it is not possible to exclude a newborn child from breathing in clean air.

An important example of a public good is safety. When the armed forces make us safe from war, this safety is non-rival and non-excludable. The same issue arises with safety within the country, which is produced by the justice system.

By definition, public goods are non-excludable. No private firm would produce public goods such as clean air as residents cannot be billed for the services rendered. It is not possible to exclude any person from the benefits. Excludability is essential for firms to obtain a revenue stream. Hence, we require state action to obtain tax revenues and provide the public good.

The term 'private good' is the opposite of 'public good'. It does not denote 'things that are privately produced'. For example, telecom services are a private good, whether produced by a government or by a private person.

The free market does not, on its own, solve these four kinds of problems. The interventions by the state should be primarily located around these four problems.

This classification sheds new light upon many things that we do in economic policy. As an example, healthcare is commonly seen as being the work of the government. But healthcare is a private good. The services of a doctor or a hospital are rival and excludable. When I am on a hospital bed, you cannot at the same time be on that hospital bed. We need to be more careful in understanding the market failures in the field of health, and designing optimal policy pathways for what the government should be doing in the field of health.

Market failures are readily visible in the microeconomic arena, e.g., when my loudspeakers interfere with your peace. But they are the ultimate justification for macroeconomic policy also. Large business cycle fluctuations are a reflection of the failure of the uncoordinated decisions of private persons.

When faced with a proposed state intervention, our first question should be: What is the market failure that this seeks to address? When market failure is *not* present, we should be sceptical about state intervention. This is a valuable way of drawing the line between central planning and legitimate intervention in the economy. As an example, from 1993 onward, in the US, federal officials were required to formally demonstrate the presence of market failure before planning interventions in the economy.

Redistribution as the subsidiary ground for coercion

Inevitably, all states engage in redistribution: in raising tax revenues and giving resources to some people at some times.

All states engage in disaster relief. After a natural disaster, the state expends resources in rescuing people and in post-disaster reconstruction. This is redistribution, as tax resources are being used to give resources to some people placed in certain states of nature.

All states also transfer resources to the poorest persons of the country. This reflects a mixture of altruism and self-interest. Helping poor people is a moral imperative, and in addition, everyone is better off when the poorest are protected from the extremities of poverty and hopelessness.

There is one important calculation in redistribution to address poverty. There are about 0.1 billion poor people in India, so when a government gives them Rs 100/day, this comes at a cost of Rs 3.65 trillion per year.

As with all government activities, there is a state capacity challenge in translating such objectives (disaster relief or a subsidy programme) into action. There is quite a management challenge in identifying the 0.1 billion poorest people, and accurately delivering Rs 100 to them every day.

Summing up

The first question in the field of public policy is: What should the state do? A great deal of good policy reform can be obtained by putting an end to certain government activities, and by initiating new areas of work that better fit into the tasks of government.

The state has a monopoly of violence. All activities of the state are grounded in coercion: either directly (when the state demands that private persons behave in certain ways) or indirectly (when the state uses threats of violence to collect tax revenues, and then spends them in certain ways). Coercion of private persons is the unique thing that only the state can do. Coercion is an unpleasant thing and can easily go wrong. Building the republic is about creating ethical control systems that contain and channel state violence for the common good.

The founding intuition of the field of public policy is the notion that freedom works pretty well. Left to themselves, free men and women achieve reasonably good outcomes in most situations.

Freedom works well most of the time, but there are exceptions: the four kinds of 'market failure'. These are: Externalities, public goods, market power and asymmetric information. On its own, the free market often fares poorly at dealing with these situations. This is where the state can add value in society, by addressing market failure.

All states do some amount of redistribution. For example, relief work done by the government after a natural disaster is a case of transferring the money obtained in coercive ways (through taxation) from the populace to the affected people.

2

The limited toolkit of intervention

The word 'policy' is often used loosely in India. The Indian government landscape is littered with documents such as a 'National Map Policy'. These documents are written by officials in the executive branch. They lack legislative backing. In a constitutional democracy, only the legislature can authorize the coercion of private persons, through laws. What can government do? There is a limited menu of interventions which can be utilized in order to address a market failure.

Coercion that modifies behaviour

The state has the monopoly over violence in society. This can be utilized to enact a rule that bans a certain behaviour, backed with the threat of penalties for non-compliance. For example, a law approved by the legislature can define a speed limit for cars, and a punishment that will be meted out to wrongdoers, by persons in the executive branch.

When civil servants give oral threats to private persons, or informally tell private people the behaviour that is required of them, this is a violation of the rule of law.

Coercion to pay taxes

Coercion can be used to force people to pay taxes, thus creating a resource base for expenditure.

The objective of modified behaviour and the objective of raising taxes can be interlinked. The state can tax a certain behaviour in order to deter it, e.g., taxing cigarettes. Subsidies can also be delivered to taxpayers in this fashion, e.g., through a favourable tax treatment of purchases of infrastructure bonds. In both cases, these adaptations of tax policy also require authorization in law. In both cases, the design of the tax system is used to modify incentives, and thus behaviour.

Using budgetary resources to produce public services

The state can use its budgetary resources in order to directly run production of certain services within a government organization, e.g., monetary policy or the police.

Expenditure programmes require the authorization of the legislature through the Finance Act.

Using budgetary resources to give out subsidies

The state can subsidize certain activities, e.g., if you install rooftop solar equipment, the state can pay part of your capital expenditure. Similarly, education vouchers leave the school choice decision to parents, and state financing flows to the school chosen by parents.

Research and higher education produce externalities, which justifies public resourcing, but this resourcing is generally devoted to high externality areas (e.g., research in all areas, or fields such as philosophy or mathematics) and not the areas with low externalities (professions such as doctors, engineers, lawyers, accountants where education is just a private good).

Subsidies can be unconnected to externalities; they can be pure redistribution.

All these kinds of expenditures require the authorization of the legislature in the form of the Finance Act.

In many fields, we see three pillars of intervention: production (e.g., government running schools), regulating (e.g., government regulating private schools) and financing (e.g., government paying kids to attend private schools). These flow from the limited toolkit of intervention.

Summing up

The state can demand certain behaviour, and threaten violence against private persons who refuse to comply.

The state can demand tax payments from the populace, backed by threats of violence against people who do not comply. The tax rates can vary based on the situation. Private persons overproduce things that impose negative externalities (such as pollution) and underproduce things that impose positive externalities; modifications to tax rates can help improve the outcome.

The state can choose to spend tax revenues in two ways. It can run state organizations such as the police, which produce certain public goods. Or, it can transfer money to private persons. These transfers can be linked to market failure (e.g., using education vouchers to address the externalities in education) or they can be pure redistribution.

The world of public policy is about these three levers: rules about behaviour, taxation, and spending money. These are generally grounded in laws that define the behaviour of government. Taxation and expenditure programmes are spelled out in the Finance Act, which constitutes the budget of each year. The Indian government often produces 'policy' documents which do not mean too much.

3

A long history of failure

During the Cultural Revolution in China, there was a cult of personality surrounding Chairman Mao. In public, everyone claimed that Chairman Mao was their great leader, who had their best interests at heart, and had the right answers to all policy questions. Chairman Mao extolled practical knowledge and denigrated intellectualism.

One day, Chairman Mao organized millions of people to kill all the sparrows in China, on the grounds that sparrows eat grain.

Suppose we are willing to ignore the ethical problems associated with killing sparrows, and suppose we are willing to agree that this is a good objective as it would increase the amount of grain available to humans. Even then, the intervention failed.

With the sparrows removed from the scene, the insect population surged, and the insects ate the grain. Chairman Mao may have had good intentions, and he may have had practical experience of sparrows eating grain, but the intellectual foundation of the intervention was faulty.

The problems of state intervention

The murder of sparrows in China may appear to be an extreme example. It is not an exception. Across a large number of situations, state intervention works poorly.

Safety of the people is the most important function of the state. But after 9 p.m., over half of New Delhi feels it is unsafe to go to an ATM, and 90 per cent believes that it is unsafe for an unaccompanied woman to be outside the house. Only 13 per cent of Mumbai believes that an unaccompanied woman is safe outside the house at any time of the day, and for New Delhi this drops to 2 per cent.[1]

In India, teacher absenteeism is at 23.6 per cent[2] and the absence rate for medical personnel is 40 per cent.[3] Immunization rates are at about 60 per cent.[4]

The expenditure per student in government schools rose from Rs 2455 in 2010 to Rs 4385 in 2016. Learning outcomes *declined* in this period. In 2010, 50.7 per cent of children in class 5 in government schools could read a class 2 level text, but this declined to 42.2 per cent in 2014. Parents voted with their feet, and switched from free government schools to private schools charging a fee. Enrolment in government schools fell by 11.1 million while it rose by 16 million in private schools, from 2010 to 2016.[5]

At the end of many decades of very large expenditures in health and education in India, we are holding dismal outcomes. This shows the difficulties of state intervention.

'Public economics' is the idealized world of economic analysis, where market failure is identified. This leads to policy analysis, about how state interventions can be undertaken in order to address market failure. These are implemented through organizations, and their design and management lies in the field of 'public administration'. In an ideal world, we would detect market failure using public economics, and then do public administration in order to intervene in society so as to address the market failure.

In the real world, many interventions are ill-advised: they are not motivated by the desire to address market failure. And many interventions fail. The state is supposed to be a machine that converts coercive power into human welfare. But human societies fare poorly in controlling and channelling the monopoly of violence into welfare and justice.

The law of unintended consequences

There is black humour in the phrase 'the law of unintended consequences'. A government intervention that is intended to have a certain outcome will very often end up yielding a very different result. Such failures happen so often that these have been elevated to the level of a humorous 'law'. It requires extreme clarity of thought to devise policy initiatives that hit the target; all too often the actual outcomes stray far from what was desired.

A coercive agent is poorly placed at solving failures of negotiation

Why does the state fare poorly at addressing market failure? Ordinarily, freedom works well, and we have negotiations and voluntary choice by individuals all across society. The essence of market failure is the channels of influence between two persons which are not governed by negotiations and choice:

- *Market power:* One party in the negotiation has little power and experiences a loss of choice.
- *Asymmetric information:* The process of negotiation works poorly as there is a lack of information.

- *Externalities:* There are channels of influence between two parties that are not negotiated.
- *Public goods:* The individual is not given the opportunity to negotiate and choose.

Market failure is rooted in weaknesses of negotiations and choice. We think we are bringing in the state to address market failure. But the state is a coercive agent, and is ill placed at addressing a lack of negotiation.

The impossibility of paternalistic policy

Paternalism is the idea that an altruistic government understands the desires of its populace and seeks to do good for them. The assumption is that a paternalistic government is like a parent. It knows what a person desires, works in her best interest, and does nice things for the person.

But the only power of a government is a coercive power. A government can force people to do certain things, and a government can force people to pay taxes. State paternalism can then only be in favour of some and not all. A government that makes person 1 happy by forcing person 2 to gift her Rs 1000 is a government that makes person 2 unhappy.

We need to change course, from viewing government as a benign paternalistic agent that means well, to a more sceptical view of government. We need the state in order to address market failure, and we must give the state the monopoly of violence; but we have to be sceptical about the things that will be done by the state.

Summing up

There is a long history of failure in the field of public policy. Over and over in history, we see governments that try to do things and fail. There is a 'law of unintended consequences', where an initiative often ends up inducing an outcome that is different from what was intended, and indeed was completely unanticipated.

The state is a coercive agent. At the heart of market failure is a failure of coordination, of a lack of negotiation. There is a tension at the core, where problems of coordination are not easily solved through the tool of coercion.

Some people might like to have a paternalistic government. Coercive power gives the state the ability to take from one and give to another, and this will make some people happy at the expense of others. Paternalism by the government is an impossibility.

Part II

Diagnosing the
Indian experience

4

Anatomy of our policy failure

Looking back

India obtained freedom in 1947 with great expectations of rapidly rising to the ranks of a prosperous liberal democracy. This did not work out. A few rare countries that were poor in 1945 have graduated to prosperity and the freedoms of a mature liberal democracy, but most did not, and we in India fall in that group.

Our founding fathers had the best of intentions, and initiated numerous policy programmes. However, good intentions do not suffice, and we have poor outcomes in a large number of areas, such as the criminal justice system, the judiciary, the tax system, and financial regulation. Social change has been quite limited; we continue to be hobbled by superstition and prejudice. As an example, women's participation in the labour force in India is much like it is in Pakistan.

In 1991, we thought we were at the dawn of a new age of freedom. The following years have been disappointing. The Indian state is too often characterized by intrusion into freedoms, with a proclivity for coercion, powers to raid and investigate and harsh punishments. A great deal of central planning at the Planning

Commission and departments of government has subsided, but the controls have found their way into the behaviour of the newly created independent regulators. The regulators look much like the erstwhile departments of government, with a philosophy of control backed by arbitrary power. Private 'under implementation' investment projects in 2019 are 20 per cent smaller than the level seen in 2011 in *nominal* terms. The optimism of 1991–2011 seems like a distant memory.

The Indian state is overwhelmed with the problems that it faces. Day-to-day crisis management tends to dominate, and there is little effort or ability to engage in the long, slow journeys that are required to genuinely solve problems. As the financial economist Harsh Vardhan says, *we work through panic, package and neglect.* The Indian state works poorly, experiences panic when faced with a crisis, comes out with an announcement of a policy package that seeks to address the crisis in a short-term way, and retreats back into neglect. Smooth, capable working on an everyday basis has not come about.

There is a conventional classification scheme, where government failure is decomposed into two parts. First, there is the political economy problem, and governments are hijacked by special interest groups to aim for the wrong objectives. And then, there is the state capacity problem, where government fails to achieve the objective that it seeks to solve. This organizing structure is inaccurate insofar as, in the first stage, it thinks that government is itself pristine, and is only nudged off course by external forces. Instead, we find it useful to analyse policy failure in four ways.

- *Situations where freedom works well:* In most cases, doing nothing is a good answer. There is no market failure, and there is no need for the state to intervene. An example of this is Securities and Exchange Board of India (SEBI) rules that force exchanges to only work in the Indian daytime. There is no market failure when exchanges stay open for business at any time of the day or night, and there is thus no case for SEBI to coerce exchanges on their trading hours.

- *There is a market failure, but the politics goes wrong:* In some situations, market failure is present, but the search for the right state intervention is hijacked by special interest groups, and the very objectives of policy go astray. An example of this is the fertilizer subsidy in Indian agriculture.
- *There is a market failure, and the objectives of policymakers were sound, but the design of the intervention was wrong:* In some situations, the identification of a market failure is correct but the intellectual clarity was lacking, and hence the wrong interventions were chosen. An example of this is the Delhi government's odd–even initiative, where half the cars were sought to be taken off the roads every day, in order to improve air quality.
- *There is a market failure, the correct intervention was attempted, but the implementation failed:* The leadership thought of the right thing, e.g., mosquito control, but was not able to execute it.

This four-part thinking is more useful than the more conventional classification scheme of 'political economy problems' versus 'state capacity problems'. It is also more useful than the concepts of 'first generation reforms' (simple stroke of the pen reforms) versus 'second generation reforms' (those that require the construction of state capacity).

The obstacle course of public policy

The three key steps in policy thinking are:

1. *Are we facing a market failure?* If not, there is no role for the state.

2. *Does the proposed intervention address this market failure?* Sometimes, we see proposed solutions which do not address the claimed problem.
3. *Do we have the ability to effectively implement the proposed intervention?* Many times, an idea might be sound but, under present capacity constraints, the implementation of the proposed intervention may be infeasible.

There is a vast unfinished agenda, in India, of market failures where not enough work has been done. The justice system should be the first priority of civilization. This requires far-reaching work in rethinking laws, police, prisons, public prosecutors and courts. We have major new dimensions of health crises emanating from air quality, road safety, antibiotic resistance and substandard medicines. All these areas require subtle understanding of market failures, and commensurate state interventions. The competition perspective is required all across the working of economic policy, to address the problem of market power.

Numerous elements of state coercion present in India lack justification, insofar as there is no market failure that can justify the use of state power. Why does the state control the time at which a stock exchange opens and closes, or the objects that it trades in? Why does the state seek to imprison a farmer if her produce is not sold at a physical market specified by the state? Why does the state plan to put young people into jail if they trade in crypto-currencies? Why is the state forcing corporations to spend 2 per cent of their profit on good works? The list of erroneous interventions runs into thousands. India will obtain great progress by identifying and removing these interventions into the working of the economy.

Summing up

When faced with a potential government intervention, it is useful to ask three key questions. Is there a market failure? Does the proposed intervention address the identified market failure? Do we have the ability to implement the proposed intervention?

A disciplined approach of carefully walking through these three steps will result in improved economic policy thinking. It adds up to a powerful and non-trivial toolkit for thinking about the world.

There are four classes of errors in Indian public policy that call for reform: (a) Situations where freedom works well, where the right thing for the government is to do nothing but the government is doing something; (b) A market failure is present, but the politics pointed state power in the wrong direction; (c) A market failure is present, the politics worked out right, but the wrong intervention was chosen; (d) A market failure is present, the right intervention was chosen, but the implementation was lacking.

A successful political system is one which is able to navigate this minefield. It should hold back from engaging in interventions where there is no market failure. It should be able to channel democratic politics away from the traps of populism or special interest group politics. It should be able to foster expertise in understanding problems and devising the right solutions. And finally, it should have the execution capacity of translating the right idea into a successful execution.

5

Why do things go wrong?

Public policy failures are born of: (1) The information constraint;
(2) The knowledge constraint; (3) The resource constraint; (4) The
administrative constraint; and (5) The voter rationality constraint.
These five problems interact, and jointly generate government
failure, of both kinds: pursuing the wrong objectives and failing
on the objectives that have been established.

Element 1: The information constraint

Why do things go wrong? Because we are flying blind.

India is in poor shape in terms of the range of information
available to policymakers, the errors in data, and the delays in data.
Policymakers just do not know what is going on.

The criminal justice system in Delhi should evolve based on
a quarterly 'Crime Victimization Survey', which measures the
outcomes of the criminal justice system based on asking a random
sample of persons. This information infrastructure is lacking in
India. Under these conditions, episodes like a horrific rape event
impinge upon the policy process and dominate perceptions.

In the modern age of electronic and social media, these outliers gain visibility and become clickbait. Practitioners tend to be well informed about outliers, and outliers exert a disproportionate influence upon forming a view of the world. This is a poor way to proceed. Systematic measurement, and the formal analysis of evidence, yields a better understanding of the world and the design of better public policy.

Our ability to undertake rational analysis of interventions and conduct post-mortems of policy initiatives is bounded by our availability of information. *What you measure is what you can manage.* We will be able to rationally reform the criminal justice system only when fine-grained data about the criminal justice system can be interrogated. This involves comprehensive measurement of crime, courts, police, prosecutors, and prisons.

A particularly disappointing feature of the Indian statistical environment is that in addition to having limited data, some of our standard public data sources are also flawed. Expressions like gross domestic product (GDP) have institutional legitimacy in the international discourse, but in India we have to be cautious about errors in measurement. Economists in India are doctors without stethoscopes; we suffer the unique agony of trying to do macroeconomics without a well-measured GDP.

Example 1: Education and air quality

A standard recipe in public policy is to demarcate between inputs, outputs and outcomes. To use education as an example, the inputs are school buildings and teachers. The outputs are students enrolled that go through the motions of being taught. The outcome is the knowledge that students achieve. We have to worry about inputs not yielding outputs (e.g., the teachers do not show up to work) and outputs not yielding outcomes (e.g., the students do not learn much).

Assessing the situation, and undertaking management changes, requires a vast statistical system. Without high-quality fine-grained data, management is impossible. Hard-won public resources are being spent in the pious belief that education is important, but the value for money is abysmal.

Consider the problem of air quality. The policy process on air quality involves pursuing a series of questions. *How bad is air pollution in India? What is the root cause? What are the interventions which can make a difference? When interventions were undertaken in the past (e.g., shifting taxis to CNG), did they deliver useful results?* Making progress on these questions requires fine-grained data on air quality at thousands of locations in India. At present, such data does not exist. *What you measure is what you can manage.* We will only be able to rationally confront the air quality crisis of north India once the requisite statistical system has been constructed.

Information constraints hamper paternalism

A paternalistic government does nice things for each person. For this, it would need to know the preferences of each resident, to know what that person desires. Paternalism is infeasible because no government has such databases.

When redistribution is done, cash transfers are particularly attractive as they leave the choice of consumption goods in the hands of the recipient. No government knows what each individual wants, but the market economy is able to present each individual with a vast array of choices within which each individual obtains a best basket of consumption goods, in exchange for cash. This encourages us to focus redistribution, in India, into cash transfers.

Element 2: The knowledge constraint

Why do things go wrong? Because we do not know enough to do the right things.

Designing state intervention into the working of human society is an act of research. Whenever the state intervenes, a high level of knowledge is required about the problems it is seeking to solve, and predictions are required about how a proposed intervention will solve those problems. The understanding of the problem and the prediction about the impact of the intervention require research. Every intervention must flow from a theory of change, and our ability to theorize in India is quite limited.

Without deep roots in knowledge, the policy process degenerates into a contest of political and business special interests that harness the coercive power of the state to their own ends. Where we do not have high intellectualism, we get raw power play.

One way in which many countries ensure that state intervention works as applied research is by mandating that state agencies justify their intervention by providing the rationale in the form of an analysis of expected impact of the intervention. For example, some countries require analysis of benefits and costs to be done before any regulation or law is finalized, and usually this analysis is to be periodically reviewed to ensure that it still stands the test of evidence. Inputs into this analysis are given by myriad studies and reports that are available in public domain or are accessed or created by the agency looking to intervene in the economy.

The kind of research that serves as input for most of policymaking is social science research. Economists, sociologists, psychologists, political scientists, anthropologists, and others apply the methods of their respective discipline and sub-disciplines to present a picture of our world in a manner that is able to help us understand the general patterns, persistent trends, and notable exceptions in social phenomena.

In a process of iterative refinement, they help policymakers make sense of their world, and understand whether their perceptions, the petitions from stakeholders, the pressures from interest groups, and other sources of ideas are consistent with what the evidence is telling. In the modern world, the policy process consists of feedback loops from intervention, into the analysis of big data (either administrative data or private data sets), feeding back into refining the intervention.

Research and evidence is essential, not just in formulating policy responses, but also in making the decision to not act. On many problems, it requires sophisticated analysis to conclude that there is no substantial market failure, or that all the feasible tools for intervention are likely to work poorly.

We in India have a dire shortage of knowledge resources to serve as inputs into the policymaking process. As argued in the chapter on the statistical system, the basic information systems in India are weak.

We produce far less research than we need to. The bulk of state-supported research tends to be oriented towards science and engineering. However, the knowledge that is required to feed into public policy comes primarily from the social sciences and the humanities. The atrophying of intellectual capabilities in the social sciences and the humanities has adverse implications for the possibility of a sound policy process.

Most committees and commissions that we have been associated with have been hard-pressed to find the data and research required to make recommendations based on sound evidence. In the absence of sound evidence, it is difficult to take sound decisions.

The process of policymaking is always about decision-making under uncertainty, but in the absence of proper data sources and sound research, the uncertainty increases considerably.

As an example of the importance of thorough policy work, demonetization was proposed as an answer to the problems of black money, tax compliance and digital payments. There was a lack of knowledge about the empirical facts, the market failures and the efficient interventions on each of these three fronts.

Analyzing social systems is hard even at the best of times. In the public policy context, however, there is an additional problem: The Lucas critique.[1] When we look at the data, it may show certain patterns. But when the policy changes, people will re-optimize, so those patterns will change. Many patterns in the data are not exploitable by policymakers. The hardest research projects are those that seek to illuminate policy thinking.

Element 3: The resource constraint

Why do things go wrong? Because every rupee of public expenditure is more expensive than we think.

We generally think of a rupee of public expenditure like we think of a rupee of our personal expenditure. However, raising one rupee of tax revenue from the economy is not a simple matter. People respond to incentives, and hence people change their behaviour when faced with a tax. Through this, every tax policy design induces distortions upon the working of the economy.

Taxation imposes a cost upon society owing to these distortions. The total cost of public expenditure is not just the Re 1 that is directly spent, but also the distortions or lost GDP associated with raising Re 1 of tax revenues.

These issues lead up to a critical concept in public finance: the *marginal cost of public funds* (MCPF). The MCPF tells us the cost to society of Re 1 of public spending. This is typically much larger than Re 1.

In India, the sources of inefficiency from the existing tax system are as follows:

1. Income tax distorts the work–leisure trade-off and the savings–consumption trade-off.
2. Commodity taxation distorts production and consumption, particularly when there are cascading taxes.
3. We in India have a menagerie of 'bad taxes' including taxation of interstate commerce, cesses, transaction taxes such as stamp duties or the securities transaction tax, customs duties, and taxation of the financial activities of non-residents. From 1991 to 2004, we thought the tax system was being reformed to get rid of these, but from 2004 onward, things have become steadily worse, starting with the education cess and the securities transaction tax. All these are termed 'bad taxes' in the field of public finance. When money is raised in these ways, the MCPF is large.
4. India relies heavily on the corporate tax, and has double taxation of the corporate form. In the last decade, corporate income tax and the dividend distribution tax added up to 35 per cent of total tax collection. The double taxation induces firms to organize themselves as partnerships and proprietorships. Production and corporate structures are placed outside India in order to avoid Indian company taxation. These behavioural distortions drive up the MCPF.
5. There is the compliance cost by taxpayers and tax collectors, which is a pure deadweight cost. Raids and litigation by tax collectors intrude upon the mind space and imposes costs upon private persons. Costs are imposed upon society by illegality and criminality owing to corruption in the tax system. When some firms get away with tax evasion, this changes the

incentives of ethical firms to invest, which imposes enormous costs upon society as the most ethical firms are often the highest-productivity firms. As India has one of the highest tax compliance costs in the world, we would be likely to have a high value for the marginal cost of public funds.

6. When we do not have a simple single-rate tax system, this has adverse consequences for GDP. For example, if there was only one customs duty (say, 5 per cent), this is much better than having different rates. Similarly, 80 per cent of the countries which introduced the Goods and Services Tax (GST) after 1995 have opted for a single rate GST. In India, various pressure groups lobby for higher or lower taxes on one industry or another, and this distorts the resource allocation of the economy. This drives up the MCPF.

7. At the margin, public spending is actually financed out of deficits which constitute deferred taxation, intermediated through the processes of public debt management. Hence, in thinking about the MCPF, we must think about deficits and their financing also. Additional costs to society appear here, as we in India do financial repression (some financial firms are forced to buy government bonds), and have many mistakes in how public debt management is organized.

8. Under a broad class of situations, there is evidence that the distortion associated with a tax is proportional to the square of the tax rate.[2] In India, many tax rates are quite high, such as the peak rate of income tax and the peak rate of GST. Some sectors such as telecom suffer from extreme taxation. These extreme tax rates tend to increase the cost imposed upon society associated with a rupee of expenditure.

All these factors induce high inefficiencies upon the economy when the government chooses to spend Re 1. There is remarkably little work on measuring the MCPF in India. We believe that the value for India may be about 2.5 to 3.5. As a thumb rule, it is useful to reckon that the cost to society for every rupee of public spending is around Rs 3.

The notion of Marginal Cost of Public Funds brings a whole new perspective upon revenues and expenses of government. It encourages us to be very frugal in spending. We should only spend Re 1 when we are sure that the gains to society exceed Rs 3.

Example 2: Market failure in health vs a socialized healthcare system

As an example, we may think that there is a market failure based on asymmetric information and market power, when a private doctor deals with a paying customer. We may have a design for a public healthcare system through which this market failure is addressed.

But public financing, in and of itself, induces a 3× inefficiency. When money flows from the paying customer to the government, in the form of taxes, a 3× inefficiency is wired in, owing to the large marginal cost of public funds.

In addition, expenditure programmes of governments are also inefficient. Where a private person will spend Rs 100, a government organization will perhaps spend Rs 200. This introduces an inefficiency of perhaps 2×, at the expenditure stage.

Putting these together, a socialized public healthcare system might introduce a 6× inefficiency. If the magnitude of the market failure in the private arrangement (through asymmetric information and market power) is smaller than 6×, the socialized healthcare system would prove to be worse than the unregulated private solution.

Example 3: Bailing out banks

In similar fashion, the marginal cost of public funds puts a whole new perspective on using taxpayer money to bail out failed banks.

Micro-prudential regulation is supposed to avoid a large-scale banking crisis. Micro-prudential regulation in India failed, and we got a banking crisis. Does this mean that between Rs 5 trillion to Rs 10 trillion of public resources should be used to recapitalize banks? We should visualize that these are costs for the economy of between Rs 15 trillion to Rs 30 trillion, using the multiplication factor of 3.

These are astonishingly large numbers. For a comparison, each Rs 1 trillion of public expenditure buys 10,000 kilometres of four-lane highways. Perhaps the right sequencing is for India to have a small banking system, and first learn how to do micro-prudential regulation of banks.

In the long run, this problem may subside

The institutional failures in tax policy and debt management, which are giving the large Indian value for the marginal cost of public funds, will take a while to resolve. In the long run, we may expect that India will achieve fundamental reforms of tax policy, tax administration and public debt management. Once these changes are achieved, the marginal cost of public funds will go down. In the best advanced economies, the numerical value for the MCPF is from 1.5 to 2.

Until those changes are implemented, however, the rule of 3 is a major constraint upon public policy thinking in India.

Element 4: The administrative constraint

Why do things go wrong? Because it is difficult to build effective management structures in government.

We in India know a lot about the management of large private firms. This makes it easy to think that such knowledge can be brought into government contexts. However, a country is not a company.

Government organizations are bigger than anything seen in the private sector. Indian Railways employs 1.3 million people, while Tata Consultancy Services (TCS) has 0.4 million.

In all large organizations, there are principal–agent problems. The employees care about their own interests, and not the objective of the organization. Management is about establishing procedures for overcoming this conflict of interest.

Public administration, the management of government organizations, is harder than management in the private sector, for three reasons. The government wields coercive power (to compel private persons) or the power to spend public money (that is, in turn, obtained by coercing private persons to pay taxes). This is not found in private firms. Private firms keep score using profits or share prices. There is no comparable dashboard in government. Private firms have competitors, and face the threat of going out of business, while the government is a monopolist that will never go out of business.

Government organizations thus contain the hardest management problem. How do we obtain good behaviour from employees that wield coercive power, while lacking good measures of performance, and having no threat of organizational extinction?

Three cross-cutting problems that are found in all organizations are human resource management, the financial process and the procurement process. In the Indian state, so far, these processes have not been properly established. This hobbles the working of all parts of the Indian state.

Large organizations require well structured process manuals, and internal audit mechanisms to ensure that the process manuals are being complied with. In the Indian state, there are process manuals governing homeostatic functions—e.g., how pencils are purchased—but organizations generally lack formal processes for the substantive content of their work. The important decisions are taken in an informal way, through meetings and files. This lack of formal processes induces reduced capability, and a high vulnerability of performance to staffing changes.

In every organization, there are front-line producers and then there is an enormous overhead of monitoring, measurement, management and strategy. A low teeth-to-tail ratio is required for the organization to work well. Too often, in India, we have organizations which are all teeth and no tail. In the Mumbai Police, the bulk of resourcing goes into hiring front-line policemen, and there is little time or prioritization for the 'overheads' of information, planning, management. This induces poor management and thus poor performance. Similar problems are found in hospitals, courts, etc., where the typical government organization is all teeth and no tail; there is negligible management capacity.

More generally, in the Indian policy discourse, we tend to glorify the field perspective, and downplay policy thinking. We tend to denigrate the knowledge obtained from the analysis of data, from meetings in air-conditioned offices. This generates poor functioning of organizations. A great beat constable does not make a good head of police.

Finally, there is a connection between administrative capacity in the country and the administrative capacity in the state. An example of this problem is seen in the GST, which calls for substantial record-keeping capabilities in all firms. When most firms by number are in the informal sector, this hampers the possibilities for building capability in the government.

These factors have induced a severe administrative constraint that hampers performance in the Indian state. The best designed policy pathways yield poor outcomes because we lack the institutionalized capabilities to build capable organizations.

Politics without romance

> *When the State trespasses beyond what is legitimately within its province,*
> *it just hands over the management from those who are interested in*
> *frugal and efficient management to bureaucracy which is untrained and*
> *uninterested except in its own survival.*

> C. Rajagopalachari[3]

Why do things go wrong? Because we have a rosy-eyed view of the state.

Many decades ago, we used to think of the state as a pristine, benevolent actor who would work for the best interests of the people. Now we think about the *incentives* of politicians and officials, who pursue their own personal objectives. Many mistakes which were made in India, in the early years after 1947, would not have been made if such an unsentimental approach was applied to all policy questions.

We in India have a lot of experience with the working of the state, and are often cynical about the motives of politicians and officials. If employees in the government were benign, we would not have had large numbers of undertrials in jail for periods that exceed the sentence that they would have received if they were pronounced guilty.

This intuition was formalized in the field of 'Public Choice Theory' which used economic analysis to think about the objectives of politicians and officials.[4]

The yearning for heroes

> *Andrea: Unhappy is the land that breeds no hero.*
> *Galileo: No, Andrea. Unhappy is the land that needs a hero.*

> From *Life of Galileo by* Bertolt Brecht, 1939.

No matter how famous or well reputed a person is, when she is hired as an official in a government agency, we are aware of the gap between her personal interests and the public interest. Public choice theory encourages us to engage in 'politics without romance'. We will not build the republic by finding benevolent people. What we need are the frameworks where various kinds of self-interest are in conflict in the public arena, through well-specified rules of the game. The objective of reform is not to hire saints, but to achieve a state which yields good outcomes when each actor is self-interested.

Public choice theory has an important implication about how we think about institutions. There was a time when we would try to hire a competent and benevolent person to head an institution, and then leave all the decisions to her. Public choice theory has helped us see that we should stop searching for heroes and that we should not concentrate power in any one person. The capability of an institution lies not in personnel choices but in the arrangement of information, incentives and power. A sound institution is characterized by checks and balances, that create forces of accountability, that push the leadership of an organization to serve the people of India and not pursue their own self-interest.

The authors of the Constitution of India thought that the Speaker of the Lok Sabha was a gentleman, who would always be ethical and fair when determining what a money bill is. For a contrast, the authors of the United States Constitution, envisioned a president like Donald Trump. They wrote a document which is not a statement of hope about what a good president can do. Rather, it is a document that is focused on limiting the damage that a bad president can do.

Example 4: The fruit of the poisonous tree

Consider the problem of policemen tapping phones. We cannot assume that policemen or their masters are benign people who mean well. We need tight restrictions upon the state apparatus for surveillance.

Suppose a policeman engages in illegal surveillance which *successfully* identifies a criminal. Should we condone the violation of laws governing surveillance, on the grounds that this illegal activity yielded a good result?

Under the 'fruit of the poisonous tree' doctrine in the US, all illegally gathered evidence is inadmissible in court, and policemen who violate laws governing surveillance are personally subject to punishment. Whether illegal surveillance found the criminal or not, the fruits of this poisonous tree cannot be used in court.

This is the only way to create incentives for policemen to live within the rules. If policemen were benign, we would not need laws governing surveillance, or we could have overlooked the occasional blemish where a well-intentioned policeman was so caught up in the pursuit of a criminal that due process was violated. Public choice theory teaches us that enforcement personnel are not benign. Strong limitations are required on their behaviour.

The lack of this doctrine in India—the implicit belief that policemen are benign persons who mean well—is a major source of arbitrary power and thus the abuse of power by enforcement agencies in India.

Who will mind the minder?

Without the toolkit of public choice theory, we tend to think that the solution to one failed bureaucracy is to set up another bureaucracy. We are willing to believe that the Lok Pal will be better than the CBI. We are willing to think that a new independent agency which reviews official statistics will be better than the Central Statistics Office (CSO).

Public choice theory encourages us to think that all officials and all politicians are cut from the same cloth. We have to construct systems of checks and balances, that will work through rational incentives of all parties, and without assumptions that any one person is a saint.

The limits of public choice theory

Public choice theory views every official and every politician as purely self interested. In reality, every individual in public life has a mixture of personal and altruistic elements. We should see public choice theory as a cautious approach: we should design institutions assuming self-interested actors, and we will do better to the extent that some saints are recruited.

A more substantive critique of public choice theory is that substantial state capacity has generally required the construction of a professional ethos, of harnessing the inherent human desire for each person in the policy process to give an account of ones work to peers and to earn the respect of peers.

At first blush, the misbehaviour of policemen will be checked by requiring that they wear body-cams which record video and audio of their every move. But going beyond that, the next level of state capacity can only come about when policemen think that they work for the common good. Being good should be important to each policeman, over and beyond the check and balance that are brought about by wearing body-cams.

Our view is that India is at an early stage in the journey to state capacity. At our levels of capability, a simple-minded use of public choice theory is particularly useful. In future decades, as capabilities develop, we would shift gears in favour of the importance of professional ethos.

Element 5: The voter rationality constraint

Democracy is the system where wicked people lie to stupid people.

Why do things go wrong? Because the people lack incentives to know about public policy.

The romantic notion of democracy involves listening to the people, but the people generally do not know much about policy. Democracy is supposed to be the rule of the people, by the people, for the people. It is easy to carry this too far, by asking the people about policy decisions. We could just put things to vote.

Incentives of voters

There is a simple economics problem about individuals and policy: the average person does not have the incentive to invest in learning about policy problems. Individuals are very interested in the knowledge that matters to them directly—e.g., a person learns about motorcycles before buying one. But the learning that is done prior to voting is limited. Individuals will not take the trouble to understand GST or Public Debt Management Agency (PDMA). This is because people respond to incentives: The improvement to the life of an average person, from devoting 10 hours to learning GST, is roughly zero. Hence, individuals will not learn about policy questions.

Consider a range of economic issues: Why do nations become wealthy; the benefits or drawbacks of markets and international trade; the role of financial markets; the effects of regulation; the origins of inequality; the benefits of soft borders and immigration. Generally there is a large disconnect between professional economists and folk beliefs on these questions. Until Donald Trump educated the world on the lack of usefulness of a wall on the border, most people in India may have supported an impermeable wall on the India–Bangladesh border. If the average person would devote time and effort to study these issues, insights will surely arise, but the problem lies in the fact that there is no incentive to obtain this knowledge.

This is not a new idea; it has been known since *The Republic* by Plato, which is 380 BC. Direct democracy does not work well. Taking policy questions to individuals, through referendums, does not work well, as individuals lack the incentive to invest in knowledge about public policy choices.

There is a lot of unhappiness that the voters in the UK or Italy chose the wrong option in the referendums of 2016. But we should not be surprised when referendums fail to give good outcomes. The Constitution of India may not have won a referendum either in 1950 or today. Similarly, demonetization was shown to be reasonably popular in opinion polls in early 2017.

> *The fact of having the majority on one's side does not in any way prove that one must be right. Indeed, humanity has always advanced through the initiative and efforts of individuals and minorities, whereas the majority, by its very nature, is slow, conservative, submissive to superior force and to established privileges.*
>
> Enrico Malatesta

Direct democracy also suffers from majoritarianism, the idea that policy should be made based on the views of 51 per cent of the population. We must question the extent to which 'the voice of the people' is the oracle that must be followed. There is much more to liberal democracy than winning elections.

The limits of voting systems

The great economist Kenneth Arrow proved an 'impossibility theorem', which shows that voting systems are not able to consistently aggregate the preferences of voters.[5] Specifically, Arrow defined three sensible criteria that a reasonable voting system ought to simultaneously satisfy, and proved that no voting system could achieve all the three at the same time. This emphasizes how voting and elections are less useful than meets the eye, in finding the right pathways for policy.

Populism, the collection of popular policy ideas

Similarly, judging a policy initiative by its popularity among the masses is unwise. There is a reason why the term *populism* is a pejorative one: pursuing the policies that have wide support among the people often leads to outcomes which are against the best interests of the people.

As an example, North American Free Trade Agreement (NAFTA) created enormous prosperity in the US, but it is generally unpopular in opinion polls. In India, opinion polls have often revealed hostility to eminently sound policies, e.g., on subsidy reform. We should not judge (say) GST by its popularity: the full general equilibrium effects will not be understood by the average voter.

Representative democracy

The strategy that, instead, works better is *representative democracy*, a republic. We as individuals elect persons to represent our *interests*. We expect municipal councillors, members of the legislative assembly (MLAs) and members of Parliament (MPs) to invest time in understanding policy questions, on our behalf. Legislators are expected to have *shared values* with voters, and obtain intricate knowledge of public policy in pursuing the best interests of their constituents.

This is not easy: there is a principal–agent problem where the individual (the principal) faces difficulties in ensuring that the elected politician (the agent) works in her best interests. Making this work is difficult, but it is more feasible than asking voters to understand policy choices.

Incentives, not technology

Some technologists think that the complicated structures of representative democracy were invented because, before modern computer technology, it was impossible to listen to each individual. This leads to design proposals where every person votes, using the Internet, on various policy questions.

The large-scale use of referendums is, for the first time, technologically feasible. Direct democracy is, for the first time, feasible. The problem runs deeper. It is not incentive compatible.

Our only way forward is to make representative democracy work. This is not to say that representative democracy always works well. But our way forward as a republic lies in learning how to make representative democracy work, and not in taking policy questions to the people.

Summing up

In an ideal world, the state is a benevolent actor, which establishes the right priorities, and is able to marshal the resources to achieve good outcomes. This is not the world that we live in. Public policy in India is characterized by a great deal of failure. We tend to establish the wrong objectives, and then we tend to fail on achieving these objectives.

What are the sources of state failure in India?

1. The *resource constraint:* Each rupee of state expenditure in India is likely to come at a cost of Rs 3 for society.
2. The *information constraint:* Policymakers mostly lack high-quality data about the society in which they seek to operate.
3. The *knowledge constraint:* Public policy is a research process, and we in India lack the foundations of knowledge for operating this research process.
4. The *administrative constraint:* We fare poorly at resolving the principal–agent problem between the individual and the state. We must approach politics without romance. Politicians and officials pursue their self-interest.
5. The *voter rationality constraint:* Individuals lack the incentive to think about policy problems, and organize themselves to influence the policy process.

Many reform proposals suffer from a clear-eyed view of the present and a rosy-eyed view of one reform proposal. By internalizing the deeper sources of state failure, we will become more realistic about our pet ideas in policy.

Part III

The science

6

People respond to incentives

Humans optimize

In 1902 in Hanoi, under French rule, there was a rat problem. A bounty was set—one cent per rat—which could be claimed by submitting a rat's tail to the municipal office. But for each individual who caught a rat, it was optimal to amputate the tail of a rat, and set the rat free, so as to bolster the rat population and make it easier to catch rats in the future. In addition, on the outskirts of Hanoi, farms came up, dedicated to breeding rats. In 1906, there was an outbreak of bubonic plague that killed over 250 people.[1]

Sometimes we think that people are stupid, or that people are hidebound in following traditional behaviour patterns. Economists have found, in field after field, that people are not wood, they are not stones. People think intelligently about their own self-interest and change their behaviour in response to changed incentives.

This is also the reason why simple laws have not been found in economics. The difference between economics and astronomy is that when Jupiter goes around the sun, he is not a sentient being pursuing some objective.

This has far-reaching implications for policy thinking. It is dangerous to look at the world, come up with a design of an intervention, and hope that it will have a narrow impact as expected.

Some Chinese universities mandated a fitness requirement measured through steps as counted on the mobile phone. A business sprang up, of firms that would shake a phone and artificially drive up the number of steps recorded on it.[2]

Human beings look at policies and rethink their optimizations. When kerosene is cheaper than petrol, we should expect that people will adulterate petrol using kerosene.

In the sixteenth century, Dutch authorities levied taxes on individuals based on the width of their houses. This has led to narrow houses. The narrowest houses in Amsterdam are 80 centimetres wide.[3]

The response to changed incentives is often small in the short run, but in time, big changes come about.

Far-reaching changes in behaviour are feasible, over the medium term, when the price system gives out the correct incentives.

India has long had difficulties in vaccine production, which were rooted in fixed price arrangements. When more remunerative production arrangements were made, vaccine production in India has bloomed, and India is now an important exporter of vaccines.[4]

Politicians and officials also respond to incentives

People respond to incentives.
Politicians and officials are people.
Therefore politicians and officials respond to incentives.

Many times, we criticize the working of a government organization, and get worked up about the mindset of the staff.

The economist Percy Mistry has always emphasized that in public policy discussions, we are not allowed to ask for a change in the mindset.

Politicians and officials are not benevolent; they are self-interested actors. What appears to be an entrenched mindset, or an entrenched organizational culture, is always endogenous to incentives. A government organization that is riven with corruption is not one which was unlucky to get a lot of corrupt people. It is one where the rules of the game facilitate corruption.

Conversely, when the rules of the game are changed, this will generate changes in the most entrenched mindset, in the most established organizational culture.

The task of public policy research is to identify the formal rules which have incentive implications for the behaviour of officials and politicians. When the rules change, the culture will change.

Politicians and officials respond to incentives. This has a big and optimistic implication. Changes in the rules of the game will generate behavioural changes on politicians and officials also.

The behaviour of politicians and officials is also malleable. The puzzle of policy design is that of finding the checks and balances, and the rules of the game, through which politicians and officials will generate good outcomes for society when they pursue their own self interest.

Example 5: Monetary policy committee

People respond to incentives.
Monetary policy committee members are people.
Therefore monetary policy committee members respond to incentives.

In previous years, monetary policy decisions in India were dominated by the Reserve Bank of India (RBI) governor. When the Ministry of Finance wanted certain things done in monetary policy, they would engage with the governor and a negotiation would take place, outside the public eye. In any such situation, the negotiation may not yield the best outcome.

The solution to this lies in handing over the monetary policy decision to a committee that is called the Monetary Policy Committee (MPC). This is analogous to going from one judge to a bench of judges. Each MPC member is asked to vote and to release a rationale for the vote in public. When individual MPC members make poor decisions, they suffer reputational damage, and thus there are incentives for each MPC member to do better in their decision making. This arrangement harnesses the incentives of individual MPC members to get them to make better decisions, and avoids the problem of centralized power with one person.

The present design of the Indian MPC still gives too much power to the RBI governor. The MPC has three RBI staffers and three external people; and the RBI governor has the casting vote. This implies that even if all of the external members have a contrary view, the RBI governor still controls the outcome. In this sense, the reform has not yet induced adequate dispersion of power, as is the case with a bench of judges where no one person dominates.

Deploy incentives with care

Caution in setting up high-powered incentives

Economists are proud of having understood how people respond to incentives. The simple-minded application of this idea into management and public policy, however, leads to many difficulties.

It is easy to propose very high monetary pay-offs in return for a simple measure of performance. In the 1860s, the US Congress paid railroad builders per kilometre of rail. This gave incentives to builders to take the longest route between two points.[5]

When such 'high-powered incentives' are set up, the agent single-mindedly focuses on achieving that measure, and sacrifices everything else. When a financial trader is paid millions of dollars of bonuses in return for high trading profit, the trader tends to take very high risks. Such risk-taking is probably not what the employer had in mind.

In the confines of simplistic microeconomic models, incentives work out nicely. In the real world, there are many objectives, and it is seldom possible to capture all aspects of performance into an incentive formula. Under these conditions, the simplistic use of high-powered incentives gives poor outcomes. In most management contexts, low-powered incentives work better.

This proves to be particularly important when transplanting ideas from advanced economies into India. In an advanced economy, there are many elements of checks and balances emanating from the legal and institutional environment. Those are often lacking in India. A high-powered incentive that works well in that environment often results in difficulties in India, because the remaining checks and balances are lacking.

Caution in setting up incentives around statistical measures

> *When a measure becomes a target, it ceases to be a good measure.*
>
> Goodhart's law, 1975

Suppose we think that a certain examination is a good measure of the knowledge of students. If we give teachers bonuses for the exam scores of their students, there is the danger that teachers will then narrowly 'teach to the test'. They will make sure the students do well in the examination. The apparent test scores will go up.

But the examination was never the end; it was the means. The examination was intended to be an instrument for measuring certain deeper knowledge. High-powered incentives that push teachers to deliver exam scores will succeed in obtaining higher test scores, but those test scores will be less informative in portraying what they were supposed to measure.

Example 6: Goodhart's law in innovation policy

At the starting point in India, researchers were like S. Ramanujan, C.V. Raman, C.R. Rao, S.N. Bose and J.C. Bose. They had very high intrinsic motivation and produced deep and original research. Despite the barriers of colonial rule and extreme limitations in resourcing, India produced remarkable scientists who mattered on a global scale.

Later, universities brought high-powered incentives into the management of researchers. Universities demanded publication orientation from researchers. This was done by counting publications in general, and particularly valuing publications in 'high-prestige journals'.

Once researchers were given career gains in return for publications, there was a strong incentive to increase the number of publications, even if this reduced the quality of research. In the extreme, 'predatory journals' have sprung up which exchange money for publications.

Similarly, many researchers choose projects which are likely to get into high-prestige journals, and have de-emphasized their own judgement about what is likely to be a fruitful line of inquiry. This is particularly harmful in social sciences and humanities, where scholars who are pursuing high-prestige journals outside India are likely to lose their engagement with the most important questions as seen in India.

Human networks are built to get into high-prestige journals, e.g., by befriending editors and referees, or finding co-authors who are well networked. Many research projects are constructed with Indian co-authors playing subsidiary roles, while co-authors abroad exert creative control.

Universities sought to spur research by creating high-powered incentives, such as jobs and promotions, in favour of publication in high-prestige journals. We now have more publications including those in high-prestige journals, but along the way we have paid a price in curiosity, creativity and innovation. We are pushing less important research into more prestigious journals. We should be more careful before unleashing high-powered incentives.

People's responses to incentives can be wonky

Typically, we think that humans have unique preferences, that are hard for an outsider to understand, and each human pursues her own self-interest. This is a very fertile line of thought which has given immense insights into the world around us.

The first thing that we learn in economics is to respect the preferences of others. When we see someone else doing something that appears incomprehensibly wrong, there is generally a good logic in favour of those decisions, based on the preferences and budget constraints of that person. Liberalism—the respect for the values, beliefs and decisions of others—is integral to economics as it is to no other branch of human knowledge.

But at the same time, there are disconcerting gaps in the paradigm. The first chink in the armour is the cost of acquiring and processing information. It is too easy to slip into the world of the model, where humans are perfect in obtaining and processing information. In practice, obtaining and processing information is costly. Humans are rational in choosing where to expend such effort.

As an example, humans think carefully before buying a microwave oven, because the gains from wisely choosing a microwave oven are large compared with the effort expended in understanding them. But humans do not bother to vote, or expend minimal effort in choosing how to vote, as there is a low link between effort spent in understanding alternative political parties and the self-interest of the voter. After 1945, voters in Europe at first carefully avoided authoritarians, but as the years went by, the memories faded. In a rational world, voters would read history books and not forget.

Consider the choice of soap. We do not live in a world where a consumer assembles all information and solves out once for the optimal choice of soap, and then stays fixed with this choice as long as tastes and prices are stable. Consumers start out somewhere, and gradually learn their way to an optimum. The key element of this process is the fact that buying soap is done frequently. Each person tends to converge upon a subjective choice of soap. This comes from an iterative process of experimentation, experience and slow learning. On the scale of a life, changes in preferences, technology and budget constraints happen to everyone, and the choice of soap shifts gradually.

This process of groping for the optimum does not come about for purchases that are made only rarely, such as a home loan. Therefore, these markets tend to work poorly.

Consider the process of an entrepreneur doing an initial public offering (IPO). The IPO is an important event in the life of the entrepreneur. She has not done it before, it is important to her, and she is keen to get it done successfully. There is no problem of rational inattention or underinvestment in information and information processing. However, there is no possibility of a learning process, as almost nobody does more than one IPO in a life. This hampers the working of the market.

The second chink in the armour lies in thinking across long time horizons. The field of behavioural economics has emphasized that humans seem to exhibit a very low regard for events deep in the future. There is a certain kind of *short-termism* that is wired into us; we tend to make decisions based on outcomes nearby in time.

These concerns about human decision making have become increasingly prominent; they have gone from novel criticism of the mainstream, with the 'bounded rationality' of Herbert Simon of the 1950s, to becoming the mainstream, with the 2002 Nobel Prize in Economics.[6]

These problems are particularly important in health and pensions. Humans have little understanding of the incremental contribution of a medical professional. We tend to be swayed by the bedside manner, and fail to understand malpractice. We fail to think correctly about how health-related decisions play out over many decades. Similarly, it is difficult for humans to make savings and investment decisions starting in the twenties that will yield income in old age, from the age of seventy to the age of 100. The optimal stance of policy is not obtained if we think of human beings as perfectly effective at understanding information and making sound decisions.

Summing up

People respond to incentives. Human behaviour is not fixed; it changes when the incentives change. When policy changes, human behaviour changes.

The behaviour of politicians and officials is also not fixed; it changes when the incentives change. There is nothing innately Indian about malfunctioning civil servants, politicians, mindset, or low state capacity.

However, changing incentives should not be done in a simplistic way. When high-powered incentives are introduced, there is the danger of individuals pursuing those incentives to the exclusion of everything else. This can often result in unintended consequences.

When incentives are established based on a certain statistical measure, there is a greater risk that this measure will be tampered with.

While human beings mostly do well in understanding incentives and doing the best for themselves, the new field of 'behavioural economics' has documented many kinds of mistakes that human beings make in understanding information, risk and time.

7

Going with the grain of the price system

The great economist Paul Samuelson narrated a fable about agriculture that is quite revealing. Suppose there is a bumper harvest and the price crashes.

If farmers make decisions based on previous years' price, this will result in reduced sowing and reduced expenditures on agricultural inputs. Now the harvest will be reduced and prices will go up.

In the next season, if farmers make decisions based on previous years' price, this will lead to increased sowing, and then the cycle goes on and on.

This 'cobweb model', a story of prices and incentives and behaviour, is an example of the intimate connection between prices and public policy problems. Economics has a great deal of understanding of the price system, and this offers four valuable rules in the field of public policy:

1. Supply and demand make the price,
2. Demand curves slope downward and supply curves slope upward,
3. There is a law of one price,

4. The policymaker should have no opinion on the price, and no
   tools to directly control it.

Supply and demand make the price

If there is a lot of demand, and not enough supply, prices will go
up. If there is a lot of supply, and not enough demand, prices will
go down.

The price will move till the market is cleared, i.e., the supply
and the demand are equal. As an example, consider the price of
salt. The per capita consumption of salt is essentially fixed; there
are no substitutes and there is no possibility for most people to
consume less. When a small shortage of salt comes about, a very
large price adjustment is required to get some people to buy less
salt, and thus remove the gap between supply and demand.

The consumption of (say) salt or wheat is price-insensitive,
therefore there will be large price fluctuations. The consumption
of (say) avocados is highly price-sensitive, so there will be small
price fluctuations.

Indira Gandhi claimed that inflation in the 1970s was caused
by hoarders and speculators. In truth, it was a simple matter of
supply and demand. Excoriating, coercing, or imprisoning the
hoarders and speculators changes nothing in terms of creating new
supply. The economic theory of people hostile to economic forces
is wrong.

Policymakers have regularly tried to ban futures trading when
the price of a commodity goes up. This is based on the mistaken
notion that futures trading causes the price to go up. The price is
made by supply and demand and not by trading. Our extensive
experience in India with bans on trading show that these do not
work in influencing the price; they only damage the working of
the market.

A gap between supply and demand is a problem. Prices move in order to remove imbalances between supply and demand. The movement in price solves this problem by inducing changes in both supply and demand. Every time a government interferes in the movement of a price, it hampers this adjustment process.

This has sharp implications in macroeconomics. The most important price of the country is the exchange rate. Every day, the exchange rate should change, to catch up with changes in macroeconomic conditions. Changes in the exchange rate impact upon capital flows and international trade, and remove balance of payments imbalances. When a government interferes with the movement of the exchange rate, this hampers macroeconomic adjustment: the underlying problem that was driving the change in the price persists.

Demand curves slope downward and supply curves slope upward

When the price goes up, less is demanded ('demand curves slope downward'). When the price goes up, more is supplied ('supply curves slope upward'). People are rational and change their behaviour. At a higher price, there is more supply and less demand.

Example 7: Minimum support price (MSP)

If a government announces a high minimum support price (MSP), farmers will see the prospect of higher profits per kilogram of output. They respond to this high price by spending more on inputs. These inputs include sown area, electricity to pump water, fertilizer, insecticides, etc.

Hence, after MSPs are raised, we get a supply response. There is a surge of production. Now there are exactly two possibilities. Either the government will succeed in running a purchase operation all across the country, to buy this enhanced production at the promised MSP, and put it away in warehouses. Alternatively, the government lacks the administrative ability to buy the product, and this glut will reach the market, where supply and demand make the price, and result in a crash in prices.[1]

This yields a teachable example of unintended consequences in public policy. The government raises MSPs because it thinks this will make farming more remunerative, but this yields a crash in prices and farmer profitability.

Example 8: Rent control

Some policymakers became unhappy at high rents, and imposed rent controls. The coercive power of the state was used to force rents to a low level. But supply curves slope upwards: when the price is driven down, the supply of housing available on rent declines. Shortages of housing will inevitably develop when rent control is imposed.

The policymaker who sets out to make rented housing cheaper for the middle class makes rented housing unavailable for the middle class.

There is a law of one price

The same object cannot command two different prices. If this is the case, there will be *arbitrage*. If gold is cheap in Mumbai and expensive in Delhi, people will buy gold in Mumbai and sell it in Delhi. This arbitrage tends to make the price difference go away.

Similarly, if gold is cheap in Dubai and expensive in Mumbai, people will buy gold in Dubai and sell it in Mumbai.

Many governments have experimented with 'dual exchange rate regimes' where the government forces one exchange rate for importers and another for exporters. These schemes never work.

Policymakers of a socialist vintage are hostile to the word *arbitrage*. However, arbitrage is the basic human instinct of removing the difference between two different prices for the same thing, and earning a profit while doing this.

The policymaker does not control the price

Every now and then, policymakers see a market price that they do not like. Perhaps the price of wheat is too low in the eyes of a policymaker, perhaps the price of wheat is too high in the eyes of a policymaker, perhaps the price of stents is too high in the eyes of a policymaker. The coercive power of the state is sometimes deployed into a price control. These never work.

A price of wheat that is too low in the eyes of the producer is a bonanza in the eyes of the consumer of wheat, and vice versa. For every exporter who gains when the rupee depreciates, there is an importer who gains when it appreciates. Once policymakers get into having an opinion on prices, they have to adjudicate conflicts between different groups of people who see prices from the buyers perspective vs the sellers perspective. There is only one objective way to think about price: the correct price is the one made by supply and demand, untrammelled with political influences.

> *The market is not an invention of capitalism. It has existed for centuries. It is an invention of civilization.*
>
> Mikhail Gorbachev

Policymakers need to learn to respect the prices that come out of the large numbers of free people buying and selling. Sometimes, prices go wrong because of market failures. As an example, a monopolist tends to drive up the price and earn supernormal profits. If so, the solution lies in addressing the root cause—the market failure. Controls on prices are illegitimate and do not work.

Policymakers of a socialist vintage feel they should have a large number of levers of control through which prices can be controlled. Modern thinking in public economics guides us into focusing on the appropriate role for policy: addressing market failures. The state is not here to control prices based on rival political influences; the state is here to address market failures.

In India, we started out with a government which controlled the price of steel and cement, and many other things. By and large, mainstream knowledge of economics in India circa 2019 has reached a point where there is no interest in price control for cement and steel. But should you bring up the exchange rate, policymakers switch back to craving for state power in setting the exchange rate, or as it is more euphemistically stated these days, in 'controlling the volatility of the rupee'.

Samuelson's story, at the start of the chapter, gives us an insight into the problem of boom and bust in Indian agriculture. The price of onions surges under shortages; this attracts sowing; the price of onions crashes in a glut; this discourages sowing; and so on.

How do we break out of the cobweb model? *Storage* (also called 'hoarding') is the technique through which goods are transported from a time point where they are cheap to a time point where they are expensive. *Futures trading* looks into the future, and produces a forecasted price at the harvest date which can be used for sowing decisions or storage decisions.[2] *Free trade* (within India[3] and across the border[4]) generates arbitrage, where cheap goods are taken away and additional supply brought in when prices are high.

We suffer from the cycle of boom and bust in Indian agriculture because the state has disrupted all these four forces of stabilization—warehousing, futures trading, domestic trade and international trade.[5] The state makes things worse by having tools like MSP and applying these tools in the wrong way. Better intuition into the working of the price system would go a long way in shifting the stance of policy.

When private persons fail to achieve the right decisions on sowing and storage, this has larger consequences. Food supply crises and inflation crises impose negative externalities upon the larger populace. If anything, addressing this market failure calls for subsidizing the stabilizing responses of warehousing, futures trading, domestic trade and international trade.

Prices, fast and slow

Some people get unhappy when prices move rapidly. A big change in the price, over a short time period, i.e., high volatility of the price, raises concern in their minds. But the one thing worse than a price that adjusts rapidly is a price that does not.

Suppose an imbalance between supply and demand builds up. Would we rather have the imbalance closed quickly or slowly? A better functioning economy is one in which a shortage *rapidly* generates a higher price. This yields reduced demand, and incentives to increase supply. In time, increased supply will kick in and help bring down the price.

If the government blocks the movement of the price, the responses of supply and demand will not come about. If the government forces the price to adjust slowly, the responses of supply and demand will come about slowly. These are inferior outcomes when compared with a rapid movement in the price.

Consider the rupee. Suppose there is a big change in economic conditions and a large rupee depreciation is called for. Suppose RBI decides to reduce the volatility only. As an example, suppose a movement from Rs 70 per dollar to Rs 80 per dollar is required, for the big change in economic conditions, and suppose RBI decides to 'reduce volatility' and spread out this change over ten months.

What would the consequence be? For every person, it is now efficient to sell domestic assets, take the money out of the country, and bring it back after this process is complete. A person would sell Rs 70 billion of domestic assets, convert them to $1 billion held abroad, wait out the 10 months, and bring them back as Rs 80 billion, which is a cool profit of Rs 10 billion in ten months. The authorities may try to impose capital controls which interfere with such movement of money across the border, but India is now too internationalized, and there are too many avenues through which these steps can be executed.

This is a teachable moment in unintended consequences: the policymaker thought she was reducing volatility of the rupee, but kicked off an asset price collapse in the domestic economy. The best functioning economy is one in which changes in supply and demand *rapidly* result in a change in the price.[6]

Summing up

Supply and demand make the price. When prices go up, demand goes down. When prices go up, supply goes up. Free men and women will buy things where they are cheap and sell them where they are expensive, and thus arbitrage away pricing discrepancies.

When there are large changes in a price in a short time, this can be disconcerting and impose problems upon some people. But if the government forces the price to change slowly, this makes things worse. Prices are the mechanism through which the market economy adjusts to shocks; by hindering price movement we postpone adjustment.

In India, the legislature, the executive and the judiciary have all repeatedly undertaken actions which go against the grain of the price system. These actions are doomed to failure. When the policymaker tries to control the price, this is harmful, and the greatest harm is done when the policymaker tries to control both the price and the quantity.

The policymaker should have no opinion on prices and not try to control prices. Policymakers must strengthen their intuition into the working of the price system, and go with the grain. The field of public policy is about identifying and addressing market failure, not controlling prices.

8

More competition, always

One of the four categories of market failure is market power, i.e., uncompetitive market conditions. The market economy yields good outcomes for society when, and only when, there are high levels of competition. Competition pushes firms to cut costs, to innovate, and to deliver the best bargains for customers. When competitive pressure is lacking, firms degrade into inefficiency but obtain supernormal profits. This works badly for the economy. Every lever of public policy should be applied to address this market failure, to reduce entry barriers and increase competition.

Every firm wants peace of mind

When competition is achieved, the market economy pushes firms to ceaselessly work hard. Every CEO is looking for a way out of the grind. Every firm is looking for a way to obtain some edge, that others cannot compete with, after which wealth and peace of mind can be obtained.

As an example, IT entrepreneurs are very focused on creating 'network effects' through which a firm like Facebook or Amazon is able to set up a position on the market that is unassailable, and then earn supernormal profits and peace of mind. The phrase 'network effects' is freely used by technologists but it should make us uncomfortable. Market power is a market failure, whether this is done by old-style cartels or new-age technologists.[1]

Creative destruction and the death of firms

Every firm constantly tries to adapt to the changing world of what consumers want and what technology makes possible. Every firm peers into the future, and speculates about the kinds of products and production processes that will prove to be profitable. Some firms will always make mistakes in this speculation and go out of business. Their departure frees up labour and capital that can go to more productive firms.

When a firm goes out of business, we feel a certain sorrow about its departure. But a key idea of economics is that birth and death of firms is healthy and desirable. The great economist Joseph Schumpeter termed this process 'creative destruction'.

In India, we have traditionally felt that all firm failure is a bad thing. As Montek Ahluwalia says, the very phrase 'sick company' suggests the need for a hospital to nurse it back to health. We need to shift gears, and marvel at the process of creative destruction. There is a great circle of life, and both firm creation and firm destruction are required for a sound ecosystem of firms.

For this to work properly, we require a well-functioning bankruptcy process. In this, the key distinction is between firms with valuable organizational capital and those without.[2]

Some firms possess value in their organizational capital. They are sound as a going concern; they just need to be refinanced through a new financing package where the erstwhile owners and creditors take a loss. As an example, European telecom companies overbid in spectrum auctions. Many companies were not able to service their debt. But they were sound organizations, and the bankruptcy process found value in the organizations. The bankruptcy process imposed a 100 per cent loss upon shareholders, a large loss upon creditors, and recreated a new all-equity ownership structure which preserved organizational capital. Customers of these telecom companies experienced no interruption of service when the old firms were put through the bankruptcy process and were recreated under a very different balance sheet.

Sometimes, the very organizational capital of a firm is faulty and it needs to be dissolved. Such a firm goes into the bankruptcy process and is liquidated. This improves the profitability of competitors, and frees up labour and capital that can go into better performing firms. The critical call that the bankruptcy process has to make is whether there is organizational capital that justifies firm survival or not.

The Financial Sector Legislative Reforms Commission (2011–15) envisaged a specialized 'Resolution Corporation' which will run a speedy bankruptcy process for dealing with some kinds of financial firms (mainly banks and insurance companies), while all other financial firms would be handled by the main bankruptcy code. The Insolvency and Bankruptcy Code (IBC) (2016) represents this main bankruptcy code, the exit framework for most firms.

Zombie firms

The Japanese experience in recent decades has inspired the phrase 'zombie firms'. These firms are the walking dead, the firms that ought to have died, but have been artificially kept alive through state or bank support. The lingering presence of these firms increases the cost of inputs for healthy firms, and reduces the profitability of healthy firms. When a policy framework encourages the lingering survival of failed firms, this harms healthy firms in that sector. Japan experienced remarkable problems through the combination of zombie banks who did *evergreening* for zombie firms. Their story of macroeconomic difficulties is an important warning in favour of sound banking regulation, blocking evergreening, and encouraging exit by banks and non-banks.

By this logic, the presence of one large zombie airline harms the viability of all private airlines. When Air India is privatized, and the flow of public money into Air India is halted, all private airlines will benefit, as the prices charged by Air India for tickets are likely to go up.

In the Indian context, zombie firms are particularly harmful given the weak discipline of the budget process. When a government faces a soft budget constraint, there is a greater temptation to support zombie firms to walk the earth for a few years more. This is one reason why public sector companies are a problem for the economy: there is a greater risk of them becoming zombie firms backed by the exchequer. This is bad for public finance and bad for the economy.

Another pathway through which a kind of zombie firms comes about is when some firms violate laws or evade taxes. In India, we see many markets where low-productivity firms coexist with high-productivity firms. The competitive market process should force the exit of low-productivity firms. This does not happen when the low-productivity firms violate laws—e.g., a low-productivity firm may emit pollution, while the high-productivity firm incurs the higher costs associated with the pollution control required in the law. In similar fashion, a low-productivity firm may survive, in competition against a high-productivity firm, by evading taxes.[3]

When enforcement capabilities, of laws or of taxes, are improved, low-productivity firms will exit. Production will shift from low-productivity firms to high-productivity firms. This reallocation will yield GDP growth, in and of itself.

In some areas, we have seen the meteoric rise of certain firms who are allied with the prevailing ruling party. For some time, such politically connected firms fare well, through harmful means such as obtaining support from regulators. When the sweetheart arrangements break down, such firms tend to collapse, as their skill lies in political manoeuvring and not in achieving high productivity. When institutional quality improves in India, the time period for which such firms will have a happy ride will come down.[4]

Economic dynamism requires closure

Creative destruction is the ceaseless process where people try out ideas, build a business, and when they find that it does not work, they close it down. Many innovations are attempted, out of which some turn out to work well. When an incumbent firm develops a high profit margin, others jump in and compete this excessive profit away.

Creative destruction requires closure in the form of firm exit. There are three kinds of frictions in firm exit. Some firms are artificially kept alive as zombie firms. Other firms face a messy exit owing to the infirmities of the bankruptcy process.[5] Finally, there is the case when the agencies come in. When business failure turns into investigations, there is no closure.

The willingness of entrepreneurs to start a business requires an economic environment of limited liability, where the entrepreneur will be able to give up, put the firm into the bankruptcy process, and walk out of it with nothing more than a bruised ego, reputational damage, and valuable experience. A society that pillories entrepreneurs, and turns business failure into protracted disputes or entanglement in agencies, is one which will have less entrepreneurship.

Business cycle fluctuations and firm failure

Bankruptcy at the level of firms or individuals is intertwined with the macroeconomics of business cycles. In good times, many firms do well, whether capable or not. Downturns are an *agni pariksha* (trial by fire) which certain firms do not survive. This has its own cleansing impact. Similar issues prevail about firm creation also: the firms who get started in bad times seem to be a bit more capable.

Conversely, there is a link between institutional mechanisms for exit and recovery from a downturn. Consider a future date when the bankruptcy process works well. Under such conditions, when a business cycle downturn commences, weak firms will go into the bankruptcy process *and get rapidly processed*, their swift exit will improve profit margins of the survivors, and the resource reallocation will generate GDP growth. The faster that this process can play out, the shorter the downturn will be. A sound bankruptcy process gives less severe business cycle downturns.

Living in creative destruction

Many of us live in the cossetted formal sector, where our salaries and pensions are assured to us. We are used to very high levels of income and organizational stability. There is a vast India out there where things are more dynamic.

As an example, India saw the rise and fall of a million-man industry in the form of STD/PCO booths.[6] All of us remember a time when they did not exist; then came a period where they took off when STD rates collapsed; and then they vanished when mobile roaming became affordable. The market economy quietly mobilized the capital and labour for this new industry, and the market economy quietly presided over its dissolution. This was creative destruction at its best.

Similarly, each visit to a mall in India shows a new set of establishments that are hawking their wares. There is a constant pace of entry and exit. This shows that small firms in India are living the economists' ideal world of a high rate of entry and exit. There is nothing special about the Indian environment which makes this infeasible.

The government as a source of market power

The job of the state is to address market failure, and in this case, to combat market power. However, all too often, we have had state actions in India that have created or fostered market power.

As an example, the powers of banking regulation have been utilized to block competition against incumbent banks (e.g., by preventing foreign banks from operating in India, and by preventing the entry of new Indian private banks) and competition against banking (e.g., by preventing adjacent industries from competing against banks for their business). In Indian banking, market power has been induced by RBI.

Similarly, the market for agricultural products has been organized around monopoly power for agricultural produce market committees (APMCs). The state has promised to punish farmers if they sell to anyone other than the APMC. In Indian agriculture, market power has been induced by the APMC Acts.

Market power results in bad outcomes, regardless of whether the actor in question is public or private. We should be as zealous about dismantling state-induced barriers to competition as we are when attacking market power created by private persons.

Policy questions in many areas have a remarkable impact upon competition. As an example, when port reforms were done by bringing in multiple competing operators at the Jawaharlal Nehru Port Trust (JNPT), this was an inspired leap of combining greater competition with private production of infrastructure services. For a contrast, when the same vendor controls the old and new Mumbai airports, this is a lost opportunity in terms of improved competition.

Summing up

The desire for vigorous creative destruction animates our interest in competition policy. All across the economy, we require a progressive outlook supporting entry and competition. Political economy generally favours the incumbent, and leads us towards stagnation where one industry after another are locked up by a few powerful incumbents.

At present, Indian public policy does not give pride of place to competition policy. Far from always promoting competition, many state actions at present *hamper* competition.

Policymakers must constantly use the power of the state to prise open closed systems, to create conditions of extreme competition, and to see the bright side of firm failure. The prolonged survival of a weak firm, based on artificial life support, induces negative externalities upon healthy firms. The exit of these 'zombie firms' is a positive for the economy. It is likely that business cycle downturns will be shorter, once the bankruptcy process is fully in place.

The Indian economy features the coexistence of high-productivity firms that abide by laws with low-productivity firms that violate laws. When law enforcement improves, and weak firms exit, GDP growth will be obtained through reallocation of labour and capital.

Creative destruction is not alien to India: for small firms, it is the everyday reality. It is only with the large firms, and the areas connected with government, where competitive dynamics is poor.

9

Trace out the general equilibrium effects

A deep insight of economics is general equilibrium: the interaction on an economy-wide scale of all economic agents. Every small shift in one firm or one industry imposes adjustments all over the economy.

As an example, suppose the world price of memory chips goes up. This will drive up the cost of computers in India. This will in turn kick off myriad adjustments. The supply function of software will shift (as software companies are users of computers); the price of software will go up slightly. Costs in user industries like finance will go up slightly and depending on elasticities of demand, these will show up as changed prices. In the labour market, persons who have skills in using computer hardware more efficiently will be paid a bigger premium compared with people who get things done while wasting resources. This will feed through into demand for books, conferences and the other purchases of highly skilled computer scientists.

We can go on enumerating a very large number of effects. The key intuition of general equilibrium is that prices change all across the economy in response to one such stimulus. The changes may be small, but they are real.

By this reasoning, the effects of a given policy change may not show up in a concentrated fashion. But if small changes are spread over a large number of economic agents all over the economy, they may add up to a substantial impact (whether benign or malign) even if they are not sharply visible at any one place.

A good thumb rule about general equilibrium effects is that there will be no feel-good newspaper story, no photographs on social media. There will be no sharp impact, no human interest angle. There will be small changes spread all across the economy, which can add up to substantial impacts.

By default, we are wired to look more narrowly. For reasons of functional specialization, the lines of turf, and the limitations of our minds, it is easier to look at one firm or one sector at a time. This is 'partial equilibrium' thinking. But every policy thinker must maintain a general equilibrium perspective in the back of her head.

When we think about tax policy, it is important to narrowly look at the incremental effects of every move. But it is even more important to see these moves in a general equilibrium context.

A great deal of the debate about GST is practical squabbles about this commodity or that location. But the best insights into GST are obtained by thinking at the level of the full economy, about how incentives of all private persons will change, how the resource allocation will be reshaped, and how production and prices will change on an economy scale.

Similar issues are faced in international economic integration. Opening up to the world is always a problem for one narrow sector or constituency, which is placed under competition from overseas. Policymakers tend to often reflexively protect the Indian persons who face new challenges emanating from overseas.

But the great insight of trade theory is grounded in general equilibrium effects. International engagement shifts labour and capital from certain industries to other industries, and in the aggregate, we become better off. This is why, to economists, 'protectionism' is a bad word. But seeing this requires a general equilibrium perspective.

Example 9: Agriculture

In the field of agriculture, we have a large number of distortions: restrictions on input prices, output prices, transportation, international trade, etc. Taken one at a time, each of these restrictions appears difficult to remove.

But the key is to apply general equilibrium reasoning, and envision the world where *all* of them are removed. In that world, India will use a different set of inputs, produce a different set of outputs, which will have a different set of prices, and India will have a major part in global agricultural trade. We will grow a lot less of wheat and rice (which are capital intensive) and do more fruits and vegetables (which are labour intensive). The overall outcome will be very good for India, but we would not see that if we think of one distortion at a time.

Example 10: Universal basic income

Suppose there is a GDP of Rs 100, and we think that Rs 4 should be used to pay out a 'universal basic income' (UBI) to everyone. Perhaps this fiscal space can be obtained by eliminating existing subsidy programmes and raising the tax rate.

The UBI will, however, play out in general equilibrium. People who get paid a UBI will be less keen to work: the supply curve of labour will be modified and the labour market will clear at some new price. Higher taxes will also result in reduced work, reduced saving and reduced investment. All these markets will interact in general equilibrium.

It is not easy to see the overall outcome that would be obtained. It is, however, a useful caution: we should at least intuitively visualize how the UBI will play out in general equilibrium.[1] The result will diverge from the simple notions about UBI.

Short term versus long term

There is a relationship between the short run vs the long run, and partial equilibrium vs general equilibrium. In the short run, we see the first effects of a policy change, which are smaller in their scope. But with the passage of time, all parts of the system adjust, and we achieve the full general equilibrium effects. Conversely, to think about the long run requires general equilibrium thinking. These themes are visible in thinking about trade liberalization, the GST reform, Direct Tax Code (DTC), customs reforms, etc. In each of these, there is a short-run effect, which is often fairly painful for a narrow section of society, but with a lag, the full general equilibrium effects kick in, which give overall gains to society.

There was a time when customs duty collections were as large as 3 per cent of GDP, and it was easy to argue that trade liberalization would present considerable fiscal difficulties. Indian policymakers were particularly clear-headed in going forward with duty reductions which apparently gave reduced tax revenues. The key idea was that deepening ties with the world would improve GDP and thus feed back into other tax revenues. This insight was borne out by the outcomes. While customs duties vanished in importance, the other taxes grew well, based on the buoyant GDP growth that was assisted by trade liberalization.

Summing up

We normally see a few firms or an industry at a time. But actually, all parts of the economy are connected together in 'general equilibrium'. Every change in one firm or one market induces ripples in every other market. The full general equilibrium effects play out slowly.

In areas like tax policy, globalization, agriculture, or universal basic income, general equilibrium thinking has a lot to offer in understanding the policy issues.

10

Go to the root cause, use the smallest possible force

In India, we have 130 fatalities per 100,000 vehicles per year. The comparable value for the UK is six fatalities per 100,000 vehicles per year.[1] We are *twenty-two times* worse.

The appropriate measure that should be used in this comparison is fatalities per kilometre, but this is not measured in India. Each vehicle in India probably travels fewer kilometres per year than is the case in the UK. In this case, road safety in India is *over* twenty-two times worse than in the UK.

Poor road safety has significant implications upon the health of the people. Would we treat the problem by building additional hospital capacity along highways?

Treat the disease, not the symptom

If a person has malaria, we do not attack the fever. The same idea holds with market failures. Market failures generate visible consequences. Practical men and women are often attracted to use the power of the state to reverse those visible consequences. But we should understand the anatomy of the market failure and address it at the root cause.

The right way to address the road safety problem is to go to the root cause, to the public goods of highway management. The lowest cost interventions are found there, by building better highways and managing highways better.

Example 11: Antibiotic resistance

Consider the problem of antibiotic resistance. There is a market failure here: When person X misuses antibiotics, and helps create antimicrobial resistance (AMR), she imposes an *externality* upon others. This increases healthcare costs for person Y, who is no longer able to get a swift and rapid solution for simple illnesses. Actions by person X have an adverse impact upon an innocent bystander Y, an impact which is not intermediated through market transactions. This is an externality, a market failure.

How could the state change things? One way is to go to the *consequence*. We could possibly pay a subsidy to person Y, to compensate for the increased cost of healthcare suffered by her. Alternatively, we could address the root cause, which is the abuse of antibiotics. It is better to change the incentives of the perpetrator, rather than redress the loss of the victim.

Occam's razor of public policy

रहिमन देख बड़ेन
को, लघु न दीजिये डारि।
जहाँ काम आवै सुई, कहा
करै तलवारि ॥

बाबा रहीम

When getting hold of a larger object, don't discard the smaller object.
Don't use a sword when a needle will suffice.

Baba Rahim

In science, there is a concept named 'Occam's razor'. When two alternative explanations are equally effective at explaining the facts, we should favour the simpler explanation. In similar fashion, we should employ an 'Occam's razor of public policy':

When two alternative tools yield the same outcome, we should prefer the
one which uses the least coercion.

There is wisdom in this approach as the use of force is always problematic. Government intervention interferes with personal freedom. Government interventions are always imperfect and have unintended consequences. If we can get something done using less coercion, that is always better.

How can we wield state power as a precision instrument, rather than as a blunt hammer? The way to find the lowest use of coercive force is to understand the source of the market failure, and go to the root cause.

Going up to the root cause generally yields a reduced use of the coercive power of the state. The two objectives—reduced use of coercive power and solving a problem at the root—are related.

Consider market failures associated with asymmetric information. The root cause of these market failures is certain gaps in information. Hence, addressing these market failures at the root cause requires interventions in the structure of information.

These are issues where economics has much to contribute. Practical men and women see a problem in society, and often come up with a simplistic attack which directly hits the *manifestation* of the problem. But we have to be careful in distinguishing between the symptom and the disease: we should not respond to bad road safety with more hospitals. Good economic analysis will often show us the upstream cause, and it is then better to address the upstream cause rather than the manifestation.[2]

Example 12: Subsidies

Too often in the Indian policy discourse, policymakers first reach for subsidies as the instrument of choice to address the consequences of market failure.

The government may think it should pay a subsidy to people who are suffering from respiratory ailments in north India. It would be better to go to the root cause, and achieve clean air.

Policymakers have responded to the difficulties of digital payments by giving subsidies to digital payment transactions. It would have been better to go to the root cause and solve the policy mistakes of the field of payments.

Practical men and women see a problem in society, and are readily able to visualize a subsidy that counters the problem. Economic reasoning helps us understand the root cause of the market failure, and use less force by focusing the intervention upon the source of the market failure.

Example 13: The problems of infrastructure financing

Infrastructure financing requires equity financing until the infrastructure asset is generating cash flows, as there is considerable political and contracting risk in the early phase. After the asset starts working, and generating cash flows, there is a role for long-term debt. This requires a bond market. In India, we have errors at the foundations of financial economic policy, and the bond market does not work. This problem needs to be solved at the root cause.

Policymakers have responded to the difficulties of bond market financing for infrastructure projects by giving subsidies to infrastructure bonds. It would have been better to make the bond market work.

Policymakers have tried to create specialized infrastructure financing companies given the failures of the foundations of finance: these included Infrastructure Leasing & Financial Services (IL&FS) (1987), Infrastructure Development Finance Company (IDFC) (1997), India Infrastructure Finance Company Limited (IIFCL) (2006) and now National Investment and Infrastructure Fund (NIIF) (2016). It would have been better to go to the root cause and make the bond market work.

Example 14: Addressing domestic distortions through trade barriers

Domestic market imperfections can hamper domestic firms when faced with international competition. This leads to demands for protectionism. But tariffs induce their own distortions. Bhagwati and Ramaswami offered a key insight into this.[3] They showed that it was better to go to the root cause: to address the domestic distortion. This old idea, from 1963, needs to be resurrected every year, when a different set of players comes up with a new demand for protectionism.

Criminal sanction

Less intrusive measures are better than more intrusive measures. How do we define intrusion? The biggest intrusions involve snooping on people in their homes, and sending uniformed personnel into homes. The most intrusive thing that a state can do is to put people in jail. We should be extremely careful before threatening criminal liabilities.

In economics, all that a person stands to gain from violating laws is unlawful profit. A penalty that is larger than the unlawful profit suffices to take away the incentive to violate a law. Criminal penalties in economic law should be viewed with great suspicion. Yet, we now have hundreds of criminal offences littering economic law.

We look back at the 1970s as a peak of the licence–permit raj, with an intrusive and powerful state apparatus. However, we now have more criminal offences in economic law when compared with the 1970s. We were supposed to have transitioned from Foreign Exchange Regulation Act (FERA) to Foreign Exchange Management Act (FEMA) in 1999. Violations of capital controls were supposed to have become a civil offence with FEMA, in contrast with the draconian FERA. However, in recent years, criminal sanctions have crept back into FEMA.

Criminal sanctions have the harshest effect in terms of reducing the freedom of individuals. Under conditions of low state capacity, criminal penalties put supreme power in the hands of enforcement agencies. Harsh punishments go with wrongful raids, arrests, prosecutions and even convictions. They set the stage for abuse of power, corruption, and a collapse in state capacity.

Forcing companies to spend 2 per cent of their profit on 'corporate social responsibility' is a use of the coercive power of the state that is not connected with market failure. Companies are rational economic actors, and if there is a problem with non-compliance, monetary penalties would suffice. When the law threatens to put individuals in jail for violating the rule, this is an excessive use of force.[4]

Summing up

We should solve the disease and not the symptoms. We should solve dengue epidemics by controlling mosquitoes and not by building hospitals; we should solve respiratory ailments by improving air quality and not by building hospitals; we should solve accident related health problems by improving road safety and not by building hospitals. This calls for an analysis of the root cause of market failure.

In the class of solutions that are available for addressing a given market failure, we should favour the one which intrudes upon the lives of private persons as little as possible.

These two ideas are related. The lowest cost interventions are often found by understanding the market failure and addressing it at the root cause.

Intruding into the home of a person, interfering in personal life, incarcerating a person, these are the most intrusive things that the state can do. These high intrusions should be used with great restraint by policymakers. In economic law, there is rarely a case for criminal sanctions: once ill-gotten gains are taken away from wrongdoers with a stiff penalty, the incentive for wrong behaviour goes away.

11

Redistribution is fraught with trouble

Difficulties with paternalism

Discussions about poverty often involve person X getting unhappy that poor people do not buy (say) music lessons. This may reflect poverty. It may also reflect preferences (poor people may not value music lessons enough). There is an ever-present danger of paternalism, of policy thinkers who feel they know how poor people should lead their lives.

Poor people have their own tastes and their own budget constraints. We should respect what they are doing. Poor people have minds and preferences and pursue their own objectives. All over India, millions of poor people are *choosing* to walk away from a free public school and pay for the services of a private school. We should respect what they are doing and try to find out the reasons for this choice.

When we organize public policy around the problem of market failure, there is the possibility of rational discussion around the identification of problems and the identification of interventions. We can debate whether a market failure is indeed present, we can debate about whether the proposed intervention is the lowest cost intervention, and we can debate about whether the costs to society are outweighed by the benefits.

Where paternalism begins, however, we are down to value judgements. When one person wants to use state coercion to give shoes to poor people, and another wants to use state coercion to give shirts to poor people, there is no rational way to settle the disagreement.

In addition, public choice theory encourages us to be sceptical when a politician or an official engages in paternalism. In addition to the lack of empathy (i.e., the policymaker is unable to step into the shoes of a poor person, and see the world from her eyes), there may also be self-interest at work.

Poverty will not be solved by redistribution

Most of us feel an urge to help the poorest. When this impulse translates into private philanthropy, this is the best of all worlds, as there is no state coercion in the picture. There is also value in creating state programmes which deliver money to the poorest persons in society.

At the same time, we should recognize that no country got out of poverty through redistribution. All countries which managed to escape from mass deprivation did so through sustained GDP growth that played out over many decades. We should never lose sight of this prioritization of growth-oriented policies.

In the main, government action should be about identifying and addressing one market failure at a time. This creates conditions for growth that is led by the accumulation of resources in private firms and productivity growth in these firms. Growth is the most powerful, and only effective, anti-poverty weapon.

The main machinery of public economics consists of understanding market failures and addressing them. Poverty is not a market failure. Certain people in every society have a low income compared with others, and this can happen in a perfect economy without any market failures present.

Alongside the main body of a sound state which is focused on market failures, there is the role for redistribution in the form of disaster relief and one lean anti-poverty programme.

Distortions in the market economy

Sometimes, policymakers intervene in the working of a market in order to help poor people. As an example, the government may use state power to coerce fertilizer companies to sell fertilizer at a low price.

While this may indeed make fertilizer cheaper for some intended beneficiaries, this also distorts the resource allocation of the economy. The overall cost–benefit analysis is generally not favourable. We are better off letting the system of markets work out, and addressing the problem of poverty through a poverty programme. When looking at a given industry, such as the fertilizer industry, the only consideration should be to identify and address market failures if they exist.

The cleanest way to do redistribution is to pay out cash. We should let the price system do its job of effectively allocating resources, so as to obtain high GDP growth. The market economy would grow the pie, the government would tax a slice of the pie, and use this money for redistribution.

Subsidy payments distort the behaviour of recipients. Poor people should be striving to obtain skills and jobs. When welfare payments are reliably obtained, this would induce some to subsist on the subsidy and not strive to climb out of poverty. This 'moral hazard' is not a problem when the subsidy is Rs 100 per day and paid out to 0.1 billion people, but it does become an issue with other subsidy mechanisms.

So far, we have taken a somewhat static view that the interventions which try to address poverty hamper the *level* of GDP. The problems are more severe when the poverty objective clashes with GDP *growth*. Many interventions of the government are done with the intention of reducing poverty, but they end up perpetuating poverty by doing damage to growth. This is short-sighted.

Fiscal risk

In an ideal world, subsidies would be paid to the poorest 0.1 billion people in India, and all others would be too proud to ask for subsidies from the government. Liberal democracies, however, tend to succumb to a competitive process of pressure groups mobilizing to demand larger subsidies for themselves.

Politicians see a ready opportunity to obtain votes by paying out cash. This tends to induce an excessive focus on subsidy programmes, and a loss of prioritization for addressing market failures. In India, we have a capacity crisis in the core activities of the state. Many politicians are despondent about the extent to which expenditures in addressing market failures might impact upon voters, and are inclined towards subsidy programmes. Fixing the police and the courts is hard, and pandering to special interest groups is easy.

There is an ever-present danger of expanding the list of beneficiaries, well beyond the poorest 0.1 billion people, and in expanding the subsidy to well beyond Rs 100 a day. When subsidy payments are sent out to a large number of people, there is a greater danger of imprudent fiscal policy.

The marginal cost of public funds (MCPF)—the cost incurred by society for each rupee of public expenditure—is about Rs 3 in India. In mature market economies, the institutional arrangements for taxation and debt management are in good shape, which yields a lower marginal cost of public funds, which makes subsidy programmes more attractive. A redistributive state is a luxury that is better afforded by countries with good institutions.

Loss of focus weakens accountability

A key flaw of Indian public policy in previous decades was to view all government actions as anti-poverty programmes. This is an incorrect approach. The assignment principle teaches us that one tool of policy should be devoted to one objective. We should not bring poverty into the picture when discussing (say) water.

Example 15: Workfare programmes

In the late 1980s, there were good experiences in Maharashtra with employment guarantee schemes.[1] The key insight of a successful workfare programme is that the only people who will show up, to earn Rs 100/day by doing manual labour, are those who are facing extreme economic stress. It was felt that the mainstream labour market would not be distorted when the state paid out a below-market wage in a workfare programme.

Policy thinkers were attracted by three key features of workfare programmes. They are *self-targeting*: Only the poorest would utilize them. They are *self-adjusting*: When there are remunerative activities, e.g., associated with an agricultural cycle, there would be an automatic reduction in workfare. Finally, they are *self-liquidating*: Once incomes in a certain region go up, through economic growth, nobody would want to do manual labour at

Rs 100/day. Over the years, these programmes would tend to fade away on their own.

These assumptions hinged on the idea that the wage in a workfare programme is lower than the wage seen in the labour market. In practice, the way the National Rural Employment Guarantee Scheme (NREGS) was implemented in India, the wage paid was higher than that seen in the labour market. There has been great economic growth in India after NREGS was born, but there has been no decline in the number of persons participating in NREGS. As a consequence, many of the beneficial features of NREGS, originally envisaged, were not obtained.

This gap, between workfare programmes in theory versus NREGS in practice, is a reminder of how the best-thought-out redistributive programmes often go wrong. Successful redistribution makes great demands upon the capabilities of the policy process.

Summing up

It is hard for the state to be paternalistic as it does not know enough about individuals. Each person is different, and only the individual can choose what is best for herself.

When the government tries to be paternalistic, value judgements are made by policymakers which are not amenable to rational discourse.

No country solved poverty through redistribution. The first priority of policymakers should be to establish a vibrant market economy, through which the size of the pie grows strongly. After this, taxation can be used to obtain budgetary resources which are then redistributed.

Distortions of the market economy, induced in the pursuit of redistribution, hinder GDP growth. That is tantamount to killing the golden goose. Subsidies distort behaviour of recipients.

The marginal cost of public funds in India is high. The cost imposed upon the economy for Re 1 of public expenditure is about Rs 3. This implies that subsidy programmes induce a large adverse impact upon the GDP.

It is easy to build state capacity for paying out subsidies such as the NREGS; it is hard to build state capacity for public goods such as the police. Competing political parties tend to enlarge subsidy expenditures as a way to win elections. The establishment of large subsidy programmes and the sense of entitlement that tends to arise around them create fiscal risk.

Fighting poverty should be the clear objective of one or two anti-poverty programmes. The objective of the remainder of government should be to address market failure, without bringing distributional considerations into the picture.

12

Private solutions for market failure

Consider the pollination services of bees. The beekeeper gets honey, but the presence of the bees imposes a positive externalities upon other farmers, who get free pollination services. The standard economic analysis teaches us that the free market will get this wrong. The beekeeper spends money on beekeeping till the point where *her* gains from bees are matched against her expenses from bees. She does not value the positive externality that her bees impose upon her neighbours. There will be an underproduction of pollination services.

The first cut of public economics lies in understanding that when there are externalities, there is a market failure. We may want to indulge in some intricate intervention into society in trying to address this. The great economist Ronald Coase brought fresh insight into this field, with what is called the 'transaction costs perspective'.[1]

Let us look at the problem of bees and externalities in a different way. It is possible for the farmer to pay a beekeeper who will place beehives at the centre of the farm. While some of the bee activities will still spill over beyond the farm, there is a strong connection between the work of the bees and the pollination services received by the customer. This creates a viable business model where some people specialize in owning and transporting beehives to locations chosen by customers.

In Maharashtra, there are professional beekeepers now charging farmers anywhere from Rs 1000 to Rs 3000 for renting out boxes for a month.[2] This presence of a private market for pollination services shows that this contractual solution is a feasible one. Through these private contracts, we have solved the externality problem, without a requirement for state intervention.

There is a general idea here. Detailed bureaucratic solutions can be brought into addressing externality problems. But there are also other ways out of the problem: Private persons can enter into contracts, which internalize the externality.

When we set up a detailed bureaucratic state intervention, there are considerable difficulties in obtaining the full knowledge of prices and technology within the government, through which optimal decisions can be made. In contrast, when private persons negotiate with each other, the full knowledge of prices and technology is brought into play by well-incentivized actors, in order to find the right solution.

The canonical example of this field concerns a steel mill and a fishery. The pollution emitted by the steel mill imposes a negative externality upon the fishery.

If the same person owned the fishing company and the steel mill, the emission of pollution would be optimal. The single owner would weigh profit from fishing, profit from making steel, and the cost of pollution control. We cannot predict what the correct answer would be, but the unified owner would understand the trade-offs and choose the optimal path, without requiring government coercion on emission of pollution. This is the simplest case.

In this simplest case, the knowledge of technology and prices that the single owner has would yield an optimal answer, that would generally be better than a government agency that worked on pollution control.

Let us now move to the case where the fishery is distinct from the steel mill, but property rights are clear. The structure of rights must be so configured that the fishery and the steel mill are forced to negotiate a voluntary arrangement. The two sides will explore all contractual possibilities and come out with a contract that works the best for both of them. We cannot predict what the outcome will be. Either the fishery will pay the steel mill to emit reduced pollution, or the steel mill will pay the fishery and emit a certain amount of pollution.

The key point is that when property rights are clear, both sides are brought to the table to negotiate, and the result is superior to any bureaucratic intervention.

Before Ronald Coase, economists viewed negative externalities as a story with a perpetrator and a victim. It is easy to slip into the assumption that the fishermen are the ones who have to be protected. However, the Coasean analysis yields an important result. Whether the fishermen have property rights, which limit the steel mill's ability to pollute, or the steel mill has property rights, which limit the other side's ability to fish, is not important. As long as property rights are clear, both sides will be brought to the table to negotiate. Coase showed us that both parties have a shared interest in finding the right solution, and minimizing total harm. The answer lies in their negotiation, and when this is feasible, we do not require state coercion.

Example 16: Windmills that emit noise

Consider a windmill company which places noise-making wind turbines near a residential community. The command-and-control approach is to view the noise as a negative externality. We would build a government mechanism which caps the noise that windmills can make. We would set up a bureaucratic procedure to identify violations and punish them.

The Coasean approach consists of bringing the residents and the company into a negotiation. The company should pay something to the residents in return for the discomfort. If the residents are intransigent, the windmill company will just go somewhere else, and the residents will get no noise and no money. The negotiation will result in an agreement that the company will pay each individual a certain sum of money per year. Such a private negotiation is the best of all worlds.

In this approach, many private adaptations will simultaneously take place. As an example, people can weigh the choice of spending money on double-wall glass windows that will diminish the noise. In other words, the recipient can also invest in pollution control. These are optimal responses, from the viewpoint of society at large, which would not easily be obtained through a bureaucratic solution.

Example 17: Trading in emission permits

A great success story of the Coasean approach is the trading in pollution permits. Under this system, scientists define a cap for the amount of pollutants, such as sulphur dioxide, that can be emitted by society at large. The government establishes a rule: Firms that wish to emit must buy permits. These permits are aligned to the cap set by the scientists. The government enforces the rule, inflicting punishment upon firms that emit beyond the permits purchased.

A market for these permits comes about. Each firm looks at the cost of the permit on the market versus the cost of pollution control, and optimally chooses what to do. At some firms, pollution reduction is easy: these firms prefer to reduce pollution. At other firms, pollution reduction is hard: these firms prefer to buy emission permits.

This results in the ideal outcome for society, where pollution control is done at the plants where the cost of reducing emissions is the lowest. For a contrast, it would be very difficult for a pollution control bureaucracy to understand which factories should reduce emissions.

The role of the state in Coasean solutions

The Coasean approach requires the state to play a role in clearly defining property rights. In the steel mill example, the state needs to establish the powers of the steel mill in controlling fishing or the powers of the fishery in controlling pollution. We are neutral between which of these two paths is taken; in both cases, the outcome works out to be optimal from the viewpoint of society. The key point is that property rights should be clear enough and that imposing an externality upon a person calls for a negotiation.

Public policy also plays another role in the Coasean approach, through the judicial infrastructure of contract enforcement. In many practical situations, the traditional UK concepts of the law of torts give rights to persons harmed, which are conducive to a Coasean negotiation. Greater effort is required in India, to lay the foundations of the law of torts, and to build the courts through which these disputes can be efficaciously adjudicated.

Once property rights are defined and private persons can search for contracts, good outcomes are obtained without requiring a heavy-handed command-and-control intervention. By this logic, policymakers should put a high priority upon the reforms that clarify property rights, and the reforms that improve the working of the judiciary.

There are many problems where a large number of individuals is involved, and it is difficult to bring all persons together into a negotiation. It is in those problems that the first cut of public economics holds true. Under these circumstances, there is a role for the state to engage in the more conventional machinery of public policy, ranging from taxes/subsidies to regulation to production.

Traditional community solutions to the tragedy of the commons

The standard idea in economics about common pool resources is the 'tragedy of the commons'.[3] We cannot easily control access, and then a scarce resource tends to be depleted by excessive usage. The classic example is the fish stock in the sea. It is hard to control fishing boats, so fishing tends to be overdone, resulting in a collapse of the fish population. Each person has an incentive to overuse the commons, which induces a negative externality upon all other users of the commons.

All non-excludable goods are not depleted by excessive usage. As an example, consider a large number of people tuning in to a radio channel. The number of people tuning in does not diminish the radio signal available. This discussion is limited to common pool resources which are depleted by excessive usage.

We could combat this market failure in three ways: state control, privatization, or a Coasean solution involving private contracts. Each of these solutions has problems:

- State control requires setting up a complex bureaucracy that will monitor, allocate and enforce. In many situations, the magnitude of the resources being allocated (e.g., pastureland associated with a village) does not justify the expenditure on the state solution.
- Privatization is infeasible in some problems (e.g., the open sea). Cutting pastureland into small plots can yield an inferior solution as the grass may grow in different places at different times of the year.

- A Coasean solution does not easily come about, as it is difficult to get a large number of people (e.g., all fishermen) to come together and negotiate.

The political scientist Elinor Ostrom discovered that many practical institutional arrangements, established by traditional communities over very long periods of time, achieve good results. Some of the examples that she has studied have been practised for hundreds of years or even for a thousand years. Her examples include communal tenure of high mountain meadows and forests in Switzerland and Japan, the *huerta* irrigation systems in Spain and the *zanjera* irrigation system in the Philippines.

Much research is required in India, on traditional arrangements that have been brushed aside in the first flush of modernization, to look more deeply about how well they perform. For instance, the moratorium on eating fish during the month of Shravan is commonly understood to tie in with the spawning season. But we have not studied the roots of such arrangements from the lens of solving common goods problems.[4]

Earlier, we in India were much more optimistic about state-led solutions. Some of that early optimism about the state has subsided. We should have greater respect for self-organizing systems that do not require state capacity. As an example, the Forest Rights Act tried to give a better place to forest dwellers. But the Act retains a substantial role for the state and emphasizes allocating rights to individuals than to communities. There may be a better pathway to a good outcome, based on researching traditional community arrangements among forest dwellers in India, in the light of Ostrom's insights.

This is another surprising dimension to modern public economics. Intuitively, we should see these organically grown institutions as being akin to the system of markets. These institutions emerge and evolve on their own, aggregate a large amount of information, and result in an efficient allocation.

Summing up

The first cut of public economics asks us to find market failures and address them. Sophisticated public economics whittles down the role for the state when compared with the first cut.

When property rights and contract enforcement work well, private persons will negotiate their way to many good solutions. And even in the extreme, where large numbers of people are involved, some traditional community solutions achieve optimality. When feasible, these pathways are superior to the traditional toolkit of state intervention, as they involve less coercion.

The conventional Indian discourse slips into moralizing, into a populist approach that favours the interests of the fishermen over the steel mill. This does not yield the optimal answer.

13

Bring cold calculations into the policy process

Toting up the costs and benefits

The public policy process involves a stylized set of questions:

1. What is the problem that we're out to solve? Are we sure that there is indeed a market failure?
2. What are the alternative interventions that could be used? What is the least intrusive intervention that gets the job done?
3. How would we implement the proposed intervention? What are the state capacity constraints that we would face? How would we build state capacity for our desired intervention? Are we certain that under our real-world implementation constraints, the proposed intervention will indeed address the malady under examination?
4. Do the benefits outweigh the costs?

Proponents of many policies are often quite convinced that they are correct. Cost–benefit analysis is the discipline of trying to tote up the numbers. The first element of costs is the direct costs borne by government. The second element of cost is the intrusion upon private persons that is caused by the policy proposal. Against this, we have the claimed benefits.

Activists and enthusiasts tend to be very convinced about themselves. Cost–benefit analysis checks the enthusiasm by demanding data. In God we trust, all others must bring data. *Did we choose the least intrusive alternative? Are we sure that the benefits to society outweigh the costs?* Such a formal process helps diminish many of the flaws of human decision processes.

Formal calculations of cost are, of course, important in economic policy. They are also useful in other areas of public policy. In October 2002, the US Congress authorized the then president George Bush to use military force against Iraq if he felt this was appropriate. In December 2002, the economist William D. Nordhaus made a calculation of the economic consequences of the war in Iraq. These calculations showed a sombre outlook. The war began in March 2003, and ran till December 2011. With the benefit of hindsight, we know that the Nordhaus calculation of December 2002 was largely sound while the arguments of the US national security establishment were not. This shows the opportunity for improved decision making through careful calculations, going beyond economic policy.

Accounting for the interests of persons not in the room

By default, human decision making tends to think about the impacts upon the persons who have been in face-to-face conversations with policymakers. This creates a bias in favour of special interest groups that are able to mobilize for lobbying. A sound cost–benefit analysis tries to quantify the overall costs and benefits to society, and not just the narrow zone of the people who are lobbying the government.

Every regulator tends to intensively engage with its regulated persons. The Telecom Regulatory Authority of India (TRAI) tends to talk to telecom service providers (TSPs), RBI tends to talk to banks. Over time, the regulator tends to adopt the worldview of regulated persons, and think of their interests. This can go beyond ordinary human nature to a more malign notion of 'regulatory capture'. Explicit calculations help ensure that the interests of the larger populace are brought on the table.

Consider the disaster resilience of a bridge in the Himalayas. In the event of an earthquake, there is a direct cost to the public–private partnership (PPP) contractor who owns the bridge, if the earthquake destroys the bridge. However, if the bridge were to be destroyed, it would also impose significant harm upon persons who live on both sides of the bridge. A sound cost–benefit analysis for improving the disaster risk resilience of the bridge would take into account the full costs and full benefits to society and not just the interests of the PPP contractor.

Long-term thinking

By default, human decision making tends to focus on the short term. A sound cost–benefit analysis would look deeper into the future, and thus green-light policy initiatives which impose costs in the short run but result in valuable improvements in the long run.

Consider a state intervention to provide or to subsidize nutrition for the young. If this is properly implemented, this yields costs in the short run and generates good results for society for decades thereafter. A similar example is found in the DTC, where tax revenues will be sacrificed in the short run, but higher GDP growth will be kicked off in the medium term.

Combating sunk costs

As humans, too often we tend to look back and are shaped by costs that have been paid in the past. Sunk cost fallacies are found in government also: Once a lot of time and effort has been put into building a scheme or an institution, policymakers are tempted to continue in the same direction. Intensification of effort comes easily to a bureaucracy as opposed to fundamental reform.

Systematic cost–benefit analysis is useful insofar as it combats the intuitive human failure of the sunk cost fallacy. Formal calculations for cost–benefit analysis help us to look forward, and thus reduce the extent to which we are deluded by the sunk cost fallacy.

Ex post review

Every legal instrument should state its objective at the outset. After three years have elapsed, an empirical examination of whether these objectives were met should be mandatory. In some situations, there is a role for 'sunset clauses' where laws are automatically repealed after a certain time period elapses.

As an example, land reform in Maharashtra, through the Bombay Tenancy and Agricultural Lands Act, 1948, was considered a revolutionary step forward in its time. We can debate whether it was optimal in its time, but there is little doubt that it is out of touch with the questions that we face today. Under this Act, even farmer-to-farmer leasing of land is prohibited. A systematic mechanism of ex post review would bubble up such laws into periodic review.

Too often in India, interventions are put into place without explicitly stating the problem that is sought to be solved. A first objective is articulated, but the moment it is clear that this did not work out, the goalpost is shifted. It is a healthy discipline to require the release of a documentation packet, associated with each intervention, where the problem that is sought to be solved is clearly stated. This will support ex post evaluation of whether the intervention did indeed help solve the problem that it set out to solve. This formal documentation will take away the possibility of shifting goalposts.

This will help reveal mistakes that need to be reversed. Clarity about objectives, and the calculations associated with cost–benefit analysis, will help the Comptroller and Auditor General (CAG) work on policy initiatives in a more effective way. The staff in an intervention, who expect such review, will be more accountable and hence do better work.

Ex post review is highly relevant in the main track of public policy: using state coercive power to change the behaviour of private persons in ways that address market failure. However, at the same time, we have to be careful when we think of crisis-management actions.

Hindsight is 20/20 vision. It is important to respect the view of the world as seen contemporaneously by the crisis manager. Many actions are taken, at the peak of a crisis, to stave off bad outcomes. Ex post, these may appear to be a waste. We should put ourselves in the shoes of the decision maker, when doing ex post analysis, and respect the fact that many of the actions that appear irrelevant in hindsight were actually expenditures on risk management.

The relevant comparison is not the overall expenditures in the path taken, but a comparison against the counterfactual, the path not taken, of either doing nothing or undertaking other decisions.

As an example, consider the actions taken by Yashwant Sinha's Ministry of Finance in response to the Unit Trust of India (UTI) crisis. The government paid a fiscal cost by paying out money to UTI unitholders. The government purchased certain securities from the problematic UTI schemes, and placed these into a new organization named Specified Undertaking of the Unit Trust of India (SUUTI). Ex post, we know that when these securities were sold, the government made a tidy profit. This seems like a successful intervention from a simple financial point of view.

Suppose this had not worked out this way. Suppose Nifty had moved in a different way, and the government had suffered a loss when selling off the SUUTI holdings. Would we then excoriate the decision makers of the time, on the grounds that their intervention in the UTI crisis was (ex post) a mistake? This would be an unfair assessment.

It is important to think in the shoes of the policymaker in 2001. A disruptive mess at UTI would have triggered off panic selling by large numbers of small investors. This is the counterfactual of doing nothing, which was on the minds of policymakers in 2001. Even if the SUUTI holdings were, later on, sold at a loss, the important thing that was averted in the UTI crisis management was a panic among individual investors.

How precise can this be?

We have no illusions about the scientific precision that can be achieved in this analysis.[1] These kinds of calculations are notoriously vulnerable to changes in assumptions. However, there are two reasons why such analysis is valuable. First, the very act of conducting the analysis forces the decision makers to improve their understanding of the problems that they seek to solve.

An integral part of a sound cost–benefit analysis is asking the question: Is there another and superior way through which we could get the job done? Could we achieve the desired objective with a lower use of state coercion? When calculations are absent, the policy process tends to degenerate into a contest of rival political influences. Systematic cost–benefit analysis encourages an exploration of alternative policy pathways, and generally yields better thinking.

Second, with all its imprecision, cost–benefit analysis is able to block some egregiously wrong initiatives. The formal step of cost–benefit analysis, in our opinion, will block perhaps a fifth of the blunders of policymakers in India.

The zone of applicability of cost–benefit analysis

Cost–benefit analysis is a valuable tool when the state intervenes in society, either through tax-and-spend or through making rules that coerce private persons. This is the zone where there is value in seeing the full picture, and toting up the costs and benefits. The costs and benefits under examination are the costs and benefits *to society*.

A great deal of work in the policy process is internal reorganization of government. Cost–benefit analysis is less useful here. For an analogy, a corporation works very carefully when testing a new product that it shows customers, but it moves more with deductive logic when internally reorganizing itself.

An institutionalized application of mind

Cost–benefit analysis is thus about creating an institutionalized application of mind. It is a way of ensuring that the right questions are asked, and alternatives evaluated, before a decision is made. This helps avoid impressionistic and casual approaches to policy formulation, and reduces the extent to which sectarian considerations dominate.

For the gains to be obtained, the key decision makers must do the cost–benefit analysis themselves. Sometimes, there is the temptation to arrive at a decision in an intuitive way, and then hand out the task of writing up an attractive cost–benefit analysis to economists who have no say in the actual decision making. It is better to apply cost–benefit analysis to a group of plausible alternative interventions, and let the calculations reveal which the best intervention is.

The release of documents with cost–benefit analysis improves the policy process as independent persons will critique the assumptions and the calculations, often bringing fresh insight into the question.

In the demonetization episode, such practices would have been quite useful. It would have helped to clearly state the objective up front. It would have helped, to undertake calculations about the costs being imposed upon society. It would have helped, to ask whether there were less intrusive interventions through which the same objectives could be achieved.

Policy thinkers have emphasized the importance of formal cost–benefit analysis and ex post review for a long time. As with other aspects of deep thinking in the policy process, there is lip service and low adherence. In the hurried real world policy process, there is an extreme emphasis on firefighting and *rapidly* pushing initiatives out of the front door. We plan in haste, and repent at leisure.

In order to do better, and obtain the institutionalized application of mind, these practices need to be codified. Parliamentary law must encode requirements for cost–benefit analysis and ex post review of laws and regulations.[2]

This is similar to the problems seen with other aspects of thorough process that induce the institutionalized application of mind. Policymakers in India generally prefer to push through a law or a regulation without introducing the delays associated with developing the required packet of documentation, releasing the materials, and engaging in public consultation.

These things will only be done properly when they are encoded into parliamentary law. From the 1980s onward, under the influence of 'new public management', laws of mature market economies have built in these provisions: cost–benefit analysis, ex post review, notice-and-comment, etc. The codification in parliamentary law, of sound processes, is the frontier of building state capacity in India.

Summing up

Going beyond the qualitative recognition of a market failure, it is important to quantify the benefit that would be obtained for society by addressing the market failure.

If the cost–benefit analysis shows that the costs imposed upon society, by the best solution, outweigh the prospective benefits, the cure is worse than the disease.

The formal process of cost–benefit analysis helps avoid emotion, respects the interests of persons who have not mobilized to campaign or lobby for their own interests, helps bring long term considerations into the picture, and combats the sunk cost fallacy.

Every new policy initiative should be launched with a clear statement of the problem that it seeks to solve, the demonstration that there is a market failure, and the cost–benefit analysis that was used to discover the best intervention. After a few years, it is useful to engage in ex post review, and change course if the original objectives were not met. Cost–benefit analysis is not a science, and there is a significant imprecision in all such estimates.

We always see things more clearly in hindsight. The idea of ex post review is not to pillory the people who looked at the information at a certain point in time, e.g., in a moment of crisis, and made a decision. It is to establish feedback loops through which a process of iterative refinement sets in.

Cost–benefit analysis is required for government *intervention* into society. It is not essential when doing internal reorganization of government organizations.

The laws that give power to government agencies to intervene in society must codify the processes of cost–benefit analysis and ex post review. Through this, it induces an institutionalized application of mind, and improves the quality of work.

14

Ask the right question

There is a vision of black money, perhaps drawn from Hindi movies, where there are suitcases of cash that are stored. Such a problem statement leads to a certain style of attack on black money, such as demonetization.

But black money is a flow and not a stock. It is paid and received every day as part of business activities that evade taxes, bribe government employees, etc. Once we pose the problem of black money as a flow, the solutions that may be attempted change considerably. We may like to remove executive discretion, improve tax policy and tax administration, remove capital controls, etc., in the attempt to address black money as a flow.[1]

When we are 'seized with a problem', we are often seized with the political manifestation of a problem. The problem that seizes you is sometimes not the problem that is worth solving.

This may appear trite, but it is actually often difficult to pose the right question. The *problem* is an elephant, and we are all blind men coming at it from various directions. There is every possibility of the policy process getting hijacked into side lanes.

In the 1970s, Indian policymakers used to compare Indian textile production against that of South Korea, and claim that India was doing better because there was lower import content. While Indian textile production did indeed have a lower import content, South Korea ran far ahead in value added and exports. It would have made much more sense to focus on value added in textiles, or export of textiles.

In similar fashion, the objective of 'Make in India' can go wrong if this morphs into an attempt to reduce import content, in which case it will become much like the old policy strategy of 'import substitution' (IS).

Common sense on taxes

In the field of tax policy, the objective is often stated in terms of a stated tax/GDP ratio. This is the wrong way to think about the problem.

Collecting taxes induces distortions upon the economy, and harms GDP. We should be asking how the tax system can yield a desired *level* of tax revenue, while GDP is as high as possible. When tax reforms reduce distortions and yield higher GDP growth, we should be delighted, even if the tax/GDP ratio were to come down.

Faced with a choice of a GDP of Rs 100 and a tax/GDP ratio of 20 per cent, vs a GDP of Rs 200 and a tax/GDP ratio of 15 per cent, we should prefer the latter. A single-minded focus upon the tax/GDP ratio is inappropriate; we must see the larger picture.

On a similar note, the emphasis on revenue neutrality in the GST, in the short run, was a mistake.

Government is an important buyer of goods and services, and a low single-rate GST would yield cost savings for all levels of government.

There are strong interlinkages between GST and direct tax collections. The value-added tax (VAT) chain induces legibility for the state, and this legibility induces higher direct tax revenues also. A successful GST reform will yield higher direct tax collections also. Looking for revenue neutrality between the new GST and the old indirect taxes is an incomplete vision.

Looking for *budget neutrality* in the induction of GST, instead of *revenue neutrality*, would have been better.

In addition, fundamental tax reforms always involves giving up revenues in the short term and making it up on higher GDP growth. Consider the reduction of Indian protectionism: There was an immediate loss of customs tax revenues, but more global integration resulted in higher GDP growth, which fed back into income tax and VAT. GST should similarly be seen as a structural GDP-enhancing reform. We should have been comfortable running up larger budget deficits in the short run. An insistence on achieving revenue neutrality in the short run was a mistake.

Not all deficits are bad

Every now and then, we get unhappy when there is a large bilateral trade deficit between country i and country j. As an example, Donald Trump has expressed concern about the bilateral US–China trade deficit. It is easy to slip into nationalism and nativism through the lens of the bilateral trade deficit.

However, international trade should always be seen in its entirety. The US imports cheap manufacturing from China, uses this to produce high-end services, and exports these to affluent countries. What must be judged is the overall trade balance of a country, and never a bilateral trade balance.

Some people view a large current account deficit as a failure to export. However, the macroeconomic identity teaches us that the current account deficit is the gap between investment and savings.

When the investment of a country is larger than the savings of a country, this shows up as a current account deficit. If the financial system is allocating resources well, investment results in GDP growth, and it is better to import capital. A reduced pace of investment is worse than a large current account deficit, where we are importing capital for the purpose of investment.

The legitimate concern about the import of capital lies in ensuring that there is a high degree of diversification. Capital should be coming into the country from a heterogeneous class of players, through many different financial channels, into many different kinds of domestic assets. This diversification will generate sustainable financing of the current account deficit. Once this is achieved, there is no difficulty associated with investment that is larger than savings.

On a similar note, for many people, large fiscal deficits are always a bad thing. The analysis of the fiscal deficit must, however, be placed in two contexts.

Macro policy is working well when the fiscal deficit is highly dynamic and managed in a responsible way. In most years, there should be a small primary surplus, i.e., in most years we should be paying down debt and the debt/GDP ratio should be declining. This establishes fiscal soundness. Once this is in place, a sharp enlargement of the deficit occasionally, when the economy is faring badly, is perfectly healthy and legitimate.

This is predicated on the underlying fiscal soundness. The government should be highly solvent. In India, we should aspire for a credit rating that is better than the edges of speculative grade. This involves putting an end to conscription of savings through financial repression, running a small primary surplus in most years, sound fiscal and macro data, etc.

Once fiscal soundness is achieved, the ability to rarely run a large fiscal deficit, e.g., as was done by the UK in 2008–09, is the triumph of a fiscal policy that stabilizes. We should not reflexively think that all big fiscal deficits are bad. It is *chronic* deficits that are a bad thing; in most years, we should have a (correctly measured) primary surplus, and the (correctly measured) debt/GDP ratio should decline.

One tool, one objective

A valuable element of the economics toolkit is 'the assignment principle', which comes from the great economist Jan Tinbergen. Each tool of policy can cater to one objective. We have to assign an objective to each instrument. After that has been done, that instrument has been 'used up'. It cannot then pursue multiple objectives. This is a simple and powerful idea. It helps cut through numerous conundrums in the field of public policy, where failure is inevitable when n instruments are being used to chase m objectives, but $m > n$.

The most famous example of the assignment principle lies in monetary policy. There was a time when we thought that RBI would pursue multiple objectives. Now we understand that the most that RBI can do for us is deliver low and stable inflation. Hence, the RBI Act was amended in 2016 to enshrine CPI inflation of 4 per cent as the objective of RBI. Once this has been done, it is no longer possible for RBI to pursue auxiliary objectives such as the level of the rupee, export promotion, financing of small and medium enterprises (SMEs), promotion of cashless transactions, etc.

On a similar note, there is a certain degree of mission creep and confusion about NREGS. Is this an anti-poverty programme, or is it about creating rural infrastructure? Going by the assignment principle, it is best to think about NREGS as a pure poverty programme, and not burden it with additional objectives.

The assignment principle links to some of the thinking in the 1950s about the role of the Ministry of Finance versus the

Planning Commission. The idea at the time was that the Ministry of Finance would think on a one-year budget horizon, wielding the instrument of the budget, while the Planning Commission would think about deeper issues in public policy formulation wielding an array of different instruments. Now that the Planning Commission has been disbanded, we will need to build a medium-term budget system that incorporates both points of view. There is a need to clearly define the role and function of NITI Aayog in this new environment, so as to fill these gaps in the mainstream policy apparatus.

The assignment principle shows a founding defect in the International Monetary Fund (IMF).[2] At the core of the IMF is a 'quota regime'. This is a single instrument which aims to pursue three goals. Quotas determine the contribution of countries to the IMF. Quotas determine the access by members to the IMF's resources. Finally, quotas determine voting power within the IMF. By placing three problems—contribution, access, voting—within one instrument, we have created a problem. An arrangement of quotas which appears sound with respect to any one objective will appear wrong on the others.

Why do organizations find themselves in situations with more objectives than instruments? Jan Tinbergen's assignment principle has been around since the 1960s; surely, everyone knows it by now.

Public choice theory predicts that public organizations will *favour* multiple objectives as this gives reduced accountability. Clarity of purpose is efficient for the principal and not the agent. It is our job, as policy thinkers, to hold the metaphoric feet of every agency to the fire, and hold it accountable for a narrow set of goals associated with a narrow set of powers. This requires drafting modern laws that clearly articulate objectives and establish commensurate accountability mechanisms.

Formal process helps

In the informal ways of policymaking, the risk of failing to pose the right question is greater. In the conventional informal ways, many things are talked about orally, a vague picture is assembled of a problem, and actions are proposed, yielding a three-page note.

The formal discipline of policymaking generates improvements by forcing a due process. We are forced to write down: What is the problem that we are trying to solve? Are we able to demonstrate that there is a market failure? Do we have an instrument through which the identified problem can be addressed? Has this instrument already been used up to pursue other objectives?

Formal documentation is required, before every move in public policy, which conducts such analysis. Without such formal statements, we run the risk of degenerating into shifting goalposts: An objective is stated, it fails to work out, the authorities then claim that the true objective was a different one.

Summing up

The first stumbling block in the policy process is posing the right question. When a policymaker wants large resources in order to run subsidy programmes, the right objective to pursue is *tax revenue* and not the *tax/GDP ratio*. The field of economic policy is littered with analytical fallacies that have set off entire policy communities in the wrong direction.

Jan Tinbergen's 'assignment principle' teaches us that one policy instrument can only be used for one objective. Monetary policy has only one instrument—the short-term interest rate—and can hence deliver only one objective, e.g., the targeted inflation rate.

A great deal of policy confusion in India stems from placing multiple objectives upon policy initiatives.

Public choice theory predicts that officials will favour multiple objectives so as to avoid accountability. A publicly stated and clear objective, on each policy initiative, improves the policy process.

15

Taking decentralization seriously

The Constitution of India is imbued with federalism: it envisions India as a union of states. It cut up all the work of government into three lists. The Union government would deal with List 1 questions, the states would deal with List 2 questions, and the two sides would amicably figure out how to deal with the concurrent list.

India is a vast and diverse country. The most salient problems vary from one place to another, and the most effective solution varies from one place to another. The constitutional scheme is a wise one. What constitutes a good solution for education policy in Kerala (where schools are closing down as the number of children is declining) is likely to differ strongly from the corresponding solution in Uttar Pradesh.

When schools are financed through the Union government's scheme *Sarva Shiksha Abhiyaan*, however, there is considerable standardization all across the country. Such centralization of policy design, at the Union government, has come about in numerous areas. In many respects, we have deviated from the constitutional scheme, and gone too far in centralizing power in New Delhi.

In the US, the phrase 'laboratories of democracy' has come to be used about states. This emphasizes the role of democratic processes in multiple states coming up with different policy strategies, out of which knowledge and experience are improved for the entire country. If there was only one powerful Central government, these gains from experimentation would be lost. In each field, 'regional role models' should emerge, e.g., perhaps southern states might look up to the solutions adopted in Karnataka on urban water supply.

We wince every time the expression 'Central government' is used in the popular discourse as this is suggestive of central planning and an exaggerated conception of the role of New Delhi. The phrase 'Union government' is an accurate description of the constitutional scheme, and a more modest phrase.

The problems of intra-India disparity

India is a continental economy, and there is very high heterogeneity within the country. As Lant Pritchett says, the ratio of the richest to the poorest parts of India is much like the ratio of the richest parts of Latin America divided by the poorest parts of Africa.

There is heterogeneity about conventional economic measures such as income and capabilities. There is also heterogeneity of political and social preferences, where the south and the west are making more progress on social issues such as the agency of women.

We may have once had a mental model that once economic development takes root in India, intra-India heterogeneity will subside. So far, there is little evidence of this convergence taking place.[1] There are other elements of the international experience, such as the poverty traps in the US or Italy, which have persisted for hundreds of years despite attempts by policymakers to change things. While we should desire convergence, we should not assume that it is afoot.

The heterogeneity of economic and social development, across the regions of India, generates heterogeneity in the public policy pathways desired by different groups of people. A policy position that is well liked in Uttar Pradesh may not be liked in Kerala, and vice versa. This creates conflict in a centralized public policy process.

These problems are addressed in a federal structure at three levels. The first involves reducing the extent to which decisions are taken in the Union government. While monetary and defence policies need to be done by the Union government, policies on drinking water and elementary schools need not. The preferences of Kerala's population, on the role and status of women, will diverge from those in Uttar Pradesh, and this should play out into policy thinking in Kerala. Kerala may create rules requiring that half of all policemen should be women before this is done in Uttar Pradesh.

The optimal design of processes *within* government also varies with locale. As an example, the price of a schoolteacher in Kerala should diverge from that in Bihar. The Mumbai municipality should have different internals when compared with the Kolkata municipality. By imposing uniformity in the working of government, we inevitably reduce the quality of working of government.

The second involves creating structures that favour migration. When wages are higher in Kerala, or when women have greater freedom in Kerala, this creates an incentive for people to migrate from Uttar Pradesh to Kerala. Alongside this, free movement within the country of capital and enterprise helps exploit the 'equalizing differences' feature of the market economy. If labour is cheap in Uttar Pradesh, firms may like to reduce costs by investing in UP. This process is limited by the extent to which basic public goods in UP are of acceptable quality and the extent to which goods and services move freely through the country.

The third involves fiscal transfers through which the per capita resources available to the state government in poor states are higher than the per capita taxation that is done in those states. This creates the opportunity for local politicians to undertake actions that make progress on policy problems within a larger budget set than would be feasible if local tax revenues were the only resource base.

Rethinking state and local government

The subsidiarity principle asserts that a function should be placed at the lowest level of government where it can possibly be performed. Mosquito control programmes can potentially be run by the Union government, a state government, or the municipality. By the subsidiarity principle, these should lie at the municipality as this is the lowest possible level.

This makes sense because at the local level, there is the best local knowledge in prioritizing problems and devising solutions. There is also greater accountability, as voters are closest to the local government.

Implicit in the subsidiarity principle is a great value for local knowledge. Social systems are not physical systems. In physics, Newton's laws work everywhere, but social systems have complex interrelationships that vary strongly with culture, institutions and history. An expert on urban transport policy in London is not an expert on urban transport policy in Pune. An expert on urban transport policy in Pune is not an expert on urban transport policy in Patna. Each place has its own rhythm, and we require deep local knowledge in every corner of the world in order to understand problems and solve them. In his book

Seeing Like a State, the great political scientist, James C. Scott, has used the word *metis* to convey deep experiential local knowledge.[2] Each of us has to study our backyard, build knowledge about it, and solve problems in it.

This approach has far-reaching consequences.

It implies that on List 2 and List 3 questions, states have to develop their own capabilities for policy planning and execution. Each state will have to cultivate its own ecosystem of intellectuals, think tanks, staff that supports legislators, debates about legislation, and policy capabilities in the bureaucracy.

Health policy in Madhya Pradesh is as complex as health policy in Germany, considering that the two countries have a similar population. This suggests that the health policy capabilities in Madhya Pradesh—data sets, researchers, think tanks, government— need to match the richness of what is found in Germany. A similar development of capabilities in the policy process is required in the large cities. After all, large cities in India match the population of many countries.

Conversely, the excessive concentration of these policy capabilities in New Delhi will have to diffuse out to locations all over India. Our institution, the NIPFP, will ultimately require offices in many states, and need to get deeply involved in public finance and policy at the level of a few major states and a few large cities.

While the constitutional scheme gives considerable latitude to the Union government on List 3 questions, the climate of opinion should move towards an environment where the Union government comes into these only sparingly.

In the field of mineral resources, there has been a long history of tension between the Union government and state government. An attractive solution is for the Union government to completely vacate this space and leave it to state governments.

Smaller states, cities as states

Uttar Pradesh is a vast and heterogeneous state. It may make sense for it to be divided into multiple smaller states, each of which would then find solutions that are the most appropriate for local conditions. Jairam Ramesh has emphasized that such actions can be taken by the Parliament acting alone.[3]

If the biggest cities become states, as has been done in China, this would help urban governance. This may be particularly appropriate as, in the future, the identity of many individuals will be tied closer to a home city than to a home state. Participation in local politics will become more natural if it is organized around a city rather than a state.

In the modern economy, cities are the engine of growth. Sustained growth in India is critically linked to achieving sound urban governance. If cities are empowered with their own tax base (by becoming states), there would be incentive compatibility in governance. City governments would issue bonds, improve local public goods, which would foster greater consumption in the city, which would feed back to the tax revenues of the city through GST, and these tax revenues would be used for debt servicing.[4]

Decentralization within states

The subsidiarity principle is the essential foundation for cities that have local political arrangements for local public goods. When we see the city governance of New York or London or Sydney, we see a large array of functions being placed at the city level, which are found in India at the Union or state governments.

The slogan of policy thinkers in this field is the need to place 'funds, functions and functionaries' at the local level. While a great deal of progress has been made in Indian tax policy, one pillar which has yet to fall into place is a foundation of tax revenues for cities. The logical place for this is to carve out a component of the GST associated with a place. The GST is based on a consumption principle. It is collected at the point of consumption. It is easy to count the GST associated with consumption in (say) Aurangabad. It would make sense to transfer a fraction of this GST revenue—attributable to consumption in Aurangabad—to the city government of Aurangabad.

State-level politicians, who preach the cause of greater autonomy from the Union government, need to consistently carry this through and devolve full powers to the city governments within their states.

The limits of decentralization

Greater decentralization is criticized on the grounds that there is low capability in many state and city governments. This is partly a consequence of our historical journey.

In an age where the Planning Commission and the Union government dominated decisions about (say) education in Maharashtra, this inevitably gave an atrophying of policy capabilities in Maharashtra. When policy thinking was centralized at the Union government, we got more field orientation at state and city governments. When the political/bureaucratic system at states and cities is asked to play policy functions, at first, there will be a gap in capabilities. As decentralization progresses, policy capabilities can be built in organizations which may presently appear to have a mere field orientation.

While shifting power to states and to cities is desirable, political system reforms will also be required. As an example, the chief minister of the typical Indian state faces little by way of checks and balances: winning one assembly election yields extreme power.

The five pillars of checks and balances—data, intellectuals, media, legislature, judiciary—all work poorly upon state governments. Strengthening of these checks and balances needs to take place alongside the traditional decentralization agenda.

Once these political system reforms are implemented, the pressure of accountability to local voters can be stronger in states and cities than is the case with the Union government. A voter sees a street lamp that does not work, and is able to translate this into an opinion about the performance of the city government. In contrast, the policy actions of the Union government are largely out of sight and out of mind.

While decentralization is a sound approach, there are two areas which we should be careful about.

The first issue is about problems that require coordination *between* states. As an example, the transportation system requires design at the level of the country, about how highways and gas pipelines and ports will be placed. The Union government can play a leadership role for this planning.

The second issue is about the possibility of severe capacity constraints in a state or a city. There is the possibility of a geographical region falling into a vicious cycle, where talented people leave, which gives a shortage of skills in the public policy process, which exacerbates elite flight. We need to keep a watch for these vicious cycles and have a set of strategies to address them.

Summing up

India is a continent, with very high heterogeneity. There is no one answer to policy questions, on most problems. The fact that many Union Territories—run by the Union government—work better than many states should not lead us to question decentralization. Decentralization of government helps produce local answers to local problems. The 'subsidiarity principle' asserts that a function of government is best performed by the lowest possible level of government where it can be performed.

The Constitution of India is imbued with federalism. The evolution of the republic shows an inappropriate extent of centralization, of schemes that are designed by the Union government and rolled out everywhere. The phrase 'Union government' is preferable to 'Central government' as the latter suggests greater control. Similarly, there is an inappropriate level of control of cities and villages by the capital of the state government. The appropriate role of the Union government lies in coordination problems (e.g., the design of infrastructure networks that cut across states) and in addressing poverty traps where the conventional feedback loops of liberal democracy have broken down.

In a truly federal structure, state and local governments will have to design their own schemes. This requires capacity building in public policy at states and cities all over India.

For decentralization to work, the political system at the level of the state and the city requires reform, in order to achieve adequate checks and balances and dispersion of power.

Part IV

The art

16

Evolutionary change for society, revolutionary change for government

The pursuit of life, liberty and happiness without interference

We must create an environment in which the public has stability. Stability means many things. Stability means the confidence of planning a life, of starting a family, knowing that there will be no upheaval in society for a lifetime, which means a horizon of eighty years for a twenty-year-old adult. Stability means the certainty that one will not face violence for the next eighty years. Stability means the ability to create savings without fearing expropriation by the state or a private person. Stability means being able to embark on a business plan knowing that no disruption in the political or economic environment will arise.

These are primordial values in their own right. We must value such stability and endeavour to achieve it. This requires a respect for each individual in society. In public policy, we should not undertake actions that will disrupt the lives of the people on a large scale.

It is all too easy, in the world of public policy, to slip into the mode of directing people on how to lead their lives. But the pursuit of happiness by each person is best achieved when the state creates conditions of stability and vanishes into the background.

The ideal non violent state will be an ordered anarchy.

Mahatma Gandhi

At its best, the state should not impinge on the consciousness of individuals. People should have the ability to pursue their own values, with complete concentration, for decades on end, without intrusion from the government. One may wish to be a painter, another may wish to be a trader, for each of them there should be the opportunity to be absorbed in the desired zone for decades, without noticing the existence or actions of the state.

Social engineering is inappropriate

This pursuit of non-intrusiveness, stability and order has one powerful implication: We should favour small impacts upon the lives of the people over large ones. Social engineering, even if for ostensibly noble goals, should not be attempted. Every political system has Jacobin elements, which are attracted to transformative projects, that need to be kept in check.

Even if we were comfortable with interfering in the lives of others, large-scale schemes of social engineering have a long track record of failure. Social systems are very complex and outcomes are generally greatly different from those that the planners may have desired. Social engineers have, all too often, ended up inducing a capricious set of upheavals in the lives of the people. There is value in a precautionary principle here: We should be very concerned about initiating a move that will cause harm. For these reasons, even if social engineering were desirable, it is infeasible.

We see social engineering as infeasible and inadvisable, we prefer gradualism. When a government tries to redesign society, to create a new man, this is overreach.

If economists could manage to get themselves thought of as humble, competent people on a level with dentists, that would be splendid.

John Maynard Keynes

The demonetization episode was a large shock upon the economy. Even if a cost–benefit analysis showed that the benefits outweighed the costs, the fact that it was a large disruption should have been a consideration in the decision.

China's one-child policy illustrates many themes of this book. It was inappropriate for a government to embark on it, because it constituted social engineering. It was also inappropriate as it involved a high degree of intrusion into the personal space of individuals. In the event, the one-child policy has induced serious problems for China. It illustrates how social engineering often goes wrong: We know too little in order to safely meddle into human society in most areas other than market failures.

This is not a defence of the status quo

Liberal democracies have achieved far-reaching change through small changes over long time periods. We applaud these changes. We favour a world where society evolves in far-reaching ways.

The values and imagination of the *people* should drive the changes of the world, rather than the values and objectives of a few central planners. Respect for each individual takes us to this notion of self-determination, which views the evolution of society as the outcome of millions of thoughts and actions by the people, rather than by a small group of rulers.

Communicate till it hurts

This pursuit of non-intrusiveness, stability and order has a second implication: a bias in favour of communication. We in the world of policy should always copiously talk about what is being done. We should prepare people for what is coming. We should never give out bad surprises. All new policy decisions should be discussed in the public domain, and once a decision is taken, the effective date should be many months or years away. This reduces the extent to which the policy decision induces instability.

Too often, we see a big policy change that was planned in secrecy, and then there is an uproar, and then we get a policy reversal. It would have been much better to have done the developmental work in the public eye. Sometimes, the early feedback would have been so negative that the decision may never have been taken. In general, people react better when they are adequately sensitized.

Revolutionary change for government

When it comes to society, we should respect every person going about her daily life in a stable way based on her own search for happiness. Policymakers should not be the source of upheavals, of crises, of disruption.

A very different approach is required when it comes to redesigning *government systems*. As policymakers, we should be quite willing to ask civil servants to do new things. There is no need to respect the stability of the life of a civil servant. There is a need to constantly redesign organizations, rearrange turf, design better operating procedures, etc., to push public bodies to higher levels of performance.

As a thumb rule, each doubling of GDP (in real terms) calls for a fairly far-reaching change in the organization structure of government. It calls for a substantial rethinking of the boundaries and functions of departments and agencies, and of government processes. In India, most of the organization design seen today dates back to the time when India had one-tenth of the present GDP. Greater energy is called for, in organization design in government.

We should prioritize the good night's sleep of the populace but not of civil servants.[1] We should pursue revolutionary change for government structures, but evolutionary change for the people.

It is when the state interacts with private persons—either by coercing them or by setting up an expenditure programme—that we should be cautious in our movement, and undertake cost–benefit analysis at every step of the way. When reorganizing management structures and organization designs in government, there is little role for formal cost–benefit analysis.

Example 18: Why did India build a large public sector after Independence?

There is an interesting connection between these debates and the strategy adopted by India in 1947, to have public sector companies occupying the 'commanding heights' of the economy. Numerous public sector companies were then created. Was this an inappropriate attempt at bringing about a revolutionary change? With the benefit of hindsight, we can perhaps understand and interpret the actions of those policymakers.

The key argument perhaps lay in a 'big push' that was required to solve the coordination problem in economic development.

The early industrialization required a large number of different elements of the economy to come about, and there was a coordination problem. The aluminium factory would not come about as the entrepreneur considering that project could not be convinced that another entrepreneur would surely build an aircraft factory, and vice versa. The big push by the government created a skeleton around which the market economy could get going in an incremental fashion. Key staff persons in most private banks have an employment history in public sector banks. Similarly, Hindustan Aeronautics Limited (HAL) incubated aerospace knowledge in India, and Indian Drugs and Pharmaceuticals Limited (IDPL) alumni laid the foundations of the private Indian drugs industry.

There was possibly a political economy logic in the establishment of public sector undertakings (PSUs) also, in the limited social base of entrepreneurship. In 1947, female literacy was only 6 per cent, and very few people were available to play senior management and entrepreneurial roles. In a purely private entrepreneurship scenario, we can potentially envision an Indian capitalism that was dominated by a narrow set of ethnicities. This may have gone on to create significant social problems, analogous to what was seen in Indonesia. It can be argued that the early decades with public sector companies helped diffuse entrepreneurial and managerial skills across a broad-based elite.

This is not a defence of public sector companies more broadly. Once the early private economy came together, it was important for the government to shift from supplanting the private sector to regulating the private sector, and this was not done. When public sector companies and their parent departments set up barriers against imports and against the entry of private firms, this was one of the most harmful things for the economy. But for our understanding of where we are, it is important to know the logic of where we came from.

Summing up

A good society is one in which individuals plan and live on their own terms, in a state of confidence over long time horizons. The purpose of public policy is to create the enabling conditions for such a life. As an example, the right way to structure monetary policy is a formal inflation-targeting system, as it rules out inflation surprises, and makes personal financial planning possible over multi-decade horizons.

The best framework of public policy is one in which the state impinges upon the lives of individuals as little as possible. This is not a defence of the status quo. Society can and should evolve, gradually, through the thoughts and actions of the people. The state should not engage in social engineering, i.e., it should take no leadership role in the evolution of society.

Non-intrusiveness, stability and order is fostered by better communication. The government must say what it will do and then do what it just said. There should be no surprises.

Within the structures of government, however, it is permissible to undertake large-scale reorganizations. We do not need to bring stability to the life of a civil servant.

17

Cross the river by feeling the stones

The phrase, from Deng Xiaoping, has gone deep into the world of public policy. What exactly does it mean to cross the river by feeling the stones? There are three elements to translating this idea into tangible policy strategies.

Element 1: No silver bullets

There is sometimes a temptation in thinking that what is required is one big bang and then the problem is solved. This is never the case. No problem is susceptible to a big one-time policy effort.

In every successful policy effort, there will be a large number of decisions, and iterative refinement based on empirical experience. We have to plan for sustained work over many long years rather than one big-bang reform. This calls for capacity-building process of a stable team within government, the organizational structure within which that team will work, and a supporting intelligentsia outside government. If any of these three elements are neglected, an initiative is likely to falter after the big bang.

As an example, the reforms of the Indian financial markets consisted of analytical work through the 1980s, and the establishment of a non-statutory SEBI in 1988. This work leaped into high priority after the Harshad Mehta scandal of 1991–92. This involved the establishment of institutional infrastructure with the closure of the office of the controller for capital issues, establishing the Capital Markets Division in the Ministry of Finance, legislating the SEBI Act, setting up the National Stock Exchange (NSE), and the emergence of data sets and an academic community in the field. This combination—a strong team within government, organizational structures in government, and a supporting intelligentsia outside government—was able to work on a sustained basis from 1992 onward. This gave fundamental progress over the 1992-2001 period.

Similarly, the 'R group' reforms in the petroleum sector took place through a stable team over a six-year period.

Policy proposals such as demonetization have a certain silver-bullet appeal. We are encouraged to take one bold decision, and after that the problem of black money will be solved. Similarly, it is claimed that the HR problems of government will be solved by bringing in 500 lateral recruits. Real-world public policy success is generally found in more wonkish territory.[1]

Element 2: Participatory and therefore slow process

Policymaking that is done by a few people in government, under conditions of secrecy, is inadvisable as it lacks democratic legitimacy. It also yields poor results. No small team knows the answers. Wider participation, from experts and from practitioners, improves policy work. In addition, the process of participation seeds the private sector with a sense of what is coming, so they can develop business strategies ahead of time.

The sound process of drafting legal instruments consists of the following:

1. Clearly identifying a problem that needs to be solved,
2. Demonstrating that there is market failure,
3. Using a systematic process (cost–benefit analysis) to identify the lowest cost intervention that would address the problem,
4. Drafting a legal instrument that expresses the chosen best intervention,
5. Releasing these draft documents for public discussion,
6. Responding to all substantive points that are made through public comment, including modifying the legal instrument in response to some comments which proved to be correct,
7. A senior-level discussion about the entire documentation packet, and the consequential modifications to the legal instrument,
8. Releasing the final legal instrument with a future date on which it becomes effective,
9. Conducting an ex post review, three years later.

This process for drafting law induces the institutionalized application of mind, through which legal instruments are slowly drafted, one by one, that genuinely solve problems, and earn the respect and trust of the private sector.

At present, one state agency in India—the Insolvency and Bankruptcy Board of India (IBBI)—uses such a procedure. Nowhere else is it used. In the absence of such a thorough process, policymaking is tantamount to crossing the river based on ideology or political compulsions. When law is drafted without such a careful and slow process, the private sector sees the government as a source of regulatory risk.

The sound process described above is encoded into the draft Indian Financial Code (IFC) as the process prescribed, through which financial regulators would write regulations. This is similar to the methods applied in mature democracies, where parliamentary law requires agencies to work in this fashion. As an example, in the US, the federal Administrative Procedures Act (APA), 1946, prescribes such a machinery that must be used by all federal agencies.

Element 3: Small moves coupled with feedback loops

Experimentation is valuable. Too often in India, interventions are unveiled without the requisite level of knowledge about social systems. That knowledge can be slowly constructed through a systematic process of experimentation.

As an example, suppose SEBI believes that there are problems in the world of high-frequency trading, and suppose there is an intent of unveiling an intervention into the world of high-frequency trading. SEBI could choose a set of twenty randomly selected medium-sized firms, and the intervention could be rolled out for a period of one year for these twenty firms. This would permit a comparison between these 'treated' stocks and a set of similar 'control' stocks where no intervention was made, to assess the extent to which the intervention was useful. Once this is known, the intervention can either be scaled up or rolled back, based on empirical evidence about what works. This is analogous to the 'beta testing' that private firms do, where new products are tested out before they are rolled out more widely.

In the US, the securities regulator, the Securities and Exchange Commission (SEC), regularly undertakes policy experimentation in this fashion.[2] As an example of the difficulties in India, consider the problem of cash-settled versus physically settled derivatives. Single stock derivatives were cash-settled from their launch in 2001 onward, and this system had worked well. In 2017, SEBI decided to force these to be shifted from cash settlement to physical settlement.

This is a major action, which has a substantial impact upon the life of market participants. The decision was taken without identifying a market failure, measurement or experimentation. There was no ex post review, so we do not know the magnitude of the adverse impact of this decision upon market quality.

The approach to experimentation is one valuable feature of the Chinese experience. The word *ShiDian* is used in China for 'Policy Experimentation' or 'Policy Piloting'. This refers to political–administrative procedures that discover and test novel instruments and thereby propel policy innovation or institutional adaptation. The Chinese have engaged in spatially, sectorally and temporally limited policy trials so as to reduce the risk and cost of major reforms.

Abhijit Banerjee, Esther Duflo and others have emphasized the importance of 'randomized control trials' in learning about economics. We see this as being a key part of the economic policy toolkit, in the process of iterative refinement.

Example 19: Bans on plastic packaging materials

There is a global problem with the use of plastic in packaging. This plastic is creating litter in the natural environment, particularly in places where the handling of solid waste is weak. Plastics are not biodegradable and the residue will linger for 500 years.

As a consequence, in 2018, single-use plastics were banned in Mumbai.[3] This is a big disruption for the packaged foods industry, which has come to value the impermeability of plastic as a tool for avoiding bacterial and insect infestations in food.

It would perhaps have made sense for the government to start by experimenting with these bans in small towns, and simultaneously establish a data-gathering and research process to measure the impacts. Perhaps the scaling up could be from a few towns to a district to a group of districts. At each step, evidence is required before making the next move. The packaging industry would also have time to develop and scale up plastic-free alternatives.

Policy reversibility

> *Do things that you can undo.*
>
> James C. Scott

In the US, one in twenty-five people who were sentenced to death were, in fact, innocent.[4] The prosecution claimed, and the judiciary agreed, that these persons were guilty of heinous crimes, beyond all reasonable doubt. And yet, in fact, one in twenty-five people killed by the state were innocent. Under conditions of low state capacity, this error rate is likely to be higher. Death cannot be undone. We in India should be even more hesitant about the death penalty as compared with thinkers in the US.

Where is greater reversibility found? The presence of measurement systems helps. If an action yields an impact that can be well measured, there is a better chance of seeing a mistake and reversing it. In contrast, when measurement systems are absent, policymaking is fraught with greater risk.

The distinction between 'first-generation reforms' (stroke-of-the-pen reforms) versus 'second-generation reforms' (those that involve establishing complex government organizations) is useful here. It may be possible to reverse first-generation reforms, when it is understood that there was a mistake. It is harder to close down a bureaucracy once it has been created. Second-generation reforms are more irreversible.

Irreversibility is thus inherent to some things (e.g., death of a person), is greater when measurement is lacking, and is greater when the action involves establishing an implementation structure in government. These are the areas where greater caution is required in state intervention.

Summing up

There are no silver bullets. The reforms that matter are complex multi-year journeys that require a large policy community.

Participatory policymaking works better than small groups working in secret.

The ideal mechanism is to have measurement systems, and make small moves. Based on the feedback from the measurement, the small moves can be refined and modified as part of a larger strategy.

Do things that you can undo.

Beware of the things that you cannot undo. When the measurement is weak, mistakes will not be caught, and there is a need for greater caution. Stroke-of-the-pen reforms are easier to reverse, but when a government organization has been set up, it is hard to undo, and there is a need for greater caution.

Many a mistake will not be undone, so there is wisdom in intervening less.

18

Adapting from the international experience?

In mature countries, one element of the privacy problem is well established: the need to restrict government access to information about individuals, i.e., to tie down surveillance by the government into rule-of-law procedures and limit the extent of surveillance. This has evolved in the UK and in Europe over centuries. The conflict between state access to personal information, and human freedom, is particularly seen in the authoritarian governments of the twentieth century. This is the prime problem in the field of privacy, and is a largely settled matter in mature democracies.

In recent years, there is fresh concern about the abuse of information about individuals by firms such as Facebook. European policymakers have pushed to the frontiers of the field with the 'General Data Protection Regulation' (GDPR) in the EU.

A simple reading of the contemporary literature on privacy in mature democracies is, then, quite misleading. Such a reader would see the bulk of the contemporary policy discourse as being the debates around GDPR and its enforcement. A reader of this literature would think that Facebook is a major problem in the field of privacy. Policy recommendations in India may flow from this study of the international experience that we have to block information access about Indians by Facebook using a legal instrument on the lines of GDPR. This position would be treated warmly by persons in India who are hostile to foreign companies.

Such transplantation of the international experience would, however, be incorrect for two reasons. First, access to personal information by the state is far more dangerous for individuals as compared with access to this information by private firms. Second, a law like GDPR makes assumptions about UK or EU state capacity. To favour creating a new privacy regulator that will coerce private firms on the question of privacy, without the checks and balances prevalent in the EU, would work out poorly in India.[1] In the Indian discourse, we have rapidly run ahead to proposing criminal sanctions, in the hands of the proposed 'Data Protection Authority'.

The interesting policy question on privacy in India is not about how to transplant UK common law or the EU's GDPR into India. The prime question in the Indian privacy debate is about reining in intrusions into the privacy of individuals by the Indian state. This requires understanding the existing surveillance system and bringing it up to the qualities of state surveillance seen in healthy democracies.[2] Alongside this, we need to ask: *What is a modest and minimal scale of coercion of private firms, to increase the privacy of individuals, which are feasible under Indian levels of state capacity, which deliver the bulk of the gains?*

There is a tremendous prestige associated with the successful institutions of the first world. However, we should not be the sorcerer's apprentice, we should not engage in what the economist Lant Pritchett calls 'isomorphic mimicry', we should not mechanically copy the international experience.

It is always interesting to review international experience. But the core thinking about public policy in India must always be grounded in first-principles reasoning that is deeply grounded in the Indian institutional context.

The policy thinker needs to envision how component X will work, in the context of all the other elements of the Indian landscape that are left intact. The policy analysis should envision how many policy alternatives will work—when placed in the Indian landscape—and then propose the possibilities that will work out best.

The problem with simple transplantation

Every bad policy has been adopted in at least one good country.

Ashok Desai

When faced with a policy question—e.g., the working of agricultural markets—one easy path is to do a literature survey of what advanced economies are doing. As an example, the policy thinker may study the working of agricultural markets in the US, the UK, Australia and Canada. Some combination of the institutional apparatus seen in these countries might then be proposed as a policy reform for India.

In this age of Google searches, many policy notes in India are written in this fashion. A problem is proposed, the experience of a few mature market economies is reviewed, a few countries are identified where the outcomes are good, and some remix of the solutions adopted in those countries is proposed. This is particularly taking place with young law students and people who have studied outside India.

We would argue that this is a faulty way to do policy thinking.

Go beyond description to understand why things work

Practitioner knowledge from other countries is generally of a descriptive nature. A UK insolvency practitioner can describe how the UK insolvency process works. But the problem in policy analysis is that of going below the 'thin description' to understand *why* something works. What are the incentives that hold the pieces together? What is the combination of norms, laws and enforcement that produce good behaviour?

For these reasons, practitioner knowledge has limited value in policy thinking. As Lant Pritchett says, a First World policy practitioner is a bit like a New York taxi driver. The taxi driver knows how to perform rides and get paid, but has no conception of *why* the taxi system of New York works. Policy institutions in advanced economies have been refined for hundreds of years, and most people in close proximity to those institutions lack an awareness of *why* things work. To do public policy in India, we need to think like an engineer (what are all the moving parts, and the incentives that hold them together) and not a driver (a practitioner who operates in a given institutional apparatus).

Seeing the invisible infrastructure at work

When we look at one narrow piece of a policy puzzle, e.g., in the health system in France, we fail to see the 'invisible infrastructure' upon which it depends. A large number of elements of state policy interact with the visible decisions of health policy to add up to the successful French health system. A front-line worker in the French health system does her job reasonably well because there is invisible infrastructure of the civil servants HR process through which she will face sanctions for not doing her job well. A visitor to France who focuses on studying the health system may admire many design elements of the French health system. But these are often not transferable into a different context, where the invisible infrastructure is lacking. Visitors tend to see elements of health-system design in France and not notice this invisible infrastructure.

As an example, we in India look at the US Securities and Exchange Commission (SEC) and think of it as roughly analogous to SEBI. We often fail to see the capability of the US *judicial* system, through which 'Administrative Law Judges' (ALJs) hear cases brought by the US SEC. Hearings at the SEC are conducted by *judges*, not by SEC employees, and the separation of powers at the SEC is protected. This is made possible by the invisible infrastructure of a well-functioning legal system. We in India have an inferior arrangement, where the SEBI Act does not enshrine the separation of powers. SEBI employees who also perform legislative and executive functions, and lack judicial independence, are performing the judicial function. The lack of this invisible infrastructure—separation of powers and judicial independence—results in lower capability at SEBI when compared with the US SEC.

Similarly, securities law is only one small part of commercial law, and many schemes that break laws go beyond violations of securities law. We tend to not see the key role played by the law enforcement apparatus of the state of New York, and the US Department of Justice 'Southern District of New York (SDNY)' office. The SEC is one piece of a complex policy apparatus. When we look at the SEC alone, we tend to not understand the remainder of this apparatus and the role played by it.

In the US, ordinary courts work well, lying in court is dangerous, and lawyers, investigators, prosecutors and judges have high capabilities. All this is the invisible infrastructure that shapes the working of the US SEC, which is lacking in India.

When we read policy papers and blog articles which engage in contemporary policy debate in advanced countries, they tend to focus on the frontiers of *their* policy environments. The US has the Food and Drugs Administration (FDA) that broadly works well, and standing on that foundation there are fervent debates about a contemporary problem such as (say) medical implants. If we transplant that worldview into India, we tend to overemphasize the problems of medical implants and underemphasize the foundations, the invisible infrastructure of a well-functioning agency like the US FDA.

Envisioning policy choices in the Indian context

Every individual state intervention takes place in a context. That context is shaped by the organization of the economy and the existing structure of state interventions. There is path dependence; the history of the country and of past actions of policymakers shapes where we are and how we see things. A policy pathway that is very successful in (say) Australia may not work in India as it is being placed in a very different setting. Envisioning how a given policy initiative will work in India requires deep knowledge of the local context. We need to visualize all the moving parts and think about how one proposed piece will fit into the larger context. This requires knowledge of history, institutions and politics.

As an example, infrastructure development is done by private persons in many parts of the world. But in India, private infrastructure development ran afoul of an array of problems that are unique to the Indian context.

As an example, we see many countries where regulators investigate violations of their law, and then initiate prosecution in ordinary courts. If that were brought into the Indian context, it may work poorly, as courts in India have many difficulties.

The international experience is a valuable source of knowledge about higher design principles. Concepts like freedom, the public discourse, human rights, the rule of law, dispersion of power, negotiation, scientific inquiry, etc., are all drawn from enlightenment values. These are universal principles. It is when we come down to practical problems (e.g., how to organize the agricultural spot market) that the portability of ideas across countries breaks down.

Example 20: Tax information network

In 2002, we proposed the Tax Information Network (TIN). This was envisaged as an IT system which stored facts about the income tax deducted at source, by the employer, and supported reconciliation with the claims by the employee about income tax already paid by her. The key insight for the TIN was related to the thought process of VAT credits, but it was relatively new when applied into the income tax context. TIN was envisaged as a system that would be run by National Securities Depository Limited (NSDL), the information utility.

When these ideas were exposed to many international experts, their first response was negative. They felt this was a complex system, and an unproven idea in the international discourse. They also alluded to the ways in which the problem does not arise in mature market economies: If an individual falsely claims taxes deducted at source, there is a small probability of getting caught and of very large penalties. Mature market economies did not have the problem that we were trying to solve.

The TIN was implemented and it was a great success. This example shows a sound approach to doing public policy in India: understand local conditions, and engage in first-principles problem solving. The solutions adopted here will often diverge from those seen elsewhere.

The way forward

We require a creative stage where we propose possible solutions. The international experience is a useful source of early-stage candidates for this funnel. As an example, when we discover that in Brazil, public sector banks have been channelled exclusively into financial inclusion work, we should think: *How interesting, could that possibly be useful in India?* We should also design from the ground up, exploring policy pathways that are unique to India.

All these candidates should go into a process of envisioning that is deeply grounded in the Indian context. In this analysis, we will often discover that a policy initiative that succeeded elsewhere is likely to fail in India, and vice versa.

The simple description of international experience, drawn from websites or from practical experience, is not useful for policy analysis in India. Sound policy analysis in India requires authenticity. It calls for deep experiential local knowledge (metis). The most valuable people in the Indian policy story are those who have authentic knowledge of India, and are able to imagine and envision how policy choices will play out in the Indian setting.

This calls for intellectual capacity in the Indian policy process. It is useful to think of three levels of intellectual capacity.

At Level 1, we come up with foolish proposals, unmoored in logic or analysis.

At Level 2, we use Google and unthinkingly copy what other countries are doing. At this stage, we will avoid mistakes like the Chinese Great Firewall which controls Internet access of the populace, which is abhorrent in all healthy democracies. It would have helped to know that no country has ever taken 86 per cent of its currency notes out of circulation in one fell swoop. It would have helped to know that no mature democracy bans cryptocurrency investment or trading. However, at this stage, we will make many mistakes, that come from inappropriate transplantation of policy designs.

At Level 3, we have acquired metis, we are authentically grounded in our backyard, and engage in creative problem solving from first principles. We would be fully knowledgeable about how the rest of the world works, we would creatively imagine new solutions on our own, we would be authentically grounded in the Indian reality in envisioning how various policy alternatives would work. We would be fully able to debate with policy thinkers elsewhere in the world, and present Indian solutions as optimal pathways under Indian conditions, while carefully warning other countries that they have to think for themselves. We would be confident about our work, but recognizing the importance of metis, we would not think that our success stories are the blueprint for other countries. The puzzle before the Indian policy community lies in nurturing the intellectual capacity for Level-3 work.

Free-riding on state capacity outside India

There are, however, some situations where international economic integration brings the possibility of simple free-riding on state capacity that exists in mature democracies.

Example 21: Regulation of food and drugs

In the field of food safety, regulation in India is weak. A market failure, asymmetric information, is present when buying boxes for food storage and transportation. The consumer cannot know the extent to which the box is made of harmful substances.

Lacking such regulatory capacity, the typical plastic box for food storage and transportation, that is sold in India, may contain harmful substances. One easy solution *for a consumer* is to buy such plastic boxes from places where food safety regulation is strong. As an example, perhaps Tupperware plastic boxes sold in India benefit from US FDA regulation on food safety. When this is done, the Indian consumer is free-riding on the US regulatory system.

In the field of medicines also, the same market failure (asymmetric information) is present. When we buy medicines in India, there is a risk that these are ineffective or counterfeit, owing to weak regulation on drug safety.

As with Tupperware plastic food storage boxes, one could think of Indian consumers buying medicines which benefit from the oversight of mature democracies and thus free-ride on their regulatory capacity. In general, a bottle of aspirin purchased in a developed country is superior to a bottle of aspirin purchased in India.

These pathways are hampered by the Drug Price Control Order (DPCO) which forces very low prices for drugs in India.

In the field of drugs and food, the US and EU authorities run active inspection programmes through which certain factories in India obtain the rights to produce drugs or food products which can be exported to the EU or the US. There is a natural opportunity for public policy in India to free-ride on this work.

Perhaps an Indian drug safety regulator can say that the privilege of selling drugs in India is limited to factories that have earned the permission to export drugs to mature democracies. Perhaps there can be a way for manufacturers to say that a certain packet of biscuits is authorized by the US FDA for sale in the US: this would improve the respect of consumers in India for the level of food safety that has been attained.

This approach also breaks down in the field of drugs owing to the Drug Price Control Order: drugs that are manufactured to FDA standards are unprofitable when sold at DPCO prices.

Example 22: Finance

In the field of finance, we have had an interesting dichotomy between firms listed purely in India vs firms that are also listed in the US. Disclosure laws in the US are better in certain critical respects, so a firm like ICICI Bank releases information owing to its American depositary receipt (ADR) listing which is not ordinarily available to Indian shareholders of banks. In addition, there is stronger liability for ADR issuers. As an example, owners of ADRs on Satyam got damages from PriceWaterhouse while the Indian owners of Satyam shares did not. Through this channel, managers associated with Indian firms that list in the US may be more careful. When this happens, Indian shareholders are free-riding on the US regulatory environment.

Example 23: Telecom

In the field of telecom, regulation is required to deal with one market failure, an externality. This is the possibility that one device may pollute the airwaves and hamper the working of another device. Regulation is required to share the scarce natural resource—the electromagnetic spectrum—and to ensure that each device works within certain rules of the game for emission of radiation. This requires a daunting level of state capacity where every device that is sold in the market needs to be tested in a government-approved laboratory to ensure that it plays fair within the rules. It is difficult to set up this state capacity.

There are other countries where this state capacity is present. As an example, the US was traditionally a large market for such devices, and the US Federal Communications Commission (FCC) does such testing. As the US market is an important one for any global devices vendor, these vendors generally obtain a US FCC approval. It is, then, possible for a regulator to free-ride on this testing process. For example, an Indian regulator can require US FCC approval for devices that are to be sold in India.

This free-riding works if and only if the policy framework for spectrum utilization in India is the same as that in the US. For example, this means that India should allocate spectrum for unrestricted use in a way that is similar to the Industrial, Scientific and Medical (ISM) bands used in the US.

Summing up

Many policy notes in India are written by reviewing what is done in a few other countries, and patching together some plausible-sounding policy proposal for India. This approach works poorly. Enlightenment values port across the world, but tangible policy designs do not.

We must go from a 'thin description' of what is done elsewhere in the world to a 'thick description', an incentive-based understanding of why officials and private persons behave as they do in advanced countries.[3]

A great deal of what happens in advanced economies relies on an 'invisible infrastructure' of state apparatus and checks and balances that is not immediately within view when focusing on a narrow problem of policy. The US SEC does certain things right because the United States Constitution establishes certain protections, but when we focus on how the US SEC works, these foundations tend to be overlooked.

To do public policy in the Indian context requires envisioning how a proposed design of an intervention or a government organization will work *in the Indian setting*, with a deep understanding of the surrounding conditions. We only change one piece of policy at a time, while everything else stays unchanged. We have to find the best given the constraints of the environment.

Ground-up design of solutions, from first principles, for the Indian environment will often look different from those seen elsewhere.

The institutions of the First World carry enormous prestige. The sum total of these institutional designs adds up to modernity and prosperity. However, when one element at a time is sought to be transplanted into India, we run the risk of being the sorcerer's apprentice (who uses the spell without knowing why it works) and engaging in isomorphic mimicry (copying the form without copying the function).

Public policy thinking in India requires metis: deep experiential local knowledge. Level-1 thinking is coming up with nutty proposals. Level-2 thinking is copying from websites. Level-3 thinking is grounded in metis, in thinking from the first principles.

There are some situations where it is possible for policy thinking in India to free-ride on state capacity outside India. When this can be done, this is welcome, as it reduces the requirements of building state capacity in India.

19

Test match, not IPL

Let's start at the classic example of trade barriers on a certain product being eliminated. This yields immediate gains for the economy at large, as the price of that product comes down, though this gain may be imperceptible to most people as the magnitude of purchases of this particular product, by any one person, is small.

The existing producers of the product suffer from a decline in profitability and greater pressure to increase productivity. The pain is focused upon these persons.

Over time, some of these existing producers go out of business, thus freeing up capital and labour. The reallocation of this capital and labour into more productive uses gradually yields gains for the economy at large.

Entrepreneurs would see new business opportunities, including possible export markets, for business plans that involve buying this cheaper product. Gradually, these new businesses arise, and give gains for the economy at large. It takes time for the full 'general equilibrium' gains to play out. Public policy work is a test match, not an IPL.

Delays in building state capacity

When the Insolvency and Bankruptcy Code (IBC) was enacted in 2016, this had no immediate impact on the ground, as the state and private institutions that were required to implement the law did not exist.

A multi-year process began, which included building the National Company Law Tribunal (NCLT) and the Insolvency and Bankruptcy Board of India (IBBI). On the private side, individuals started specializing in the field of bankruptcy, and the slow development of 'information utilities' and 'insolvency professional agencies' began.

It takes years for these changes to play out, for adequate capabilities to develop on all these fronts. For this reason, the gains for the economy, from enacting the IBC in 2016, are obtained at a later date.

The bulk of the gains from the bankruptcy reform come from *modified behaviour* of private persons, taking place in the shadow of the law. The threat of the law is expected to induce modified behaviour on the part of borrowers and lenders. This also takes time. At first, the threat of the law has to change. In time, this will induce changes in culture, in the ways in which contracting and negotiation take place. The full impact unfolds over time.

Lags of policy impact

The most important reforms impose pain that is concentrated upon a few people, and gains that are diffused over the entire country. The pain comes early and the gains come with a lag. The political puzzle of reforms lies in managing these two tensions.

The art of politics lies in understanding the map of interests and pulling off such reforms. This involves understanding who will lose in the short run, negotiating with them and influencing their view of the world, modifying the reform in non-fundamental ways so as to reduce the pain upon these persons, and sometimes compensating them through other instruments. It involves harnessing the support of the gainers from the reform.

Policymaking on the election clock

The clock that counts the years to the next elections weighs heavily upon this thinking. The art of politics lies in thinking through these time horizons, launching a portfolio of reforms in year 1 and year 2, which induce pain (attenuated by specific transfers to affected parties) in year 2 and year 3, and yield overall gains by year 4 and year 5.

This requires extreme capability in the team that wins power. The incoming team cannot just land up in power, take control of the levers of power, and wield power in random ways based on political compulsions and ideology. They need to have a portfolio of policy proposals, backed by teams of experts, with fully articulated planning of actions, anticipated impacts, design of the measurement system to monitor the process on an ongoing basis, identification of the persons negatively impacted, and possibly the design of compensatory transfers to defuse the unhappiness.

There is a crucial role for the communication strategy that is put into play from the date the cabinet is formed. In this age of Twitter, 'communication strategy' consists of catchy slogans and choice abuse. The true role of communication, however, lies in improving coordination on an economy scale. The political and technocratic leadership must have a shared strategy and shared messaging, through which the full picture is consistently and strongly communicated. This would help align expectations and ensure that private persons change their strategies in ways that are coherent with the strategy of reforms.

If there is no strategy in reforms, or if it is not properly communicated to the private sector, businesses and financial investors will make mistakes in the formulation of their strategies, which will result in reduced economic performance. This will increase the time lag between the policy change and its full beneficial impact.

Example 24: Cutting the peak customs rate by 5 percentage points every year

In 2000, the Vajpayee government chose a path : the peak customs rate would drop by 5 percentage points every year. Everyone in the administration understood the strategy and consistently communicated it.

At first, there was an uproar from incumbent firms, and the government had to deal with their anger in year 1. From year 2 onward, firms understood that the peak rate was going to be down by an additional 20 percentage points by year 5. This set off India's firms on paths of fundamental productivity growth, and improved the choice of investment projects. Every step of the way, as customs duties were cut, tradeables in India became cheaper, and this kicked off an export boom.

This combination of communication and staggered introduction of the reform induced synchronization between the government and the private sector. This was critical for the economic boom which started in 2003.

Before the first year

In the world of business, there is a balance between building a great product and selling it on the market. An extreme emphasis on a sales and advertising team can yield a brief surge of customer interest, but this does not translate into sustained success if the product is not of high quality and the machinery of production and distribution is not in place. In other words, a firm needs not just sales and advertising, it also needs research, design and operations management. It needs a great product and the capability to produce and distribute the product, on top of which the sales and advertising offensive is essential.

There is an analogy with the world of politics. Running an election campaign is analogous to the sales and advertising problem. To win power, this is essential. But if this is all that is done, sustained voter satisfaction will be elusive. Political parties need to prepare to govern, alongside campaigning to get elected. Once the election results are in, every day lost in establishing the team and kicking off a portfolio of reforms is a costly delay. We are doing too little transition planning in Indian politics.

When out of power, political parties should have a shadow cabinet. There should be a sustained process of engagement with think tanks, academic institutions, data sets and intellectuals, in order to cogitate about what is going wrong. The emphasis in an opposition party should be not just on criticizing what the ruling party has done, but on developing a set of plans for what would be done when in power.

The incumbent ruling party equally faces this problem. At year 5, a successful ruling team is jaded, and an unsuccessful ruling team is demoralized. Yet, it needs to think through the possibility of re-election, and find the energy for transition planning.

This preparatory work would be particularly valuable when it is fed into the manifesto of the political party and, when coalition governments are formed, the negotiation for a common minimum programme. The paragraphs in such documents matter disproportionately, but receive inadequate attention ahead of time.

Long-range thinking and capacity building are required in each political party to develop the capability to succeed in the event of winning elections. When such developmental work is not done, ahead of time, we translate remarkable election outcomes into failures on policy.

Playing the long game

A cult of *jald baazi* is taking root in India. This is the notion that a problem can be understood in a few days, and solved in a few weeks. Powerful policymakers tend to whip up a frenzy of getting things done quickly. Every expert in India has gone through the surreal experience of being ignored for years, and then asked to deliver a reform document overnight.

> *You rush a miracle man, you get a rotten miracle.*
>
> *The Princess Bride*, 1987 film

This is a harmful approach. In some rare situations, a team is available in India, which is fully imbued with a problem, has the right understanding, has the right human networks in the country, has learned how to work with each other, and can move at high speed in executing a reform. Even under these conditions, drafting laws and building state capacity takes a long time.

In most situations, there is a starvation of intellectual capacity in the country. We lack data, knowledge, experts and teams that know how to work with each other. There is thus a slow process of understanding problems, designing solutions, going up from individuals to teams with esprit de corps, and implementing reforms.

The cult of speed yields failure in both cases. Even when the best teams are assembled, if the work which requires two years is compressed into a few months, this will be done badly. With weak teams, the pressure of solving a problem in a few months surely yields failure.

There is a pipeline in the policy reform process: data to research to policy proposals to consensus to government decisions to policy implementation. It is not possible to short-circuit this process. Some fields are at a weaker stage, where the basics of data and research are not in place. In these fields, the only horizons over which meaningful policy reform can be achieved are a long time horizon.

The cult of speed is ultimately derived from management failure in government. We are faring poorly on establishing institutions which contain harmonious teams that impound information and expertise; we are unable to make long-term plans and stay focused on them. We suffer from a strong pace of personnel changes, which prevent the development of knowledge and rapport within policy teams. We suffer from three-page notes of individual reform measures, typically written by interested parties, which lack strategic thinking. We fluctuate from one topic to another, based on the crises that engulf us each day. When a government flits from one issue to the next based on the news cycle, there is no strategy.

It would behove the policy process to be sceptical about the solutions that are hawked in three-page notes, to be slow and cautious. We should set a high bar on the minimum level of knowledge and evidence required before embarking upon even a modest intervention into the lives of private people.

Example 25: The bankruptcy reform

Parliament enacted the Insolvency and Bankruptcy Code (IBC) in May 2016. There was a great rush in quickly getting the Insolvency and Bankruptcy Board of India up and running, and in declaring the IBC open for business. Many corners were cut in getting to a quick launch.

By early 2019, we have seen many difficulties in the working of the IBC. The big cases have proved stubbornly hard to process. Consider an alternative history. Would it have made sense to lay the groundwork from May 2016 to May 2018, and only then declare the IBC open for business? We suspect that things would have looked better by early 2019, if that slow path had been taken.

Example 26: The Rhine was not cleaned in a day

In 1986, a blast at the Sandoz chemical plant in Basel, Switzerland, leaked tonnes of toxic chemicals in the Rhine, Europe's longest river. The 1233-km-long transboundary river, passes through Switzerland, Liechtenstein, Austria, Germany, France and Holland. This presented complex multi-nation problems of policy coordination, in order to clean the river.

In 1987, the Rhine Action Plan was drawn up, with a simple and bold target: *By the year 2000, there would be salmon in the Rhine again.* The implementation plan employed a variety of measures and instruments to clean the river—from expanding and equipping biological sewage treatment plants, to working with non-profits like Greenpeace to monitor emissions levels, and industrial regulation and enforcement. While the original plan had a bold target of an outcome in thirteen years, in reality, it took thirty years and 45 billion Euros, and the fish were back.

After this, the Rhine Action Plan was reformulated as the more ambitious goal, over a ten-year horizon, that the riverine ecosystem would become a thriving environment for all creatures.[1]

Building a bridge vs building institutions

Policymakers in India now understand how to build a bridge. They know that building a bridge is expensive, that it requires professionals to build, that there will be a project plan, that many steps have to be undertaken, and these take time, and only then can a bridge be inaugurated.

The same approach is required with state capacity! When a new government organization is required: (a) It will be expensive; (b) It requires professionals to build it; (c) There must be a formal project plan in order to build the organization and its capabilities; and (d) Implementing this project plan will take time. Only when the project is completed, can a new organization be declared open for business.

We have repeatedly seen new organizations being launched in the Indian state in a casual and informal way. The present ways— of hiring a few people and declaring a government agency open for business within a very short time horizon—are downright harmful. Right at the outset, the organization is crushed with demands that it is ill-prepared for. The fledgling organization is underfunded and under-resourced in every possible way. It gets into a firefighting mindset, makes mistakes, and generally never recovers from the early failures.

We in India have learned how infrastructure projects require time and money. We need to carry this professional approach into building state capacity in government organizations.[2]

The equity market reform started at the G.S. Patel Committee report in 1984. A humble researcher in this team, R.H. Patil, was central to the establishment of NSE. SEBI was begun as a non-statutory organization in 1988. The pieces of the equity market fell into place by 2001. There was an exciting journey of ideas and action, with the establishment of SEBI, NSE and NSDL, which ran from 1984 to 2001. This gave fundamental progress in the equity market.

We may have thought that once completed, this would stand in place. In the event, there was a dissipation of the institutional memory. The experiences of the 1980s and 1990s, which shaped decisions of the 1990s, were forgotten. In numerous aspects, there has been a retreat in the capabilities of the financial markets in the recent decade. As an example, the first settlement failure in the history of the NSE, and the first settlement failure in the Indian equity market after a gap of nineteen years, took place in 2019.[3]

Similarly, the pension reforms began with Project OASIS, led by Surendra Dave, in 1998. This led up to the decision in December 2002 to implement the New Pension System (NPS) for new recruits into the government. Pension Fund Regulatory and Development Authority (PFRDA) was set up, and the law enshrining PFRDA was only enacted in 2013. However, there was a dissipation of the institutional memory. The experiences of the 1990s, and the logic of the NPS, were forgotten in many important ways.

These experiences underline the importance of building stable teams which are able to engage with the reforms process over long time horizons. Each area of work is a complex problem with many moving parts. As policy projects unfold over long time horizons, we require teams and policy continuity over long time horizons. When staffing is unstable, and when institutional memory is lost, we lose ground.

Building the republic takes time

It took hundreds of years to build the US, the UK and the other mature liberal democracies of the world. As an example, the US Constitution was written in 1776, but the 'fruit of the poisonous tree' doctrine—which is absolutely fundamental to limiting the power of investigative agencies—only came together in the early twentieth century, i.e., 154 years after the founding of the country. It was only in the 1970s that US lawmakers shut off domestic operations by the CIA, and brought electronic surveillance by investigative agencies under the rule of law.

Similarly, it took seventy years from 1947 for India to decriminalize gay sex. Assuming there is progress towards freedom and the rule of law in the future, it will prove to take over seventy years to get to basic elements of civil liberties including decriminalization of defamation, removal of sedition from the IPC, and placing electronic surveillance of the populace under a rule of law framework. These are long and slow journeys.

We should not look for the newspaper headlines, the quick wins, the buzz on social media. We should instead dig into the long and slow process of genuinely building the republic.

Summing up

When a policy reform takes place, the full gains are obtained through the reallocation of resources in the economy. Policy reform requires private persons to fully internalize the new environment, and re-optimize for it. Many policy reforms require the construction of institutional capacity within government and in the economy. These adjustments take time. For this reason, the pain is front-loaded and the gains come with a lag. Policymakers need to understand who will lose in the short run, negotiate with them, and find compromises with them.

After elections take place, and the leadership faces a five-year horizon, it is useful to think of year 1 as the time to launch complex initiatives, which will mature through years 2, 3 and 4, and show positive impacts by year 5. This imposes demands on the team formed after the elections. It needs to choose the major projects, staff them, and communicate this to the economy so as to reshape expectations. This requires considerable work within political parties before winning the election.

Such thinking over long time horizons diverges from the cult of speed that is often found in Indian public policy, where three-page notes are written over a weekend and implemented over the week. Such actions tend to be superficial and achieve little.

There is a pipeline of the policy process, from measurement all the way to policy execution. The institutional memory of each field is contained in a community of intellectuals and policy practitioners. The pipeline and the community need to be nurtured, in order to play the long battles of policy reform.

We in India now know that a bridge across a river is a project that has to go through certain steps. It takes time, money and professional capacity in order to build a bridge. We have to see policy reforms in a similar way. There is no short cut from the date on which it is decided that a bridge shall be built, to the date on which the bridge is inaugurated.

Building the republic takes time. It will take many decades of hard work by the policy community for India to rise to the ranks of the advanced nations of the world. Policy reform is slow, hard work, and not amenable to quick wins on social media.

20

What is hard and what is easy

When we think of a given government intervention, we need to judge how hard it would be for successful implementation. Suppose the Indian state is evaluating a universal human papillomavirus (HPV) immunization programme for children. While we know that this is hard, it is in the zone of feasible policy pathways. But suppose the Indian state is evaluating a programme where officials will interview unemployed individuals and decide which of them should get welfare payments every month. This seems beyond the reach of the implementation capacity of the Indian state.

What are the general principles through which we can engage in such reasoning?

Four dimensions of complexity

Lant Pritchett and Michael Woolcock first posed this question and offered elements of the answer.[1] They predict that implementation is hard when there is more discretion and when there are a larger number of transactions. In addition, implementation is harder when there is more at stake for private persons, and when there is more secrecy.

Number of transactions: It is easier to achieve state capacity on a problem where there are a smaller number of transactions. A vast sprawling machinery involves greater agency problems; it is difficult to be sure that every element of the administrative machine is working correctly.

Discretion: It is easier to achieve state capacity when there is low discretion. An immunization programme is a good example, where there is a population-scale outreach, but the work that has to be done by each civil servant is fixed and there is no discretion.

Stakes: It is harder to achieve state capacity when there is more at stake for private persons. Problems like the criminal justice system, the judiciary, the tax system and financial regulation are the hardest puzzles. Here, the decisions of state agents have enormous consequences for individuals, and private persons will devote considerable effort in trying to influence the outcome.

Secrecy: The bulk of the working of the Ministry of Rural Development takes place in the open. Policy documents and data sets come out into the public domain. This makes the feedback loops of analysis and criticism more effective. In contrast, the secrecy that surrounds a ministry, such as the Ministry of Defence, can serve as a cloak for poor performance.

Example 27: Monetary policy is easy, financial regulation is hard

By this reasoning, monetary policy is a relatively easy problem:

- *Low discretion:* Once inflation targeting is embedded in the law, there is a clear accountability mechanism. Individuals who make the decision have relatively limited discretion. Individuals who make flagrantly wrong decisions will be exposed in public and will suffer lifetime reputational damage.

- *Low number of transactions:* There is no citizen-facing part to monetary policy. It is only four to six decisions a year.
- *Low stakes:* Raising or lowering the policy rate has important consequences for the economy as a whole but it is of extreme importance, at a personal level, to nobody. Not much is at stake as far as private persons are concerned; there will be relatively little tangible lobbying or pressure in trying to influence the outcome. It is interesting to see that when the monetary policy transmission is weak, the stakes are even lower, as small changes in the policy rate have a negligible impact upon the economy. It is easier to establish independence of the central bank under conditions of a weak monetary policy transmission.
- *Low secrecy:* A sound central bank has essentially zero secrecy, so there is the full potency of analysis and criticism in the public domain, thus giving strong feedback loops from failure to improvement.

Hence, monetary policy is a relatively easy puzzle in state capacity building. A small elite is required that writes the rules of the game, that gets the country up to a modern central banking law. A small elite is required which mans the monetary policy committee. Central banks can be fairly small, lean organizations. The complexity of solving principal–agent problems in a large organization can be avoided.

In contrast, financial regulation is a difficult problem.

A lot of behaviour lies in the shades of grey; there is *discretion* for the investigator and the prosecutor in classifying a certain activity as a violation or not.

There are a large *number of transactions*; there are thousands of financial firms and there is a requirement for perhaps a thousand investigators and prosecutors in India.

The *stakes are sky high*. How regulations are drafted and enforced makes a difference of trillions of rupees in terms of the payoffs to private persons. Billionaires have a great incentive to reshape the working of financial regulation in their favour, and they will use every trick in the book in trying to impact on the policy process.

There is *a good deal of secrecy*. Supervision, investigations, enforcement and the quasi-judicial process of financial regulators is cloaked in a good deal of secrecy.

Hence, financial regulation is a difficult problem in constructing state capacity.[2]

Solutions that reduce complexity in some dimensions

There is a great deal of optimism about the extent to which modern IT solves problems of governance. We are able to see one zone where IT systems are truly transformational: in the removal of discretion.

As an example, when there is an IT system through which railway tickets are sold, the discretion of the front line sales person is eliminated. IT systems ease the construction of state capacity by offering process engineering through which discretion can be removed.[3] This is a recurring theme running across many great opportunities for utilising IT in building state capacity.[4]

Example 28: Judicial reforms

In the working of courts and tribunals, there are two distinct elements which can be seen as pillars of intervention. There is the highly discretion-intensive problem of the thinking of the judge. Alongside this, there is the low-discretion and transaction-intensive problem of running the operational processes of the court. This is also termed 'the registry' of the court.

It is possible to bring modern business process re-engineering into the working of the operational procedures. This approach is likely to give substantial gains in the operational efficiency of courts, while leaving the independence of the judiciary intact.[5]

This is a useful vertical split, between high-discretion and low-discretion parts of the working of a court. Using modern IT systems, the low-discretion part can be rapidly transformed.

Solutions that change from one dimension of complexity to another

Many government offices in India find it difficult to achieve clean toilets. Cleaning the toilets is a transaction-intensive problem, which calls for considerable state capacity in being able to recruit and manage a cleaning crew.

This is a well-defined service function, which does not involve the use of coercive power upon the people, and hence it can be contracted out. Our first impulse might thus be: *Why not replace tenured janitors who do not clean the toilets by a private contractor who will not give tenure to her employees?* This appears to offer gains in one dimension: We are replacing a transaction-intensive function (janitors cleaning) by a small number of transactions (procuring and monitoring the private contractor).

In the process, however, we do run up to larger stakes. A tenured janitor gains about Rs 150,000 a year (her wage) from doing no work. In contrast, a private contractor that undertakes cleaning services for an entire building may be paid Rs 1.5 crore (Rs 15 million) a year. The private contractor now stands to gain a bigger amount by doing no work. The stakes are higher. It now requires a large amount of state capacity, albeit in a different dimension, to ensure the contract goes to the right person, using a fair process, and is adequately monitored.

When PPP was first proposed as a way to improve upon low-quality infrastructure built by government departments, this was hailed as a big step forward. With the benefit of hindsight, we see that PPP contracting is hard, as the stakes are high.

The four hardest problems

The criminal justice system, the judiciary, the tax system and financial regulation suffer from the problem of high discretion, high number of transactions, very high stakes and varying amounts of secrecy. How the front-line policeman behaves can make a difference of life and death for a person. This gives extreme discretionary power to the policeman. The hardest problems in state capacity are the criminal justice system, the judiciary, the tax system and financial regulation.

Learn to walk before you run

Once we see that high stakes harm the construction of state capacity, a natural tool for sequencing is to initially start at low stakes.

If the fine for driving through a red light is Rs 10,000, there will be pervasive corruption. Jobs in the highway police will be sought after; large bribes will be paid to obtain these jobs. There will be an institutional collapse of the highway police. It is better to first start with a fine of Rs 100, and build state capacity. Once a country has learned how to run a highway police at a fine of Rs 100, we can think of going up to larger fines.

A low tax rate induces low stakes. High tax rates are a high load upon the state, as the personal incentives of tax administrators (to take bribes) become highly divergent from the objectives of the institutions that they represent.

Public anger about the failures of the criminal justice system in India has often given a sharp escalation of punishments. This leads to higher stakes, and thus *reduces* the capability of the criminal justice system.

When we are at the early stages of learning how to be a state, it is wise to start out at low stakes (e.g., low tax rates, low punishments). Once capabilities are fully established, there can be a mature debate about whether the right policy pathways involve higher stakes (e.g., higher tax rates, higher punishments).[6]

Summing up

When we face a problem in public policy, it is important to assess how difficult it will be, to build the requisite state capacity. Four factors shape this:

1. *Transaction intensity*: If something involves a large number of transactions, by a large number of front-line civil servants, it is harder.
2. *Discretion*: If something involves more discretion in the hands of the civil servant, it is harder.
3. *Stakes*: If there are high stakes, it is harder.
4. *Secrecy*: When there is greater secrecy, it is harder.

Monetary policy is easy while financial regulation is hard because the latter involves a larger number of transactions, a greater use of discretion, high stakes and greater secrecy.

Complexity in this four-dimensional space is not immutable. We can often undertake actions that reduce the complexity in some of these dimensions or trade off complexity in one dimension for another dimension.

The four hardest problems are the criminal justice system, the judiciary, the tax system and the financial regulation. They suffer from high transactions, high discretion, high stakes and high secrecy.

If a government organization is asked to suddenly achieve capability on a difficult problem, it will collapse in an organizational rout. A natural way to sequence the construction of state capacity is to first start with an easier problem, to achieve success, and then escalate the complexity. At an early stage in the republic, it will help to reduce discretion, reduce secrecy and most importantly, reduce the stakes. At first, agencies should be given low powers to investigate and the punishments that can be awarded should be low. This will create better conditions for achieving state capacity.

21

Confident policymakers work in the open

In public policy, we don't just dine with friends, we must also sup with fiends.

Ashok Desai

There is a long tradition of secrecy in public policy in India. Too often, in India, a reform is pushed through as a sudden *fait accompli* upon the losers. As the complexity of the economy has grown, and as Indian democracy has matured, it is increasingly unwise to maintain this level of secrecy.

Secrecy harms planning and execution

Exposing early drafts to the persons who have a lot at stake may often yield improvements in the work. Particularly when we have low state capacity, the most well-meaning reform is often marred by technical mistakes in the execution. A more open policy process catches more errors and it improves the resulting work.

As an example, most draft laws in India are faulty owing to gaps in capabilities for drafting law in government organizations and in their supporting law firms. A thorough and genuine process of consultation will find mistakes.

One of the reasons why the demonetization decision suffered from difficulties of policy design and implementation was the secrecy in which it was surrounded. The areas of Indian public policy which are shrouded in secrecy (military, intelligence, trading in the RBI treasury) may have the biggest flaws.

The full gains from a reform require a great deal of advance planning and preparation by myriad private persons. This developmental work takes place if there is ample advance warning. The same reform will deliver better results if the overall economy has been primed for the idea adequately.

Losers from a reform require fair warning

Every reform hurts certain firms and certain persons. With more advance warning, they can plan their life better. This would reduce the costs for the economy as a whole.

As an example, consider the simplest reform: trade liberalization. Certain Indian factories, in areas where India does not have a comparative advantage, have to close down when the trade liberalization is done. We as a country have two choices: to present them with a surprise big-bang trade liberalization, or to talk about it every step of the way and give ample warning. By giving ample warning, for many years, firms will cut back on investments in physical capital and organizational capital into the businesses that are not going to survive trade liberalization. This reduces the destruction of capital that always accompanies trade liberalization.

The policy process is one of negotiation

There is a valuable political economy perspective upon this question, where we see all reforms as a process of negotiation. Healthy democracies are those where various interest groups are able to sit together, engage in discourse in good faith, and emerge with reasonable compromises. The essential foundation for the democratic process of negotiation is trust—a certain presumption of good faith.

We as a society need to experience decades upon decades of decent behaviour with each other, in order to learn how to trust each other to negotiate in good faith. This will yield a political system in which we are able to rise above partisan hatred and enter into bargains that make everyone better off.

The trust building that is required for this is hampered when policy measures are hatched in secrecy and suddenly unveiled upon the populace. The persons who get hurt feel that they were not treated fairly. This adversely affects the trust capital of the country, and holds back our emergence as a mature political system.

Give people time to change behaviour

Let us go back to the example of trade liberalization. So far, we have emphasized the presence of people who lose from the reform. But sheer fairness requires that they need to be able to plan for this ahead of time.

But the full impact upon the economy works through a series of adaptations. Some of the affected firms may choose to wind down their business or sell it. Others will choose to push up their productivity. Some firms that *use* goods that have lower tariffs will now see new opportunities to make things for the local or overseas market, as a consequence of lower prices. This may, in turn, kick off technological changes.

The full impact of a policy measure plays out in reshaping the work of the private sector. It is better for this work to commence as early as possible. For this reason, an open and consultative process works better.

If private persons have ample warning, their adaptations commence at an earlier date. Through this, the lags of the policy process are reduced. The gains for the economy are obtained in a shorter period.

It is easy to deride 'paralysis through analysis'. For many people who are not instinctively comfortable with intellectual discourse, the slow process of public debates and government committees seems like a waste of time. Reaching out to critics is tactically costly as this increases the say that critics have in stalling or subverting a reform. The authoritarian impulse, to favour action over talk, is fashionable.

However, the best policy work gets done in the open. The participatory policy process, grounded in intellectual debate, generates a better reforms process. It helps avoid a policy process that is pure power play. The work is better rooted in the landscape of people and institutions. The mistakes are more likely to be taken out. The negotiations and compromises create support and legitimacy. Policy implementation works out better.

Example 29: Petroleum reforms, the 'R group'

An example of this is the 'R Group' which worked on petroleum policy reform starting in 1995. This involved all parties to the thinking, worked in the open, negotiated short-term vs long-term elements of the reform, and laid the foundations of an important and successful reform.

A group of young leaders from public sector oil companies— all below age thirty—was formed, to prepare a road map to international competitiveness. The idea was that these individuals had a long-term stake in the success of the reform, and would be less invested in the present ways. This was termed the 'below thirty group'.

The 'R group' was set up under the chairmanship of the secretary, Petroleum and Natural Gas (Vijay Kelkar). The members were the leaders of public sector and private sector firms, and independent experts.

Multiple conferences took place with the leaders of trade unions on the benefits from the liberalization programme chosen by the 'below thirty group'.

The reforms began by replacing administered prices by international oil prices, for all upstream companies including Oil and Natural Gas Corporation (ONGC). This was coupled with competition in new exploration. ONGC simultaneously got better revenues and greater competition. ONGC also got the freedom to operate in the world, just like any large oil company would.

The next step was open competition in the downstream industry, along with replacing the cost-plus pricing regime by international parity pricing. This was introduced sequentially. It began with industrial inputs such as naphtha and fuel oil, and then for transportation fuels such as petrol and diesel, and finally for the household fuels, kerosene and liquefied petroleum gas (LPG).

Finally, the price of natural gas was linked to international fuel oil prices, instead of a cost-plus pricing regime.

This entire story took place over a six-year period. It led to increased investments in upstream, midstream and downstream sectors, productivity gains and higher accretion of domestic oil and gas reserves.

There was no political friction in this process. As the reforms were extensively discussed, there were no unpleasant shocks either to consumers or to producers, and the gains for consumers and for trade unions outweighed the pain. The entry of private firms was done through carefully designed auction procedures, so as to avoid accusations of corruption.

Example 30: Inflation targeting

Inflation targeting was talked about by some intellectuals in the early years of the first decade of the millennium, as a response to the difficulties that RBI was then facing with monetary policy. This public debate at an intellectual level led to the first recommendation in a government committee report by Percy Mistry, titled 'Mumbai as an international financial centre' (MIFC), in 2007. This was followed by a similar recommendation in Raghuram Rajan's report in 2009. This was followed by a draft law for inflation targeting by Justice Srikrishna's 'Financial Sector Legislative Reforms Commission'.

There was a great deal of debate in newspaper columns, blog articles, research papers and conference panels. This was followed by an RBI committee, headed by Urjit Patel, which also recommended that inflation targeting be adopted. The implementation was done in two steps: first, the 'Monetary Policy Framework Agreement' that was signed between the finance secretary, Rajiv Mehrishi, and the RBI governor, Raghuram Rajan, on 20 February 2015, and next, the amendment to the RBI Act in February 2016.

This was not a small reform. This was the biggest milestone in RBI's history. It is fitting that alongside the introduction of a 4 per cent consumer price index (CPI) target into the RBI Act, the text in the preamble to the RBI Act which established the RBI in 1934 as 'a temporary measure' was simultaneously deleted.

This was a long and slow journey for the RBI—from a temporary measure in 1934 to the first intellectual clarity in the early years of the millennium to the modified RBI Act in 2016. Policymakers developed a strategy and gradually executed it, in a completely open process, to the point where, at the end, it was an inevitable non-event.

From date of announcement to date effective

From these points of view, it is particularly important to ensure there is a substantial lag between the date of a policy announcement and the date on which it becomes effective.

One of the most harmful things that is taking place in the Indian state is announcements that show up on a website in the evening, without any previous notice, and are effective next morning. These impose huge costs upon private persons, and drive up the ex ante fear of policy risk in the minds of firms.

Professional capabilities in public policy

There is a pattern in the Indian story, where weak policy teams tend to operate in a more secretive way. There seems to be a lack of confidence in being able to win arguments in the public domain. The weakest ideas are hatched in secrecy and suddenly sprung upon the economy.

This is related to the problems of knowledge partnerships and the comfort with intellectual discourse. The best policy teams in India are well connected into intellectual capabilities, are comfortable with criticism, and are able to debate with their critics as part of the public discourse. Weak policy teams are more likely to be disconnected from intellectual capabilities, work in secrecy, react in a hostile way to criticism, and deliver poor results in policymaking.

When a policy team is comfortable with articulating and debating a reform in public, and listens to other points of view in order to engage in a process of iterative refinement, this sends a signal to private persons that there is genuine capability in the policy process. This improves the legitimacy of the policy process and increases optimism that good work will be done.

Summing up

वादे वादे जायते तत्वबोध।

Good debate to good debate, knowledge grows.

Ancient Sanskrit proverb

Secrecy harms policy planning and execution.

In a liberal democracy, the relationship between the policymaker and the individual is not the relationship between a ruler and a subject. The policy process is a process of negotiation. The losers from a reform require fair warning. When there is ample warning, the adaptations of the private sector kick in early, and the gains for the economy are obtained in a shorter time.

Confident policymakers work in the open. Working in the open signals capability.

The most harmful events are those where a policy announcement shows up on a website in the evening, without any prior warning, and is effective next morning. The best episodes are those with an open consultative process, where the legal instrument showing up on the website is a non-event, and there is ample lead time between the date of announcement and the date effective.

22

Criticism and conflict have great value

निन्दकाचे घर असावे शेजारी।

संत तुकाराम

Your critic should live right next door.

Sant Tukaram

Our traditional self-image of India consists of seeing us as a healthy liberal democracy. There are, however, many disturbing features which have crept in gradually. As an example, we may think that India has a free press, but India is now ranked 140th out of 180 countries on press freedom, by Reporters Without Borders. As a consequence, there is much less criticism of the establishment than is required.

As policymakers, we tend to develop a point of view. We should, however, be humble. We are not omniscient, and we are frequently wrong. It is wise to listen to our critics as they are likely to often be right.

Good for fairness, good for self-interest

A healthy democracy is one in which diverse points of view are able to engage in civil discussions, engage in give-and-take, and search for common ground. Critics see the world from diverse points of view. All these points of view are legitimate elements of the democratic process of negotiation and compromise.

In this point of view, acceptance of criticism is integral to norms of good behaviour in liberal democracy, and is a noble thing.

Respecting and valuing criticism is not just about fair play. As the Marathi aphorism by Sant Tukaram at the beginning of the chapter says, it is also about the self-interest of the policymaker. As our information and wisdom are always limited, it is useful to have people in our midst, who will identify mistakes in our reasoning.

Neuroscientists have described a phenomenon called 'the power paradox': persons who possess power appear to become more impulsive, less risk-aware, and less adept at seeing things from other people's point of view.[1] This makes mistakes more likely. Encouraging and respecting criticism is the key path to avoiding hubris.

Another dimension of the gains from nurturing criticism is related to the idea of crossing the river by feeling the stones, using feedback loops. The best way to make progress is to take small steps, and to listen to the statistical evidence. A distributed system of criticism can tap into a larger knowledge base, and create valuable feedback through which course corrections at intermediate stages can be achieved.

The peculiar twist in India is that in many areas, the statistical system is weak. We are down to gathering anecdotal evidence by talking to people. No one individual can talk with a large number of people.

Each critic is valuable insofar as she represents information from a different subset of the system under examination. Critics of public policy strategies are a valuable part of society, and essential for the process of crossing the river by feeling the stones. The critic is not a bad human being; the critic is not an enemy; he is someone who has given you free advice that helps strengthen your work.

> *We must love them both, those whose opinions we share and those whose opinions we reject, for both have labored in the search for truth, and both have helped us in finding it.*

> St. Thomas Aquinas

We need not agree with our critics, but our critics can help us see the flaws in our thinking and make improvements. We should not attack critics, and we should not encourage sycophants. We should foster an intellectual landscape featuring honest analysis and discussion. When person X praises the policymaker and person Y criticizes the policymaker, it is more useful for the policymaker to meet person Y and understand the logic of the criticism. This conversation may result in course corrections.

In an environment where critics are attacked and harmed, these feedback loops will be harmed. The government will then encourage sycophants, who will always praise the government. Mid-course corrections will not take place. Lacking in the support system of criticism, the government will stumble from one mistake to the next.

Authoritarian regimes, that neglected the value of feedback, have repeatedly failed in the human experience of thousands of years.

Conflict in the public domain is the healthy state

Authoritarian regimes look well organized and powerful, like the clean formations in a military parade. There is a great leader, and everyone is deferential to the positions of the great leader and the inner circle of power. Once a position is taken, everyone falls in line, in public, with a great deal of flattery. The great leader is incapable of making mistakes and must always be praised. There are disagreements and conflicts, of course, but they take place outside the public gaze, and tend to degenerate into pure power play.

> *No government can be long secure without a formidable opposition.*
>
> Benjamin Disraeli

> *The absence of a true opposition has led to the rapid deterioration of democracy into a kind of totalitarianism.*
>
> C. Rajagopalachari[2]

In contrast, democracies *look* messy. They are riven with debate, dissension, and a tug of war. Power is dispersed across many individuals and many elements of the government. Neutral and intellectual voices weigh in on the conflicts that are played out in the public domain.

This policy process is a world of ideas and rational thinking, and not merely an exercise in power play. The continuous debate in an environment of dispersed power is the *reason* why democracies work well. The continuous process of criticism and debate finds and solves mistakes.

In the best of times, most people are greatly influenced by voices around them. On most subjects, we do not have deep expertise, and tend to go with the mainstream.

Conversely, if novel proposals are not vigorously contested, there is the danger of oddball ideas taking root. This problem is particularly seen in authoritarian countries. When the establishment takes a certain position, and there is a great deal of sycophantic applause, the climate of opinion shifts. This is also why authoritarian governments work badly.

When we think about criticizing the government, it is important to see that government is not a monolithic creature. Government is made up of many individuals and agencies, all of which have different points of view.

Criticism of the stated position of an agency generally strengthens the hand of the reformers within the agency. An environment where all criticism is attacked or proscribed is a recipe for policy paralysis. The really important initiatives will never achieve traction without an extensive reshaping of the larger discourse, in which criticism of the status quo is of central importance.

In some ideal world, government is like a nice NGO. Everyone is imbued with a shared sense of what is good for the people, and all cooperate in harmoniously building a utopia. Conflicts melt away because everyone appeals to the common good. This is an idealized world of agitprop documentaries.

Public choice theory encourages us to see that everyone involved in government works for herself, and all policymaking is marred by conflicts. Conflict is the normal state, and we should not be uncomfortable about it. Differences between persons and agencies are normal and healthy, and should be played out in the public domain. Differences arise out of conflicting interests, differences in information sets, and legitimate differences in how information is analysed.

The protagonists of a conflict criticize each other. The media creates rancour by playing up conflict. We should disagree in polite language, maintain good personal relationships, and work through formal procedures for resolving conflicts. But we should be comfortable with conflict as the normal state. In fact, it is only in an authoritarian regime that conflict is squelched, as persons are too fearful to speak up. *If two people agree on everything, only one is doing the thinking.*

The under-supply of criticism

We must recognize that in every society, there is a market failure in the form of an under-supply of criticism. Criticizing the government imposes costs upon the critic.

The gains from criticism are diffused; the entire society benefits from the criticism. The self-interest of the critic leads her to ignore the gains for society at large, and thus to under-supply criticism.[3]

In July 2018, Xu Zhangrun, a law professor at Tsinghua University in Beijing wrote a tough review of the hard-line policies of Xi Jinping, the revival of communist orthodoxy and the adulatory propaganda surrounding Xi Jinping and the regime. Prof. Xu Zhangrun's essay has text such as: 'People nationwide, including the entire bureaucratic elite, feel once more lost in uncertainty about the direction of the country and about their own personal security, and the rising anxiety has spread into a degree of panic throughout society.' Such writing by intellectuals is the essence of building a civilized society, and imposes positive externalities upon the Chinese populace.

However, Prof. Xu Zhangrun is alone in facing the attacks from the regime. He has been suspended, barred from teaching, investigated and barred from leaving the country.[4] The externalities do not accrue to Xu Zhangrun, while the costs do. A few academics are courageous and speak up like this, but most would prefer silence.

This is similar to the standard economics argument about individual incentive leading to an underinvestment in higher education, as the decision maker does not value the spillovers, the positive externalities for society at large.

When an Andrei Sakharov goes up against a regime, the critic instantly earns respect. When an individual goes up against a billionaire, the details are more intricate, billionaires are able to resort to tactics that governments cannot employ, and there is less moral clarity. There will thus be an even greater under-supply of criticism of billionaires.

In a village economy, everyone knows everyone else, and economic relationships are efficiently organized under conditions of high information. In a modern market economy, however, many key relationships take place under substantial asymmetric information.

In an environment where information is suppressed, there is greater fear about what lies beneath. This hampers trust and arm's-length relationships.

As an example, in 2012, the research firm Veritas Investment Research Corporation wrote a research report about a firm. Two years later, the authors of the report were taken into custody by the Gurgaon police. After such an event, arm's-length investors became more concerned about the possibility that there is bad news about firms in India that is not being honestly revealed into the public domain.

Voting turns conflict into better decisions

Consider a formal or informal meeting where multiple persons, with diverse interests, come into a room to make a decision. How can the conflict be channelled most effectively, so that the knowledge and the interests of all persons in the room are well represented and a good compromise is obtained?

When multiple viewpoints come to the table, they are normally intermediated by informal systems of power. The persons in the room are all in a repeated game, and there is a give and take across many different elements of these relationships. It is all too easy for this process to collapse into an autocratic arrangement, where all power is placed with one or two people. Our cultural mores in India tend to give disproportionate power to the oldest or richest person in the room.

The give and take which occurs in these informal meetings is part of a larger game between these individuals. A person may sacrifice the interests of a certain constituency in one particular meeting in return for pay-offs in unrelated settings. Each person who gets a seat on the table has the opportunity to non-transparently make certain trade-offs. In the limit, persons in the room sacrifice the interests of constituents or the public interest in return for personal gains.

How can conflicts be channelled into better decisions? Formal voting systems are a great tool for improving the quality of the discourse. It is useful to think of three stages of a meeting. Stage 1 is an approximate statement of position, by various persons, and a free-format debate. Stage 2 consists of defining sharp propositions. Stage 3 consists of voting on them. What prevents persons in the room from arranging side payments in exchange for votes? Public disclosure of each vote, with a rationale statement, helps ensuring personal accountability of each person for the position taken.

In India, two formal voting systems are in place: benches of judges in the judiciary, and the Monetary Policy Committee (MPC).

In the MPC, the stage 2 is clear. Every meeting of the MPC has a narrow range of discrete choices that can be taken. In this case, the propositions that require voting upon are well understood. An MPC meeting then involves only stage 1 and stage 3.

The Indian MPC has three votes for RBI staff and three votes for outsiders. When there is a tie, the RBI governor has a casting vote. This suffers from the problem that the two RBI staffers are likely to be deferential towards the third vote, which is the RBI governor's. Thus, in effect, the governor controls the outcome of the MPC. A better design would have one vote for the RBI governor and four votes for independents. In that design, in order to have her way, the RBI governor would need to persuade at least two out of the four independents. This seems like a healthy reduction in the power of the governor.

Decision making through a vote, with genuine dispersion of power, qualitatively improves meetings. When one or two persons dominate a room, others tend to be listless and uninterested. The knowledge and interests of all person are not vigorously brought into the room. When a certain set of persons have a vote each, each of them is fully energized to participate in the discussion, knowing that she has equal power and that her vote counts. This improves the very *discussion* that precedes the vote.

When a meeting ends in a vote, everyone in the room thinks better and participates more. This idea can be used in a wide variety of meetings in order to improve the dispersion of power and the brainpower that is brought to bear on a question.

Formal voting systems, backed by transparency, provide a powerful mechanism for aggregating knowledge and resolving political conflicts. Particularly in an early-stage liberal democracy, where the art of give and take in political negotiation is only weakly understood, formal voting systems can often mark a big step forward from the autocratic ways.

Summing up

We should recognize the scarcity and value of criticism, and create an environment where we disagree without being disagreeable. Every critic is engaged in altruism, and harming her own self-interest, by speaking truth to power. There is a market failure, in the form of an under-supply of criticism owing to positive externalities.

It is in the self-interest of the policymaker to engage with critics, so as to improve by discovering areas of weakness in the policy work. When the policymaker is short of time, meeting the critic is more useful than meeting a supporter.

Conflict and negotiation is the healthy normal state of a liberal democracy. Liberal democracy is the endless search for a middle road.

Informal meetings run the risk of collapsing into the power of one or two people. Formal voting systems are a good tool for improving the arrangement of power in the room.

23

Coming out right, always, is too high a bar

In most situations, policymakers in India are excessively risk-averse. The phrase 'policy adventurism' is a lethal one, which can kill off any proposal. Policymakers would like to cultivate an image of being all-knowing, of occasionally championing an idea, and of coming out right every time. The incentives of officials tend to be asymmetric: success is not particularly important, but failure can be career threatening.

There is a particularly harmful combination of low capabilities and low risk taking. When policymakers have poor knowledge, they are less confident. This creates a bias in favour of inaction. The fear of failure feeds into this bias for inaction, or for action in the form of campaigns on Twitter. To solve public policy problems, and build the republic, requires taking actions that involve risk.

Real-world policymaking is extremely complicated. If we are very risk-averse, and move only when we are absolutely sure, this will generate excessive conservatism.

This was a problem in the past, and this will be a greater issue in the future. In the past, Indian policy reform consisted of low-risk projects like dismantling industrial licensing and dismantling barriers to globalization. The analytical clarity on those issues was strong and there was little that could go wrong. But as these first-order ideas are used up, future policy work will not be as unambiguous.

What is normal in the field of public policy is 'complex systems failure'—where there are many moving parts and they came together in an unexpected way. Failure will happen, and when failure occurs, there is no simple concept of identifying the decisive mistake and the key person who made that mistake.

Humility in public

We must necessarily peer into the unknown when we choose between multiple solutions to a visible problem. In most cases, it is not entirely clear what solution is superior. To avoid paralysis, we have to be willing to make mistakes.

This requires creating an environment that is more supportive of failure. We need to put aside the machismo, be honest in saying what we know and what we don't know, and approach every policy initiative as a process of hypothesis testing.

If a policymaker lays claim to omniscience and benevolence, this can lead to two outcomes. On one hand, the policymaker can be afflicted by hubris, and suffer from unintended consequences and failure. On the other hand, the policymaker may achieve a genuine understanding of the complexities that are faced, and retreat into paralysis owing to fear of failure that is incompatible with the public claims about omniscience.

A key part of this is the allocation of credit. In authoritarian regimes, all achievements belong to the leader, which makes it difficult to ever admit that a mistake was made. When credit is given more accurately, to the cast of thousands that work on any one policy initiative, it is easier for the leadership to accept that things have not worked out well and to introduce course corrections. The best management culture is one in which we *get credit for not taking credit*. This helps create a healthy environment of trying things, accepting that some did not work, and abandoning or fixing the troubled ones.

The mass media sensationalizes success or failure. It puts frail humans on a pedestal, and attributes godlike powers upon them. There is a need for greater maturity on both sides, in the media and in the policy community. Policymakers need to speak clearly about imperfect knowledge, and others need to recognize the trial and error that is required of any successful policy process. We start on a journey, and improve things based on criticism and empirical evidence. Bona fide errors are an integral part of any sound policy process. A policymaker who is not making mistakes is not trying hard enough.

It is better for the policymaker to honestly depict the lack of knowledge, to speak openly about all policymaking as a research process, and to embrace the process of crossing the river by feeling the stones.

A policy process that makes mistakes and learns from them

When we insist that no mistakes were made, the process of learning stops. Wherever humanly possible, new policy initiatives should first be rolled out on a small experimental basis. This will create experience based on which we can make more rational moves in the future. And, if something does not work too well, we can back away from it without having suffered too high a cost.

This is connected to an open and participatory process. If the policymaker claims to know how to cross the river, there is the danger of mistakes or inaction. If, on the other hand, the policymaker only claims to know how to feel the stones, and approaches the larger community with a sense of humility, this gives an environment that is more conducive to taking risks, learning from mistakes, and refining policy strategies based on evidence.

The capability of the policy community is a resource, that needs to be nurtured. An approach of acknowledging the uncertainties, and discussing and drawing lessons from failure is the key to obtaining improvements in the capability of the policy community over time.[1]

Summing up

Officials of the Indian government tend to be averse to changing things. This is rooted in the bureaucratic incentives that penalize failure. In order to make faster progress, we need to create an institutional culture that is more accepting of failure.

Part of the problem lies in the official line, which does not recognize or discuss failure. But most public policy work is characterized by failure, and we would all be better off by discussing this in a comfortable and realistic way.

When a policymaker lays claim to omniscience, it is difficult to admit that a mistake was made. It is better to honestly speak about the uncertainties that are being faced, and embark on policymaking as a process of discovery.

24

A country is not a company

Before 1991, most firms in India were managed poorly. We now have a large number of extremely well-run firms in India. The key persons in these firms are legitimately proud of their ability to run large complex organizations. Alongside this, we see the shambolic Indian state, which is unable to get the basics right. Can management skills and techniques carry over from the Indian private sector into government? Unfortunately, the skill and rhythm that is required in the public policy landscape is different from what works in for-profit firms.

Government lacks feedback loops

All big private firms are listed for trading on the stock market and see a stock price. The vast machinery of speculation in financial markets produces a real-time measure of the performance of the firm. Internally, private firms see operational management information system (MIS) statements that are updated daily. Revenue and profit are simple tools to distil the working of the firm down into a numerical yardstick.

Are there comparable measures which can be used in public policy? Is GDP growth a good measure of how the government is faring? Later in this book, we show concerns about chasing the yardstick of GDP growth. In any case, in India, we are at the early stages of learning how to measure GDP.

Is the performance of Nifty a good measure of how the government is faring? The movements of the stock market index express *surprises* in the outlook for corporate profitability; this is only weakly related to the achievements of the leadership.

Is the rupee–dollar exchange rate a good measure of how the government is faring? The fluctuations of the exchange rate have nearly no link with how the country is faring. Depreciation is often beneficial for the economy. When a leadership starts viewing the exchange rate as a measure of its performance, this is generally harmful.

There is thus no information system that generates feedback loops for government, in the way that accounting data and stock market data generates feedback loops in private firms.

Government agencies are monopolies

The customers of private firms generally have choices about whom they buy from. State agencies are generally monopolies. The only place that you can get a driver's licence is a government office; the customer has no choice. The policy thinker Manish Sabharwal once said that RBI's bond exchange, the Negotiated Dealing System (NDS), 'has hostages, not customers'. Nobody chooses to be a member of the NDS, they are forced to use it. This diminishes organizational performance.

The leadership of a private firm fears financial non-performance, which will ultimately lead to the loss of jobs and empire. Persistent weak performance can induce a sale of the firm to a new shareholder, who can impose painful changes upon the firm. Private firms face the threat of a bankruptcy process where the firm can be shut down or fundamentally reorganized.

None of these possibilities influence employees in the government. There are rare events where a government agency is closed down. Politicians fear losing elections. Officials have no fear.

The RBI was created in 1934. Consider the thousand-odd large private firms which also existed in 1934. By 2019, most of these firms had gone under, in the face of competitive pressure. The survivors (e.g., Tata Steel) were unrecognizably different, in 2019, compared with their organizational capabilities of 1934. But the RBI of 1934 has survived into 2019 without facing any competitive pressure, while having small changes in its organizational capabilities.

With private firms, we see something remarkable in the organizational culture of a Tata Steel or an IBM—firms that have managed to stay relevant over very long time periods. In government, in contrast, the oldest agencies are likely to have the most outdated internal arrangements.

Government's coercive power is qualitatively different

In a private firm, the levers controlled by the management cover products, production processes and the internal organization of the firm. In government, there is similar decision-making power about the internal organization of government. But the surpassing feature of government is the monopolistic power to coerce.

The state has a monopoly on violence. It is able to coerce private persons, either to pay taxes or to change behaviour. This yields a fundamental arrogance about state organizations, that private organizations do not suffer from. The puzzle of public policy lies in reining in employees who have the power to coerce, to prohibit, to raid and to imprison.

Government has greater complexity

A big firm in India has 25,000 employees. Compared with this, state structures are vast. Indian Railways has 1.3 million employees. Even if the efficient staffing at Indian Railways is half this size, it is a vast and complex organization when compared with what we see in the private sector.

The public policy process plays out not just through employees but through everyone, as coercive steps by the state induce changed behaviour by the people, which feeds back into the working of the state, and so on. This further increases the complexity of decision making. Policy decisions have to take into account the internal behaviour of large complex government organizations, and then the responses of the general public which in India's case is above a billion people. This is a scale of complexity which is just not found in private firms.

Government has to prize rules over deals

In a private firm, there is ample room for discretion. The idea is to make many tactical decisions— 'a hustle here and a hustle there'— that add up to profit.

As an organization becomes larger and more complex, there is greater use of formal rules. In a ten–man firm, every decision is tactical. By the time we get to a 1000-man firm, there will be an HR policy that will shape and constrain HR actions. If a firm has three franchisees, each of the three contracts can be negotiated separately. But if a firm has a thousand franchisees, there will be a policy framework that determines a few standardized contracts that are applied in all settings.

In government, this evolution towards rules is carried forward to an extreme extent. Given the unique features of government, it is pragmatic to work through policy frameworks and not tactical actions. We establish sound general frameworks, and work within them for a long time. We avoid transaction-specific decisions, even when we see a particular situation where the general policy is yielding the wrong answer.

In addition, Article 14 of the Constitution of India requires the Indian state to treat identically placed persons identically. There is no such constraint upon private firms. Private firms can make deals, but states need rules.

Governments must disperse power

The management of a private firm is often quite autocratic, partly because its internal staff is all that it controls. In contrast, public policy requires dispersion of power. The job description for a role in public policy is a package of policy knowledge, team building and nuanced negotiating ability. These are often elusive for persons with a background of leadership in autocratic firms.

Successful governments feature a long and slow process of debate, negotiation and compromise. The leadership in the world of public policy requires the traits of listening, respecting and negotiating middle roads. This is a very different organizational culture when compared with what is found in most private firms.

It is interesting to see that the organizational DNA in the largest and most complex firms veers towards the strategies of government. The largest and most complex firms have reduced power of the CEO, dispersed decision-making structures, and a greater emphasis on rules rather than discretion. The challenge of public administration lies in carrying this organizational evolution, from small firms to the biggest firms, further up a hundredfold.

Governments operate on longer horizons

Many in the world of business have come to revere the alpine-style assault, where a firm builds something very big in almost no time. Instagram got to 10 million users in a year and was bought for $1 billion in two years. A world-straddling company like Google was only founded in 1998. Successful management teams are often imbued with the idea of saving time.

The rhythm of public policy is quite different: to do good things requires a long slow ascent. Big sudden phenomena in the world of policy are generally harmful and/or failures.

Summing up

We in India revere success and wealth, and there is a lot of respect for business folk. We tend to assume (say) that sound HR practices in TCS will work well in government. But we should be cautious when thinking about transferring expertise into the world of public policy.

Companies have feedback loops where the daily MIS shows how things are faring, where quarterly financial statements are put out, and the stock price is updated in real time. When mistakes are made, they kick off corrections. Governments have no comparable feedback loops.

Most firms operate in competitive marketplaces. When mistakes are made, they lose customers. Governments have hostages, not customers, and there is no choice.

Firms wield no coercive power. They have to be nice to customers all the time. Governments wield coercive power.

The danger of functionaries that mistreat individuals is ever-present. Process design for government organizations involves establishing checks and balances against this threat.

Big firms are small compared with government organizations.

A lot of decisions in private firms can be tactical. Governments become the most effective when they establish rules rather than discretion, and eschew day-to-day tactical responses. Governments are bound by equal treatment (Article 14 of the Constitution of India) while private firms have no such constraint.

The management of a private firm is often quite autocratic. Successful governments, in contrast, do not have a CEO. Success comes from a long process of debate, negotiation and compromise.

Firms tend to work on short time horizons. The best governments work on long time horizons.

For all these reasons, the expertise on the working of private firms does not carry over into public policy, and vice versa. A country is not a company.[1]

25

System thinking

When a government gets involved in the working of society at the level of detail, this tends to go wrong. If a government is shaping products and processes, and favouring one technology over another, we are doing something wrong. If a government is 'picking winners'—one firm over another, one industry over another, one technical standard over another—we are doing something wrong. We have to be sceptical about engineers bearing industrial policy. Social engineering works badly as the real world is too complex, intervention is ridden with unanticipated effects and state capacity is limited. The most advanced economies do the least industrial policy.

The government should restrict itself to addressing market failure, while being mindful to only pick a few battles given its low capabilities. The economy and society should evolve as a self-organizing system, driven by the innovations of free men and women.

Solving coordination problems

There are, however, some situations in which there is a cautious case for 'system thinking' in public policy. System thinking addresses traditional market failures, in the form of asymmetric information, externalities and market power. In fields such as healthcare and pensions, where consumer behaviour may suffer from limited rationality, there is a greater case for system thinking. But it involves a new and daunting level of intrusive intervention, which goes well beyond the main work of public policy.

Consider a two-way street where people face no restrictions. This will frequently yield traffic jams. When one person drives on one side of the road, this hampers incoming traffic on that side of the road. The adverse impact from one person to another works through channels other than market transactions and voluntary agreements. It is an externality.

What is required in addressing the externality is a negotiation between many people, about who will use what parts of the road when, and a tidy solution is surely feasible. But it is difficult for all users of the road to find each other and negotiate such an agreement.

It is important to see that there is no complex political economy in this negotiation. Nobody particularly gains or loses from rules of coordination; all we have is a pure Coasean transaction cost of putting people together and negotiating.

A 'Keep left' rule, imposed by the state and backed by state coercion, nicely solves the problem of coordination by opposing traffic. It is a creative leap, a piece of system thinking, to envision this solution to the coordination problem.

Does this smack of central planning? When a government imposes a 'Keep left' rule, we can think of this as solving this problem of negotiation. The citizenry has chosen representatives (legislators) who would undertake the negotiation on their behalf, and the outcome of this negotiation is 'Keep left'.

Coercive unbundling

Economies of scope are about utilizing a customer relationship to sell an adjacent product, and about the reduced cost of producing an adjacent product. When governments use coercive power to *prevent* a firm from doing adjacent things, they are generally in the wrong.

As an example, the Indian financial markets were forcibly cut up into three sub-industries: commodity futures, regulated by the Forward Markets Commission (FMC); equities and long-dated corporate bonds, regulated by the Securities and Exchanges Board of India (SEBI); and currencies, government bonds and short-dated corporate bonds, regulated by the Reserve Bank of India (RBI). Firms in each silo were prohibited from doing business in the other two silos. This hampered economies of scale and economies of scope. In general, the coercive power of the state should not be used to hamper firms that exploit economies of scope.

In some situations, however, bundling and tying raises concerns about a market failure in the form of market power. As an example, consider the Life Insurance Corporation of India (LIC), which has a dominant position in the brand awareness and distribution of insurance products. Suppose a new firm is born, with high skills in the production side of insurance products. This firm would not be able to reach consumers, as LIC has a lock on distribution and sales. LIC can get away with very poor manufacturing, as it owns the distribution.

Using state power to force an unbundling, between manufacturing and distribution, can solve this problem. Consider the New Pension System (NPS). Project OASIS, led by Surendra Dave in 1998, saw that the overall pensions problem contained three distinct industries : managing money, owning customers, and record-keeping.[1] It suggested an unbundled architecture where pension fund management was separated from interaction with customers. Record-keeping was centralized at an information utility, to harness economies of scale, and to ensure that it was easy for consumers to switch from one pension fund manager to another.

This design caters to heightened competition. On the strength of better fund management, a new pension fund manager can steal away customers, as switching is always possible. Similarly, the front-end firms would live or die based on their friendliness to customers, and not on the quality of their fund management.

In the conventional world, finance professionals generally focus on the deal making required to get a new product to the customer. These finance professionals are a little shocked when, in the NPS environment, incumbent manufacturers do not control the distribution. All distributors are equally keen to push all products; all manufacturers have equal access to all distributors.

Similar arguments are found in electricity where governments have pushed in favour of breaking up monolithic electricity utilities into three distinct industries: generation, transmission and distribution. This creates opportunities for entrants in generation and transmission. Until this unbundling was done, the firm that owned the distribution was the only game in town when it came to transmission and generation.

Forcible unbundling backed by state coercion is a harsh intervention. What is an alternative, softer strategy? Suppose a new-generation company came up, and was denied access by an old-style integrated electricity utility. It could have used conventional competition law to litigate, and could have won, on the surface. However, there are too many levers, through which the monolithic utility could have rigged the game to disfavour the new entrant. It would take very high state capacity for a

Competition Commission of India (CCI) to track down such misbehaviour and enforce against it.

When state capacity is low, simple and transparent interventions are favoured. A simple unbundling rule is easier to articulate and enforce, when compared with the complexity of fighting with an integrated utility that is trying to hamper access to a new entrant.

In the field of technology policy, at heart, net neutrality regulation is about forcing an unbundling between the content industry and the data pipes. The content industry is analogous to a manufacturer. What is best for society is that content firms slug it out against each other to produce better content. Under net neutrality, content firms are not allowed to do deals with the data pipes in order to create privileged distribution for themselves. Similarly, data pipe companies must slug it out against each other to give us fatter pipes at lower prices. But they are not allowed to do deals with content companies in order to create complicated bundles of content and pipes for customers. The separation protects competition in both industries.

A firm that invents a new biscuit puts 10 per cent of its effort into the biscuit and 90 per cent of its effort into figuring out the distribution. Incumbents always have deep pockets, are entrenched in the distribution, and try to choke off competitors there. Every practitioner living in this world treats these anti-competitive barriers as an everyday reality. The Internet is a unique open market; the moment a new shopfront comes up, it is instantly connected to all customers who are on the Internet. This implies superior competitive conditions when compared with the old economy. A new e-commerce firm puts 100 per cent of its effort into innovation, as it knows that all pipes are of equal access. Net neutrality regulation is about keeping it this way.[2]

These examples are related to the common law concept of a 'common carrier', which is a firm that transports (say) goods in a non-discriminatory manner. The state coerces common carriers to force them to treat all customers equally.

The need for caution in system thinking

System thinking is very attractive to engineers. Every engineer feels she can redesign society in certain ways that are good for everyone. But system thinking is fraught with danger.

It is important to underline the use of state power, of the monopoly of violence that the state possesses, when policymakers do system thinking. When a government imposes a 'Keep left' rule, this is done by putting policemen in the street who impose punishments upon persons who drive on the right-hand side.

System design in public policy is unlike engineering design done in a private firm. A private firm that designs a product tries to put it on the market, and if there is a lack of voluntary buyers, the firm loses money, realizes this was not a good design, and goes back into debating the next design. In contrast, when system design is done in public policy, the citizenry has no choice, the solution is forced upon them backed by threats of violence, and there is a limited chance of discovering that the design was a mistake.

In the optimistic view, the engineer in the government is omniscient and cares about the welfare of the people. In the real world, both these assumptions are questionable.

It is very difficult to think about design questions on the scale of society. Human systems reflect the interactions of a large number of sentient persons, and attempts at intervention are plagued by the law of unintended consequences. We may emphasize that social systems involve the interactions of many *people*, and envisioning these complexities requires knowledge of the social sciences and humanities, and not just engineering. Hence, the policymaker can easily be wrong.

In addition, public choice theory reminds us that policymakers are just people, and are likely to pursue their own personal objectives, which may or may not align with welfare of the public.

For these reasons, it is useful to approach system thinking with high scepticism, and use the coercive power of the state in reshaping society only rarely. For most situations, the self-organizing system that is the market economy works better. This reflects a trade-off between the cost of some situations where system design in public policy goes wrong versus the cost of some situation where the self-organizing system gets trapped in the wrong equilibrium.

The self-organizing system works better than state-led design of society when state capacity is high. It is even more attractive when state capacity is low. When state capacity is low, there is a greater chance that state power will be used to impose the wrong designs upon society. There is a greater chance of this power being hijacked to serve an agenda other than public welfare.

Hence, while mature market economies avoid system thinking, we in India should avoid it even more.

How to do system thinking

If system thinking must be done in the public policy process, how should it be organized?

The first threat is that of the designers within government having the wrong design. To avoid this problem, a strong policy pipeline is required, with evidence, debate and the development of consensus in the expert community. If a design is made by any small group of people, without ample debate over elongated periods of time across a broad expert community, there is a greater risk of being wrong.

As an example, in the international engineering community, many important technical standards have been developed by the

'Internet Engineering Task Force' (IETF). This is an open process through which rival firms, academics and enthusiasts are able to debate and develop standards. Such a process has a better chance of avoiding errors and of achieving democratic legitimacy.

The second problem to address is the views of affected persons. A design that appears attractive to its creators might impose tremendous difficulties upon the economy. Broad-based consultation is required, with a large number of affected persons, in order to hear diverse views. Social systems are complex, and a design that appears clean to an engineer might induce unpleasant unintentional consequences for some individuals in society.

As with all government intervention, it is important to clearly state the problem that is sought to be solved, define what constitutes success, and set up a measurement system to watch how the economy is responding to the initiative. It is important to be humble, to recognize when things have not gone as planned, and be ready to change course.

A thumb rule that we would advocate runs as follows: Each policy thinker should permit herself a budget constraint of supporting no more than one policy proposal, that involves system thinking, in her life.

Summing up

Industrial policy works badly. Government should not pick winners. The purpose of government is to address market failure. A government should not be making decisions on which firm is better, what technology is better, or what technical standard is better.

There are some situations where addressing market failure (asymmetric information, externalities and market power) can be done by using the coercive power of the state to design society.

A 'keep left' rule, imposed by the government, brings order to traffic; it puts an end to the negative externalities of roads without such a rule. This can be rationalized as legislators engaging in a Coasean negotiation, and agreeing upon a contract that solves the problem of externalities.

When a government engages in system thinking, and uses the coercive power of the state in order to impose a design upon society, there are many ways in which this can go wrong. In public policy settings, coercion is applied and there is no feedback loop through which the design is rejected by customers or improved in response to customer feedback.

Social systems are very complex and there is a high risk of unintended consequences. Social engineering is thus difficult to do. The engineer may pursue objectives that diverge from the welfare of the public. The self-organizing system of the market economy generally evolves towards better solutions on its own.

There are some rare situations when a certain touch of system design is useful. One of them is a forced unbundling between industries which improves competition. Net neutrality is the use of the coercive power of the state to force a separation between two industries: the content industry and the carriage industry. Firms that make data pipes only compete on how well their pipes work, and all content providers are able to carry their product on all pipes. Such non-discriminatory treatment by the pipes is related to the 'common carrier' principle in common law. System thinking is more important in contexts like health and pensions, where we are at the limits of the rational decision-making of the typical individual.

If system thinking must be done, there are some good hygiene principles that are required. The development of the design must be done through an open process. The development of Internet protocols, through the IETF, is a role model for such an open process. Engineers may often tend to ignore the views of affected persons. Humanities and social science knowledge is of essence in thinking about questions from the viewpoint of the individual.

Social engineering is fraught with danger. As a thumb rule, we suggest that each policy person should have a budget constraint of supporting one policy proposal, involving system thinking, in one life.

26

Beware the rule of officials

During World War II, the British rulers established extreme restrictions upon the Indian economy. After Independence, these evolved into a central planning system. From the late 1980s onward, this has morphed into an 'administrative state', the rule by officials who have fine-grained control over the decisions of private persons, with functions that veer into legislative and judicial roles. This involves excessive interference in the lives of private persons. However, for the major part, this is the structure of the Indian state, and to do public policy in India is to operate within the contours of this administrative state.

Our first-order concern in Indian public policy is to improve state capability within this setting. It is useful, however, to re-examine the administrative state from first principles.

The traditional case for strong contract enforcement

Let us start at the objective of contract enforcement by courts. This is generally seen as being the foundation of business. Firms cannot contract with firms, and governments cannot contract with firms, if contracts are not honoured. Through this, an efficient and independent judiciary is an essential foundation of the market economy.

Economists have, however, been relatively lukewarm about the importance of this contract enforcement. How does poor contract enforcement matter?

- Under conditions of weak contract enforcement, people would limit their contracting to friends and family. Repeated games would spring up, where good behaviour is optimal. There would be an efficiency loss, because markets would become less competitive. A new player would not be able to dislodge friends and family from one's contracts.
- When contract enforcement is weak, firms would specialize less, there would be greater internal production and reduced use of contracting. This would adversely impact upon transactions and thus productivity.

These effects are present, but they are not particularly large. In this first cut of the analysis, the adverse impact of poor contract enforcement is relatively limited. The role of the judiciary, however, runs much deeper: it impacts upon the very requirement for an administrative state in addressing market failures.

Private solutions that solve market failure

When person A inflicts a negative externality upon person B, this is termed a 'tort' in common law. Under common law, person B is able to go to court and ask to be compensated for harm. Many negative externalities can be handled through this mechanism. If person A faces the credible threat that person B can win damages, this will constrain person A's behaviour.

This would remove the need for a state apparatus to coerce person A in ways that do not harm person B. All that is required is the common law of torts, and courts that enforce this law.

This pathway addresses a large part of the market failure associated with negative externalities and asymmetric information. This pathway breaks down when the courts do not work.

What about the problem where the persons adversely affected are many? A factory may emit pollution which may harm many individuals, none of whom have adequate incentive to undertake the expenditure of litigation. This collective action problem is solved using 'class action litigation' through which a group of people are organized to demand damages. This pathway breaks down when the courts do not work or when class action lawsuits are infeasible.

This vision of enforcement relies on the aggrieved person taking recourse to courts. It involves *private enforcement* of law. As an example, if a person or a group of persons were adversely affected by securities fraud, *they* would gather evidence and sue.

In this book, we have emphasized the power of private negotiation, as envisioned by Ronald Coase, for arriving at private solutions to many externality problems. These private solutions can flourish when, and only when, the courts are swift and competent. Otherwise, these contracts are not enforceable and the Coasean approach to addressing certain market failure is infeasible.

In this perspective, a great deal of market failure can be addressed through contracts, torts, class action lawsuits and private enforcement. Looking back into Indian history, this pathway was ruled out when, after Independence, there were difficulties in judiciary.

Example 31: SEBI's monopoly on enforcing securities law

Consider the establishment of SEBI, during 1988–92. In the early drafting of the SEBI Act, it was felt that if private persons could sue, on the grounds of violation of securities law, there was a greater risk of harassment. Therefore, the SEBI Act, unlike the US Securities Act, prohibits private persons from suing for violations of securities law. Only SEBI has the right to initiate such actions. Victims of securities law violations do not have this right.

Alongside this, India lacks a class action lawsuit mechanism, so there is no mechanism for (say) the shareholders of Satyam to sue. The design that was adopted in building SEBI was that *only* SEBI can initiate enforcement actions against a person. This is how we got to the administrative state. Now the difficulties of public management impact upon the enforcement process. Thus, persons who have experienced harm are supplicants before SEBI, requesting SEBI to enforce securities law.

Consider the judicial wing associated with regulatory actions. Securities regulators in other countries fuse the legislative and executive functions. They write regulations and they conduct investigations. But the cases brought by the securities regulator are heard in an ordinary court. In India, given the delays in judicial enforcement, we placed a judicial function at SEBI also. With this, the doctrine of separation of powers is absent in a regulator like SEBI. SEBI has become a very powerful organization, by the fusing of legislative, executive and judicial functions, and having a monopoly on enforcing securities law. In the memorable phrase of M. Sahoo, now chairman of the IBBI, regulators in India are 'mini-states'. This concentration of powers hampers the emergence of state capacity.

The policy possibilities for a country with high judicial capacity

India today is at a polar extreme, away from mature common law jurisdictions, with the domination of the administrative state.

We are weak on contract enforcement, torts, class action lawsuits and private enforcement. Organizations like SEBI are increasingly stepping into the shoes of the erstwhile central planning system.

In the late 1980s and the 1990s, the leadership in the Ministry of Finance and in SEBI was engaged in building SEBI in a practical way. They treated courts as flawed and looked for ways to make progress. While such strategies are useful in the short run, at a deeper level, they have limitations. When power is concentrated at organizations like SEBI, these organizations will find it difficult to achieve state capacity. The detailed interference by the administrative state in the economy saps economic vitality. There is a need to rethink this construction of the administrative state, in order to set India on a path of sustained economic growth into becoming a mature market economy.

The detailed licence–permit raj, and the fear of investigation agencies, are arguably at a peak in India today. How do we restore freedom? The agenda of liberalization and economic freedom requires going back to the foundations of common law: to a world of contracts, torts, private enforcement and class action lawsuits. This is what is required to scale back the administrative state.

The traditional conception of economists on contract enforcement has been that courts are required to enforce contracts. When the courts fail in this, the implications are relatively modest: there is reduced specialization and there are repeated games. Our perspective, however, runs deeper. When the courts fail, we get the rule of officials.

After Independence, we fared poorly on development of the judiciary. The coping mechanisms adopted by policymakers, in response to the failure of the judiciary, have their own harmful consequences. We need to address these failures at the root cause, through fundamental change in the judicial branch. We need to push back on the new central planning system, this administrative state, and graduate to a world of much greater reliance on the judiciary, a world of contracts, torts, class action lawsuits and private enforcement.

Summing up

The 'administrative state' is the rule of bureaucrats. This is a state where the officials manning the executive creep into controlling legislative and judicial functions. In the administrative state, politics—the process of negotiation between interest groups—has a limited role. The Indian approach to central planning of the economy, where officials have considerable control over the life of private persons, is uncomfortably close to the administrative state.

Economists have emphasized the role of the judiciary in contract enforcement, which enables the market economy. While contract enforcement is important, the more important role for judicial capacity lies in private solutions to market failure.

Negative externalities can be solved through the law of torts, as long as litigation is efficacious. Many classic problems of asymmetric information, where we do consumer protection, can be addressed through torts. When many people are adversely affected in a problem like pollution from a factory, the collective action problem can be solved through class action suits. When private people are able to sue, and state agencies do not have a monopoly on enforcing laws, this reduces the reliance on state agencies for enforcing laws.

The agenda of economic freedom in India is ultimately about scaling back the administrative state. This journey runs through great improvements in the courts.

Part V

The public policy process

27

Policymaking is siege-style assault

In mountaineering, the climbers choose from two strategies. In the siege-style assault, a large team establishes a base camp, which sets up the second camp and establishes the logistics for resupplying it, and so on. In the case of Mount Everest, there is a base camp at 5400 metres, camp 1 at 6100 metres, camp 2 at 6400 metres, camp 3 at 6800 metres and camp 4 at 8000 metres. Finally, from here, a few climbers try to get up to the top, which is at an altitude of 8848 metres. The siege-style assault is slow, expensive and reliable.

In an alpine-style assault, on the other hand, there is none of this preparation. One or two people try to walk up at the fastest possible pace. When the alpine-style assault works, the result is always remarkable. But it requires superhuman capabilities, and the probability of failure is high.

We think that the public policy process requires a siege-style assault. Every now and then, there are situations where an alpine-style assault yields some dramatic gains, but in time, these gains tend to be impermanent.

Example 32: The UK policy process on in vitro fertilization (IVF)

The world's first test-tube baby, Louise Brown, was born in the UK on 25 July 1978. There was a great deal of hostility to the concept of a test-tube baby at the time.

In 1982, the UK government established a committee headed by the moral philosopher Mary Warnock, to think about the associated public policy problems. The Warnock report was delivered in 1984 and led up to the 'Human Fertilization and Embryology Act' of 1990. This Act created the 'Human Fertilization and Embryology Authority' (HFEA) to adjudicate and license all work on human embryos, whether for IVF or for scientific study.[1]

How might things have worked out in the Indian policy process? We can see a few potential pitfalls:

- Right in 1978, when there was public criticism, there is a likelihood of a simple ban coming about. There is a bias, in India, for muscular responses to current newspaper stories. Letting the field unfold under laissez faire for four years is an unlikely event in the Indian policy process. As the securities expert Ashish Chauhan pleads, 'First you have to have a market, and only then you can regulate it.'
- If a committee had to be created, it would have been hard to find a moral philosopher to head it, as the humanities have atrophied in Indian universities.
- The translation of the report into the Act would have been done badly.
- The translation of the law into state capacity at HFEA would have been done badly.

This example encourages us to see the full pipeline of the policy process, and work on strengthening all elements of it.

The policy pipeline

Stage 1 of the policy pipeline is the establishment of the statistical system. Facts need to be systematically captured. Without facts, the entire downstream process breaks down. Our only hope for truth to matter is for truth to be recorded and widely disseminated.

In the modern world, few actors in the economy have an incentive to do a good job of measurement. As an example, academic economists are quite comfortable doing research with faulty data, because the academic economists who will review their work do not ask questions about data quality.

Stage 2 of the policy pipeline is descriptive and causal research. This requires a research community which will study the data, establish broad facts and regularities, and explore causal connections.

This work should be primarily grounded in the Indian locale. Academic researchers are too often swayed by the curiosity of journal editors and referees in a different continent. This hampers the choice of questions to pursue and the quality of research design through which those questions are sought to be answered.

Stage 3 of the policy pipeline is the creative phase of inventing and proposing new policy solutions. A large menu of choices needs to be at hand, for possible policy pathways. The republic is always short-changed when 'there is no alternative' (TINA) to one mainstream idea.

At present in India, there is no community which systematically looks for fully articulated solutions. Academic journals do not publish policy proposals, hence academic researchers are not keen to invent policy proposals.

Stage 4 of the policy pipeline is the public debate where rival solutions compete with each other. This requires a vigorous process of debate and discussion, in writing and in seminars.

A broad consensus needs to come about on what will work, within the analytical community.

In the Indian context, this is often assisted by the expert committee process. The purpose of the expert committee process is to sift through an array of possible policy pathways that are in the fray at the end of stage 3, and filter down to a few which make sense. The best expert committee reports help mainstream novel ideas in policy reform, and pull together the state of the art into a report. As Isher Ahluwalia says, nothing gets done by writing it in a government committee report, but nothing ever got done without it being repeatedly written into multiple government committee reports.

Stage 5 of the policy pipeline is the internal government process of decision making. This is where ministers and senior bureaucrats take stock of the range of possible policy pathways and make decisions. This is the zone of political economy, and the creative trade-offs that make progress possible.

Stage 6 of the policy pipeline is the translation of the decisions into legal instruments. Most policy decisions must be implemented through law that is enacted by the legislature, or subordinate legislation in the form of rules or regulations. High technical quality, and subtle detail, of this drafting process is of great importance.

In India, all too often, the drafting of law is done by persons who have a superficial understanding of the prior stages of the policy pipeline, which leads to poor drafting of law.

Finally, *stage 7* of the policy pipeline is the construction of state capacity, in the form of administrative structures that enforce the law.

Looking back into our history, the successful reforms in India were those that fared well on all seven elements of the policy pipeline. This, in turn, required capacity building in all the stages. It is only when there were human capabilities on all seven stages of the pipeline, and enough time had been given for working through these stages, that we got a sound reform.

An alternative depiction of the policy process

The economist Satya Poddar has a different conception of the policy process, which is also illuminating. He thinks in terms of a four-part story:

1. Defining the future state, or the preferred policy outcome,
2. Preparing a blueprint for the design and specification of the future state,
3. Defining the transition path from the current to the future state, and
4. Building political consensus or garnering public support for the change.

These elements are intertwined and are rarely sequential phases in the implementation process. Yet, they serve as a useful framework for project management.

The four parts require different skill sets. For example, we need visionaries and saints for the first element, who can rise above the morass of information, scientific knowledge and cacophony of self-interests. Preparation of the blueprint is science, engineering and public administration. A poorly designed transition path is often the main cause of policy failures, and thinking through a sound transition is more art than science. Consensus building is predominantly an art.

The opportunity in crisis

> It's a mistake to believe that the change that has not yet come will never come. On 9/11 the world changed; on 10/26 the PATRIOT Act

*was passed. The Patriot Act was not written in 46 days. It was simply
the instrument that was ready when the moment arrived.*

'Persuasive Language for Language Security: Making the case for
software safety', conference talk by Mike Walker, 24 May 2018

The US politician, Rahm Emanuel, famously commented that
'a crisis is a terrible thing to waste'. Crises are important events
where the 'Overton window' is enlarged, and there is a larger
zone of possibility in stage 5 of the policy pipeline. Policymakers
should be alert to these opportunities. More generally, there is
a lot to be said for a policy process where a community chips
away at stages 1 through 4 of the pipeline, and waits for the right
moment when stage 5 will use the ideas and stages 6 and 7 will use
the human capabilities.

The relationship between crises and reforms is, however,
highly exaggerated. There are three contrary points of view that
have to be kept in mind.

First, the possibilities in a crisis are the product of previous
work that has been done in the early stages of the pipeline, and
the human capabilities for stages 5, 6 and 7 that have been built
ahead of time. The apparently high marginal product of crisis is
partly grounded in misattribution; a lot of the credit has to go
to the investments by the policy community of previous years.
When we see the correlation between crisis and reforms, we are
exaggerating the role of the runner who carries the baton across
the finish line.

Investments in the early stages of the policy pipeline, and
in human capacity, have to be in place. Otherwise, a crisis will
be wasted. As an example, the rape in Delhi on 16 December
2012 created a political moment for reform of the criminal justice
system. However, as the early stages of the pipeline had not been
constructed ahead of time, and human capabilities for stages 5, 6

and 7 were weak, the response that was obtained in that terrible moment was weak.

The second concern that has to be kept in mind is that when the range of possibilities is enlarged, this includes some very harmful ideas. We should not think that the leadership is always benign and intelligent. Crises are dangerous moments when placed in a fragile liberal democracy like India.

Authoritarian rulers chafe against the checks and balances of a free press, the legislature, the courts and independent statistics. Democratic politics is about the hard work of negotiation, and when it works, heads of state routinely experience defeat. Authoritarian leaders find this a frustrating process; in fact they are often inexperienced in the culture of democratic law-making. They lack the temperament of sharing power, and are uncomfortable with the traditions of criticism and compromise.

Crises offer aspiring authoritarians an escape from constitutional shackles. When security threats arise, it is easy to label all critics as anti-national. When national security is at risk, the press, the courts and opposition parties are more deferential. We have numerous examples of crises that gave damaging outcomes. Hitler exploited the Reichstag fire in 1933. In Peru, an insurgency and economic crisis gave Fujimori the opportunity to dissolve the Constitution in 1992. Erdogan imprisoned thousands of opponents and intellectuals after a failed coup attempt in 2016. Indira Gandhi used the economic and political crisis of 1976 to declare Emergency.

> *The confusion, anxiety, and the profound sense of bewilderment about market forces are inevitable when breadwinners must worry whether income will be enough next week to feed the family . . . You cannot think straight in the midst of hyperinflation. The society becomes unglued.*
>
> Jeffrey Sachs

Let us shift gears away from a fundamental threat to the republic, in a crisis. When there is low state capacity, the day-to-day firefighting in a crisis can yield poor results. For example, India repeatedly had inflation crises in the past decades, and each inflation crisis triggered off a fresh batch of harmful command-and-control measures. The reform which actually mattered—inflation targeting through the Monetary Policy Framework Agreement (MPFA) of 20 February 2015—was not triggered off by an immediate inflation crisis.

Similarly, RBI produced seventy-four regulations in the first fifty days after the demonetization of 2016, and these crisis-management actions were not RBI's finest hour. The 2013 currency crisis had sustained policy activism over a period of months, with many adverse effects upon the economy.[2] Given weak institutions in India, we should dread a crisis.

The third concern is that focusing on opportunities for reform in a crisis tends to understate the value and possibilities from incremental reform. A lot more is possible from the slow process of improving things every day, than is commonly given credit for. The UK got to liberal democracy without anything like a French Revolution. We should not be entranced by dramatic wins; we should have the endurance to engage in 'the slow boring of hard boards' over long decades.

In India, it is often argued that deeper reform will only come about in a crisis. A flip side of this belief is a demoralized view that under normal circumstances, policy reforms are infeasible. We see the policy process as a process of building knowledge and conducting hypothesis tests every day, and we dread a crisis.

Example 33: The reforms of 1991

The reforms of 1991 are linked, in the minds of many, to the balance of payments crisis and consequential IMF conditionality. A closer examination of that period, however, shows the policy pipeline that was established through the 1980s and made this possible.

The decades in which India grew at 3.5 per cent, while East Asia did much better, had made an enormous impression upon the policy community. The intellectual foundations of the 1991 reforms were laid by Jagdish Bhagwati, Padma Desai, T.N. Srinivasan, Arun Shourie, Manmohan Singh, Anne Krueger, Ashok Desai, Montek Ahluwalia, and the other pioneers of market-oriented policy thinking in India.

The government committee process had established key pillars for reform, including the Dagli Committee on controls and subsidies (1979),[3] the P.C. Alexander Committee on import-export policies and procedures (1977), the Abid Hussain Committee on trade policy (1984), and the G.S. Patel Committee on stock market reform (1984).

By the late 1980s, there was a community of key persons in a dozen ministries who were envisioning a market-oriented India. There was an entire community that was ready to play a leadership role in economic reforms. Indeed, it was the ideas of *this* community which were written into the IMF conditionalities of 1991.

If these elements of the policy pipeline had not been in place, ahead of time, the crisis of 1991—on its own—would not have induced the positive changes that it did. For a contrast, Pakistan has had twenty-one loans from the IMF from 1958 to 2019, but lacked the policy community and the early stages of the pipeline, through which these moments of crises could be turned into accomplishments for policymakers.

Assessing the state of maturity of the reforms process in a field

For people who take interest in a field in India—e.g., agricultural reform—it is useful to score the state of maturity at each of the seven stages, every year. At each link in the chain, we should ask: What is the state of knowledge, literature and community? Can we identify ten highly capable persons (of all ideological persuasions) in each stage of the pipeline? A field is in poor shape on stages 1, 2 and 3 if we are not able to envision ten wise persons who can usefully be members of an important expert committee (at stage 4).

This classification system can be used to systematically identify the weak links in the chain in a field of interest, and strengthen those.

Capacity building for the Indian policy process

> The best time to plant a tree was 20 years ago. The second best time is now.

Chinese proverb

Capacity building for Indian policy reform requires fostering capabilities in all seven stages. Successful reforms tend to take place when there is maturity in all the seven areas. Activities that do not fit in the pipeline have limited usefulness. Alpine-style assaults are a high-risk strategy; they will often fail or be reversed.

The pipeline flows from left to right, and therefore there are prerequisites. The early stages have to be complete for the late stages to fare well. A systematic strategy of identifying the gaps—e.g., 'in field X, there is a particularly important weakness at stage 3'—can lead to constructive strategies to address these gaps.

The seven elements help us think about areas that are ripe for reform versus those that are not. The first four stages of the pipeline are of particular interest. When these early stages are strong, there is a possibility of making significant progress in actually doing reforms. The leadership which finds itself in such a situation should thank the people who put in the requisite investments, in previous years, to build the early stages.

When these early stages are weak, there is little opportunity to achieve significant reforms. It is quite inexpensive, to nurture these stages of the pipeline, and create reform opportunities for the future. But when a leadership is short-sighted and skimps on this nurturing, this has harmful effects in ways that are not visible at the time.

Summing up

Progress in policy involves a pipeline that runs from data to research to multiple policy proposals to public debate about rival proposals to decisions to legal instruments to implementation. If we use the key ' | ' to denote a pipe then the policy pipeline is data | research | proposals | debate | decisions | legal instruments | implementation. This is a slow, siege-style assault.

There is a widespread beliefs that crises are an ideal opportunity for reforms. However, crises are difficult times. If the pipeline is not mature, ahead of time, in the heat of the crisis it is not possible to overcome the gaps in knowledge and human capacity. When crises enlarge the range of possibilities, this includes some harmful ideas. Checks and balances are less effective in a crisis. Things can more easily go wrong. Institutions that are weak in normal times are unable to deal with the day-to-day events of a crisis. We should dread a crisis.

For a given field (e.g., property rights), it is useful to formally assess the state of capability in each stage of the policy pipeline. Each stage requires mature knowledge and a strong community. This will help guide the most valuable subsequent actions that need to be undertaken to obtain reform in a field.

28

Choosing from pillars of intervention

In many fields, it is useful to think of state activity under a few pillars of intervention. A government can *produce* education services by running schools. It can *regulate* the working of private schools. It can *finance* private persons buying the services of private schools. These are three pillars of intervention—producing, regulating, financing.

Each of the three pillars involves different kinds of management mechanisms. Positive externalities justify financing. Negative externalities, asymmetric information or market power justify regulating.

Conflicts introduced by public sector production

When a government is both umpire and player, this induces difficulties. The people in charge of production by the state have a bias in favour of capturing all the resources available for financing. They try to ensure weak regulation for themselves, and would like to place regulatory barriers upon private producers. In the Indian experience, there are many examples where the mixing of regulatory and production functions within one organization has worked poorly.

As an example, in the old structure of the Department of Telecommunications there was a fusion between monopolistic public sector production and regulatory functions. It is difficult for a state monopoly to regulate itself, which gave poor services. The telecom reforms of the late 1990s separated out regulation into the Telecom Regulatory Authority of India (TRAI), ended the public sector monopoly, and created multiple private providers.

This mixture of a public sector monopoly with regulatory functions is also found in many aspects of the RBI. Critical bond market infrastructure is owned by RBI which is also the regulator of the bond market. In the field of payments switching, there is a monopoly (National Payments Corporation of India [NPCI]) which is owned by a group of banks, where RBI has significant control. The recent proposal to build a 'Public Credit Registry' raises the possibility of an additional monopoly producer controlled by the RBI, while the RBI also performs connected regulatory functions. In all these cases, the strategy of mixing public sector production with regulation works poorly, and we would obtain improved outcomes through multiple competing private producers coupled with RBI regulation.

Example 34: Banking

There are two pillars of intervention in banking in India. On one hand, the state *regulates* banking. In addition, the Indian state *produces* banking services through the ownership of banks.

While there may be a case for privatization of banks, at a practical level, the state is a producer of banking services and will be in this business for some years. The public administration problem can then be phrased as two distinct questions. First, how should state capacity be achieved in the regulation of banking? Second, how should state capacity be achieved in the production of banking? Regulatory capability requires setting up a sound banking regulator and commensurate capabilities in a department of government. Owning banks is about setting up structures for the governance of public sector banks.

There are conflicts between these two lines of thought. Regulation by the state may be indulgent towards its own entities. The persons tasked with production may request a non-level playing field: regulatory restrictions upon private banks but indulgence towards public sector banks. This calls for strong separation between the two pillars.

Example 35: Education

In the field of school education, there are three pillars: funding, regulating, producing:

- There is a market failure in the field of education—positive externalities—where the person who obtains education does not take heed of the gains for society that come about as a consequence. This leads to underinvestment in education by each individual. Governments fund education in response to this market failure. This calls for the public administration design of the funding pillar. The simple and equitable way to organize this is to pay Rs X per year per child to parents. The more precise way is to link the rupee value transferred to the incremental knowledge obtained by a child.
- Parents would find it difficult to understand the true contribution made by alternative school providers. This calls for a regulatory strategy. On one hand, regulation may coerce

schools to do certain things. In addition, regulation may work through information release which helps parents make decisions about school choice. A public administration strategy is required to design this state capacity in regulation.

- Finally, there may be certain locations where private schools fail to come about. In these locations, the government may choose to be a direct producer of school services, by running government schools. The key tool for obtaining sound functioning of government schools is to ensure that the flow of resourcing into public schools only runs through parents: funding would flow to parents only, and through them, to the schools chosen by parents. A public administration strategy is required for running government schools, or contracting out the running of government schools, in underserved locations.

There are natural tensions between these three pillars. The people who do production of government schools would like to monopolize the funding, ask for weak regulation and raise entry barriers against non-government schools. This calls for strong separation between the three pillars.

Example 36: Skills

Increased skills induce positive externalities, and each individual is likely to underinvest in skilling. This motivates funding by the state. There is a market failure in the form of asymmetric information between the buyer and seller of skilling services. This motivates regulation. Finally, it is possible to have public sector production of skilling services. These three elements constitute clear verticals—regulating, financing, producing.

In India, state production is about running the Industrial Training Institutes (ITIs). Funding is about the flows of public money to private persons who add skills. Regulating is about ensuring high-quality training by all providers, public or private. This three-pillar thinking helps us organize the work in our minds, and encourages us to see the tensions within the three areas of work.

Example 37: Infrastructure

In the field of infrastructure, a useful classification is planning, contracting, regulating and producing. Planning pertains to the overall design required in both transportation and energy infrastructure. As an example, it is an act of planning to envision a container terminal at Nhava Sheva, and then the array of connections of roads and railways that have to be made to it. There is a greater role for the Union government in planning infrastructure assets that span many states.

Contracting is about establishing the PPP contracts through which private firms are given contracts to build this infrastructure. Regulating is about addressing the market failures of infrastructure monopolies in operation, which involves using state power to uphold quality of service and combat monopolistic pricing. Finally, the state does produce by virtue of owning some infrastructure assets, and an organizational framework is required for the governance and operations of those assets.

At the outset, we had pure state systems. The government would plan a road, the Public Works Department (PWD) would build the road, and roads were neglected after they were inaugurated. The first-level increase in skill lay in establishing the contracting capabilities for a private firm to build the road. This required a one-off transactional perspective. The complexity goes up greatly for a PPP contract, where the relationship between the government and the PPP vendor has to work out for many decades. This requires a higher level of capability and good behaviour by the government.[1]

Example 38: Healthcare

In the field of healthcare, it is useful to think in terms of the pillars of funding, regulating and producing. Funding pertains to channels through which public money goes to individuals who require healthcare. This may include expenditures on public hospitals, or on the new-age insurance schemes. Regulating pertains to establishing fair play by all healthcare providers, public or private. Finally, producing pertains to the ownership, governance and management of government hospitals. Once again, we see the tension where the persons involved in producing would like to monopolize the funding and have weak regulation upon themselves.

Example 39: Digital identity

On the problem of digital identity,[2] the pillars are regulating and producing. It is possible to envision multiple private persons who produce identity services. It is also possible to think of a public sector enterprise (possibly even a monopoly) that engages in production. Regardless of how production is organized, there are regulatory problems associated with regulation of monopolistic pricing, fair play to users, privacy, etc. In the case of identity infrastructure, monopolistic production creates a single point of failure, which is an unwise design strategy.

In the Unique Identity Authority of India (UIDAI), we have merged a monopoly public sector producer with a regulatory function. This leads to concerns about the extent to which the regulatory function will be performed properly. Monopolistic, taxpayer-financed public sector production also closes the possibilities for technological change and competition.

Example 40: Bond market

RBI owns and operates the bond depository, the subsidiary general ledger (SGL).

RBI owns and operates the bond exchange, the NDS.

RBI is the regulator of the bond market.

RBI is a player on the bond market.

The conflicts introduced by these functions have induced poor performance. For a contrast, SEBI regulates the equity exchange infrastructure, NSE and Bombay Stock Exchange (BSE) are the exchanges, and NSDL/Central Depository Services Limited (CDSL) are the depositories. SEBI does not trade on the exchanges. This has laid a better foundation, and helps explain the difference between the Indian story of the equity market versus the bond market.

Summing up

States are generally able to intervene in society in three ways. Coercive power can be used to modify the behaviour of private persons, which constitutes *regulation*. States can *produce* certain services. Finally, states can *finance* the purchase of certain services by private persons from private producers.

The organization design required for each of these three pillars is quite different. A funding organization is very different from a regulating organization, which, in turn, is very different from a producing organization.

State *production* creates incentives for light regulation of public sector production, an attempt at monopolizing public resourcing for only public production, and attempts at utilizing the regulatory power to create entry barriers that impede private production. Where possible, it is better to operate regulatory and financing pillars and not a production pillar.

29

Walk before you can run

In each field of reform (e.g., land market) there are many things that need to be done. In what order should they be done? This is the sequencing question.

Sequencing discussions in India often degenerate into choosing low hanging fruit to begin the work, and proclaiming that an important reform has begun. Sophisticated thinking on sequencing involves five elements:

1. Capacity building in the policy process: We have shown seven elements of the policy pipeline. There is a natural sequencing, going from left to right, of the order in which actions should be undertaken.
2. Prerequisites: When x is a prerequisite for y, we have to get x in place before y.
3. Learning by doing: Start with simple problems, learn public management, and gradually escalate complexity.
4. Political economy considerations: Weigh the gains and the costs imposed by various alternative components, and take the ones with high economic gain but low political cost first. Early

moves should create a constituency for the late moves. Early moves should not walk into a political economy trap.

5. Stinginess: Start on a low scale on coercive power and spending, escalate only when capabilities are proven.

Element 1: Capacity building

Consider the problems of Indian pension reforms in 1995. There was no data, there was no research, there was no policy community incubating ideas for reforms.

Under these conditions, the right thing to do should have been to build these early stages of capability in the country. To enact the Employee Pension Scheme (EPS) (1995), under these low conditions of capability in the early stages of the pipeline, was a mistake. It is no surprise that, with the benefit of hindsight, we now see that the EPS was a bad element of Indian pension policy.

There is a terrible air quality crisis in India today. The right policy response, as of 2019, consists of setting up measurement systems that will gather data, and setting up research centres. To try to rush ahead with solutions, such as odd–even in Delhi, is a mistake. We do not have enough knowledge for the most well-meaning policy process to emerge with the right answers.

Element 2: Prerequisites

The simplest inputs into the sequencing decision come from the question of prerequisites. What systems i, j, k are required for system x to work?

Example 41: Electricity reforms

Fuel is required by thermal-power-generation plants, and electricity generators need to be able to sell electricity to distribution companies. The natural sequencing for the reforms is then to first reform electricity distribution. At this point, we would have financially sound distribution companies. The next step should have been to reform the energy sector, so that a market for fuel was in place and generation plants would be able to buy fuel. The last step should have been to reform electricity generation.

In the Indian experience, we set about creating a new private industry of electricity generation, without having solved the problems of distribution or of fuel. Very large amounts of capital are blocked in new-age generation plants, which are stranded with the lack of fuel and/or the lack of financially sound buyers for their electricity.

With the benefit of hindsight, we see a simple failure of sequencing in the reforms of this sector. Problems in distribution and the energy sector should have been addressed before or at least in conjunction with generation reforms.[1]

Example 42: Float the exchange rate before trade reforms

Exchange rate reforms should come prior to trade reforms. This involves removing administrative barriers to the exchange rate, and getting up to a floating exchange rate. This gives a continuously self-adjusting price which counteracts changes in competitiveness.

Once this is done, and the local economy is opened up, there will be continuous adjustment of imports and exports in response to changes in the exchange rate. The exchange rate will be a shock absorber which will move in response to the short-term and long-term consequences of trade reforms.

Example 43: Finance comes first

As economist Joshua Felman says, if a great earthquake destroyed Mumbai, the first thing that we require is the financial firms, as they will provide the capital for rebuilding the rest of the city. A capable financial system is the primordial requirement of the market economy.

The infrastructure financing debacle in India is a reminder of finance as a prerequisite. The bond-currency-derivatives nexus was not in place, and therefore infrastructure financing could not be done in a market-based way. Policymakers were in a hurry, in the early years of the twenty-first century, to get to infrastructure investment, and felt that financial reforms were a luxury which could be postponed. Infrastructure investment was done, for the short run, by forcing banks to hold infrastructure assets. This lead to the worst outcome, visible after 2011, of stalled infrastructure investment and a large stock of stressed banks. It would have been much better to build the bond-currency-derivatives nexus, before embarking on infrastructure investment.

In a similar fashion, we must place financial reforms before macro reforms. This is because macro policy requires the machinery of a sound financial system. Inflation targeting requires a monetary policy transmission, which requires the underlying financial reforms in the form of competition in banking, the bond-currency-derivatives nexus and capital account liberalization. Fiscal reform requires debt management and the bond market.

These preconditions generate a natural sequencing: First we must build a capable financial system, and then we must undertake monetary and fiscal reforms. In India, we seem to be coming at this in the reverse order.

Example 44: Statistical system prerequisites

Building a factual foundation is the first step of the policy pipeline. Improved measurement will feed into all areas of decision making in the private sector and in the policy process. Hence, improvements in measurement should be prioritized for the early stages of building the republic.

If the CPI had not been well measured, it would not have been possible to do inflation targeting. Some people are excited about the value of nominal GDP targeting as a superior framework for monetary policy. We cannot consider this possibility in India, given the state of GDP measurement.

For most people in the country, GDP measurement has little practical importance. There is one place where numerical estimates of GDP play a direct role: fiscal planning. In January, when the budget is made, numerical targets for tax collection and the borrowing of the government are calculated based on estimated GDP. When the statistical system overstates GDP, this leads to tax targets that are excessively high and a borrowing programme that is excessively large. This suggests a natural sequencing: A country should build trusted GDP estimates before it uses GDP values in fiscal planning.

Element 3: Building capability gradually

Our first objective should be to establish *easy* objectives for state capacity, and fully succeed in building this state capacity. Only after this is done should we try for a more complex problem. 'Easy' here is in the sense described in our treatment of what is easy and what is hard. Simple problems are those that involve a fewer number of transactions, less discretion, low stakes and less secrecy.

In the case of taxation, high tax rates kick off much greater attempts by private persons to avoid or evade taxes. It is much harder to build a tax system with high tax rates. Hence, it makes sense to first learn how to do tax administration at low tax rates. Only after a high compliance environment is achieved at low tax rates, can we examine the possibility of higher tax rates. If, on the other hand, we try to jump to high tax rates, this induces an 'organizational rout', a collapse of the tax administration into high rates of corruption and evasion.

Similarly, a simple single-rate GST is easier to implement, as opposed to a complex GST system with multiple rates. It would make sense to first build a single-rate GST, achieve a high compliance environment, and then examine the possibility of having multiple rates.

On a related note, at the early stages of learning how to build a tax administration, the officials should have low powers of investigation and punishment. If high powers are given to officials, alongside the poor checks and balances of an early-stage organization, this will yield a collapse into intimidation and corruption. Only after a tax administration is working at high levels of probity with low tax rates, low powers of investigation and low penalties, can we consider gently raising these powers.

These are the natural sequencing opportunities: to build the easy pieces first, to learn state capacity on simple problems, and then come to the more difficult ones.

Example 45: The Indian pension reforms

Sequencing issues were central to the Indian pension reforms. There were three elements to the Indian pension reforms problem: mandatory pensions for private firms (that was done by Employees' Provident Fund Organisation [EPFO]), mandatory pensions for civil servants, and the vast uncovered unorganized sector.

Policymakers chose to build the New Pension System starting with the civil servants. This was motivated by many elements of reasoning. New institutional infrastructure needed to be built and proven, and civil servants' group was a compact problem where this could commence. The credibility of the reform would be heightened with the 'eat your own dog food' character of the reform starting with civil servants.

Once the NPS worked, the employees of private firms would clamour to exit EPFO. Finally, word of mouth through civil servants (who are credible parties in their engagement with the larger populace) would gradually draw in voluntary unorganized sector participation into the NPS, without requiring the reduced returns for pensioners that are associated with expensive sales campaigns.

Example 46: The Indian bankruptcy reform

When a country embarks on setting up a bankruptcy process for the first time, as India did in 2016, at first the state capacity will be poor. A well-functioning bankruptcy process requires numerous actors to play their role correctly, and at first this ecosystem will not be in place.

Hence, in the early stages of the bankruptcy reform, it is better to carry small bankruptcies through the system. These constitute a smaller load. With larger cases, there will be expensive legal teams in the fray, trying to find any loophole. The collision between high stakes and low state capacity will give poor answers. For this reason, the decision to put twelve large cases into the fledgling Indian bankruptcy process was a problematic one.

Placing a high load of high-stakes cases upon a fledgling bankruptcy process can lead to an organizational rout. Economist Joshua Felman has a good insight on one channel of influence, which runs as follows.[2] The essence of the bankruptcy process is the sanctity of process. The process creates the right incentives, so even if in one case there can be a higher value realization by sacrificing the process, we should still uphold the process.

Early in the life of the bankruptcy reform, judges are themselves relatively unsure about how this works. If a Rs 10 million case appears, it is more likely that a judge will favour the sanctity of process. But if a Rs 1 trillion case appears, and the prevailing jurisprudence is weak, the judge is more likely to say that the process can be overruled as the sums of money to be gained are so large. A few rulings like this can create jurisprudence that permanently hobbles the bankruptcy reform.

Element 4: Manage political economy

Successful reform is about dealing with the allocation of gains and losses, and creating and sustaining winning coalitions. We should think about the most vulnerable, and push costs to them into the future. A good sequencing is one that gives gains to the economy early, and thus boosts GDP growth.

Anne Krueger, Jagdish Bhagwati and T.N. Srinivasan have emphasized the connections between internationalization and the local elite. In the initial condition, we are trapped in a domestic political economy, where large domestic distortions go with a narrow elite that defends those distortions. Policy actions that open up the economy in all possible dimensions are a good first step because they reshape the incentives of the local elite in favour of taking on the domestic barriers to high productivity.

A powerful theme in this political economy thinking lies in early actions that reshape the map of interests. Initial actions should build a new coalition of beneficiaries, who will support the completion of the reform.

Example 47: The problems of managing the exchange rate

Suppose the government manages the exchange rate. Private persons will see the power of the government in changing their profit rates, and organize themselves to lobby for a favourable exchange rate policy. As an example, in China, a large export sector sprang up under a distorted exchange rate, and lobbied to preserve the distortion.

These problems are avoided if the first stage in the reform is to achieve a floating exchange rate, i.e., to get the nascent pockets of internationalization to think that lobbying for exchange rate depreciation is not a choice.

A related trap in sequencing is the order in which exchange rate reform versus foreign currency borrowing reform takes place. If domestic agents build up large foreign borrowings early, they tend to lobby in favour of restrictive exchange rate policy. The correct sequence is to first get to a floating exchange rate, and only then open up to foreign currency debt by local firms.

Example 48: India's petroleum sector liberalization

The liberalization of petroleum pricing in India shows an interesting success story in sequencing. First came the decision to do this in stages and not induce any sudden shock. The actions began by giving ONGC the international price for crude oil, so as to establish parity with incentives based on global price for exploration and extraction. This was an easy first move which did not impinge upon the population.

Petroleum products are universal intermediates, and the short-term elasticity of demand is very small. There is a large low-income population for whom, low price inelasticity implies that fuel price hikes are tantamount to an income shock. Hence, price liberalization for consumer products, kerosene and LPG, should be back-ended. Therefore, the sequencing for price decontrol that was adopted was industrial products (naphtha, fuel oil) followed by transportation fuels followed by cooking fuel.

Example 49: India's trade policy reform

The story of trade policy reform in India is also similarly interesting. When our policymakers worked on trade policy reforms in 1991, they shrewdly designed the sequencing to counteract the opposition of the 'Mumbai Club'. The sequencing of tariff cuts was designed so as to first improve competitiveness of incumbents, through trade liberalization of industrial inputs such as capital goods and intermediates.

The first stage was the liberalization of capital goods imports, where the only losers were incumbent public sector companies such as HMT. This was welcomed by private manufacturers as they got better and cheaper equipment. The second stage was to liberalize intermediate goods. This was also welcomed by private manufacturers. This helped many Indian firms gain confidence about dealing with import competition. Indeed, there was a great surge of Indian firms who began *exporting*, when given cheaper inputs and capital goods. At the time, we coined the slogan: 'Each time we cut tariffs, exports will go up'.

This strategy helped dilute the organized opposition of Indian industry against tariff cuts. The private sector was now armed with global-quality capital goods and buying global-quality raw materials. The stage was then set for liberalization of imports of consumer goods.

A related element was the announcement by Yashwant Sinha that every year, the peak customs tariff rate would go down by five percentage points. This was an extremely wise move. Each decline, of five percentage points, was not big enough to kick off a furore. But the remorseless application of this rule, year after year, created certainty in the minds of the private sector that they had to gear up for a world of free trade. At the same time, they were given time to gear up with globally competitive technology.

Element 5: Restraints against abuse of coercive power

Some of the hardest sequencing problems involve creating organizations that wield the coercive power of the state. At early stages of development, individuals in organizations such as enforcement institutions, will perhaps have poor checks and balances. This will create the possibility of arbitrary use of the coercive power of the state.

> *I look upon an increase in the power of the state with greatest fear, because although while apparently doing good by minimizing exploitation, it does the greatest harm to mankind by destroying individuality which is at the root of progress. State represents violence in a concentrated and organized form.*

> Mahatma Gandhi

When large punishments can be inflicted upon the people, the power of individuals in enforcement institutions becomes extreme. There is a danger that enforcement organizations become roving bandits, engaging in extortion. There is then the risk of being trapped in the wrong equilibrium, as these incumbents would resist the creation of checks and balances.

A fledgling tax administration agency with a high tax rate and the power to raid will yield an 'organizational rout'.[3] The agency will collapse into corruption and abuse of power.

In the field of customs duties, the 'collected rate' is customs revenue divided by the value of imports. In a perfect state, this should be exactly equal to the official tariff rate. In Pakistan, for goods where the customs rate is below 40 per cent, this broadly works out: the collected rate is near the official ad valorem rate. By the time we get to an official rate of 80 per cent, there is a gap of about 30 percentage points between the official rate and the collected rate. At a customs duty of 120 per cent, the gap rises to 70 percentage points. High tax rates induce a bigger failure in weak organizations.[4]

Once this organizational rout has taken place, there will be grave opposition against well-meaning reforms, by the insiders who are profiting from the abuse of state power.

High powers to obtain information, raid, arrest, imprison, and award draconian penalties are found all across the Indian policy landscape and constitute a serious problem.[5] A government agency should be given such powers only when it has achieved high levels of institutional capability. Swedish-style powers of electronic surveillance by an income tax agency can only be given to an income tax agency that has achieved Swedish levels of the rule of law.

For these reasons, it makes sense to legislate only modest coercion at the early stages of state capacity. In the early stages of development, the focus should be on building a competent organization featuring checks and balances and the absence of extortion. Only after this public policy knowledge has been mastered, can powers become larger.

How state capacity declines

We seem to go through a cycle in India which runs roughly as follows. An agency is established with low capabilities and excessive aspirations. Things do not work out, and there is a visible crisis.

We have excessive bureaucratic capture in India: the incumbents in an agency generally have a disproportionate say in the course corrections required after a crisis. It is in the interests of this bureaucracy to amass more personal power. Hence, crises lead to greater powers to do surveillance, greater powers to raid, and greater powers to punish.

Each crisis thus leaves the agency with greater discretionary power, which in turn fuels a decline in the capabilities of the agency. This perspective yields interesting insights into the decline of capability at many organizations in the last decade.

As an example of this phenomenon, RBI was the regulator of non-banking financial companies (NBFCs), and there was a large crisis of NBFCs. In response, RBI's powers were increased. Similarly, when politicians ask for greater tax revenues, the tax bureaucracy asks for more coercive power.

From dirigisme that is irrelevant to dirigisme that binds

The Indian state is littered with a variety of repressive laws and subordinate legislation. In the early years, these constraints often did not bind, as the enforcement capacity was not present. The development of state capacity, and the formalization of the Indian economy, are generating new problems with old tools of repression.

As an example, consider the Essential Commodities Act (ECA). When warehouses were owned largely by individuals, the ECA did not matter too much. Every now and then, a local policeman would use the ECA to raid a local businessman, but for the rest, the impact upon the economy was limited.

This changed with the rise of large corporations in warehousing. These corporations have a higher compliance culture. They have more at stake and cannot violate a law. Here, for the first time, the ECA has come to be a binding constraint. New life has been infused into an old piece of the repressive apparatus through the development of a capable private sector.

For another example, consider the laws about electronic surveillance. The Indian state used to have considerable power to snoop on individuals, going back to British times. These laws did not amount to much, as the Indian state did not have the capability of listening in upon too many calls. Things changed, however, with the rise of modern computer technology. For the first time, the Indian state now has the ability to record and analyse a large volume of electronic communications. The old laws can now be used to even engage in mass surveillance. New life has been infused into an old piece of the repressive apparatus through the development of state capacity.

Summing up

The policymaker has to do many things. In what order should they be done? Too often, in India, policymakers pick one of two easy things, 'the low-hanging fruit', and after that the reform peters out. Doing the easiest thing first is generally not the optimal sequencing.

The policy pipeline shapes sequencing. If the data is lacking, it will not be possible to make progress on policy design. Therefore, when the data is lacking, the first thing in the sequencing should be improvements in the data.

In the working of real-world systems, there are prerequisites. An inflation-targeting central bank will require a capable bond market, in order to do the monetary policy transmission. Reforms of electricity generation will not work if the electricity distribution does not work. We have to identify these choke points and solve them first.

State capacity does not come about easily. It is better to solve easy problems first, that put us on the path to higher state capacity in the future. Capability emerges out of the process of learning-by-doing. This calls for low transaction-intensity, less discretion, low stakes and less secrecy, at the early stages.

It is important to think through the political economy. This is not just about buying out the persons who lose from a reform. The early steps should create gainers who will then support and sustain the reform.

In the early stages of building the republic, low coercive power should be given to government organizations, particularly the powers to raid, investigate and punish. Through this, we reduce the stakes. Only after high success is achieved, in wielding low coercive power, can there be a discussion about whether higher coercive power is desirable.

In India, we are often seeing a negative spiral. An agency has excessive coercive power, and so it fails in its work, but the political response to failure generates greater coercive power for the agency, which further reduces capability. The right response to failure by an agency should be a reduction in its coercive power.

30

Low state capacity changes policy design

The grand story of infrastructure in India is instructive. By the late 1990s there was universal mistrust of public production of infrastructure services, and the policy community moved towards private production. It was felt that a private person will run infrastructure assets better, as we lack the state capacity to run these assets.

With the benefit of hindsight, we know that contracting and regulation of private infrastructure providers *also* require considerable state capacity. The simplistic notion—of shifting infrastructure provision away from a low-capability state to private providers—was wrong.

How then should we think more carefully about the optimal pathways when we have low state capacity?

How does our thinking about public policy change when we possess low state capacity?

Just a down-sized Sweden?

Consider the contrast between Sweden and India. The expenditure/GDP ratio in Sweden is about twice that in India.

The management capability in public policy in Sweden is much superior to that seen in India. If the Swedish leadership decides to establish universal HPV immunization for children, it's easy to translate this intent into action. But in India, it is quite a challenge for the leadership to implement such a decision. Sweden has more state capacity.

How would we think about public policy differently, when placed in Sweden as opposed to how we would think in India?

The simplest idea is to think of an Indian state that does everything that Sweden does, with inferior resourcing. The Swedish central bank has 360 employees, so we should aim for a central bank with 180 employees.[1] We would look at the unemployment insurance system in Sweden, and come up with a design in India which requires roughly half the expenditure.

We think this is the wrong way to think about the consequences of low state capacity. The consequences of low state capacity run deep, and require fundamentally different answers in a place like India, when compared with a high-state-capacity country like Sweden.

A higher price and a lower budget constraint

One way to think about state capacity is as a layer of inefficiency in all state activities. Low state capacity is like a modified price of engaging in a certain activity.

Sweden gets a central bank done in 360 employees, but we may require 720 people in a central bank, as low state capacity induces greater inefficiency. Here, the cost pertains to financial resourcing but even more to the scarce time of the policy leadership.

It is also useful to think of state capacity as a finite *resource*, as a low-budget constraint. The financial resources available in a low-capacity state are more limited. The scarcest resource of all is the time and attention of the senior political and bureaucratic leadership, and of the experts.

The short-term question lies in utilizing these scarce resources wisely. Doing policy under conditions of low state capacity is about making decisions where prices are higher and budget constraints are smaller.

The deeper question lies in how to increase state capacity. How can a country put itself on the journey to increasing state capacity, so that over time, the cost of undertaking a certain activity goes down, and the aggregate resources available to the state go up?

Market failures that should not be addressed

In theory, the world contains many market failures and we use state intervention to address them. In practice, we have an imperfect state. In the real world, the outcomes with state intervention are always worse than originally imagined. The policy decisions that flow from the real-world political process are suboptimal. State capacity is limited, so the implementation of a policy objective is flawed.

It is useful to think of three cases:

Market failure solved, but at a high cost: Under conditions of low state capacity, there is a greater risk of extremist policy actions.

For example, consider the market failure (externality) associated with acid rain. It is possible for a government to ban coal-fired thermal plants. This action does put an end to the market failure. But this is an inefficient solution, as the cost imposed upon society is too high.

Banning an activity is done too often in India. Public choice theory predicts that bureaucracies will favour the peace of mind and laziness. Given the lack of accountability associated with present laws, there is a bias in favour of bans.

Regulatory response, but high cost and low effectiveness: Sometimes, the Indian state pursues a market failure by trying to write regulations which reshape the behaviour of private persons. In this, owing to capacity constraints, the regulations that are written fare poorly on the cost–benefit analysis. They impose high costs and achieve low results.

The market failure is not solved, and the costs imposed upon society are excessive.

Redistribution, but high cost and low effectiveness: Government interventions through running government schemes or paying out subsidies are particularly daunting, under conditions of low state capacity, because of the high marginal cost of public funds. The cost to society of public expenditures is very high, so even a well-run programme is less attractive under these conditions.

Further, low state capacity hobbles the working of the scheme or subsidy programme, and that further hampers the net gain to society.

Put together, schemes of the Indian state fare poorly on cost–benefit analysis owing to high cost to society and poor results.

Through these pathways, the cost–benefit analysis associated with government intervention works out differently when there is low state capacity. There is a loss of welfare associated with a certain market failure. Under conditions of low state capacity, the costs associated with the intervention will be large and the market failure itself will be inadequately addressed. We are often better off living with the market failure, rather than trying to address it in an imperfect way.

Under conditions like those prevailing in Sweden, where state capacity is high, we would be more optimistic and set out to address many market failures. But under conditions of low state capacity, it would be efficient to choose a smaller class of problems worth solving.

By this reasoning, we would not do half the effort on addressing all the market failures that Sweden is fighting. The Indian state should not just be a mini-Swedish state. There would be many zeroes in the Indian optimization: We would try to go after a smaller set of market failures, where the welfare cost of the free market outcome is particularly large, and where the state capacity required in addressing the market failure is relatively small. Given our capacity constraints today, to quote Kaushik Basu, we have to engage in 'libertarianism of necessity'.

More intrusive interventions are more dangerous

When state capacity is low, there is a greater chance of making mistakes. In this case, the damage that can be caused by a more intrusive action by the state is greater.

When we live in a low–state–capacity environment, there is a greater chance that the government is wrong. In this case, we should favour small moves, small powers for the government, small punishments, small sums of money. The bigger and more dramatic the action, the greater is the harm inflicted upon society when government is wrong.

The phrase 'the government is wrong' seems like a sterile one. Our mental model may be one in which at random, there is a certain probability of making a mistake. However, the probability of being wrong is itself driven by the incentives of politicians and officials. Under conditions of low state capacity, an official has the power to raid any person, with weak checks and balances. Public choice theory teaches us that the government is not just wrong through random errors; there is malign intent in the errors. Weak checks and balances operating upon the official who controls raids will *induce* a higher probability of malign raids.

Under conditions of low state capacity, a big disruption such as demonetization should be subjected to greater scepticism than it would face in a high-state-capacity environment. This is because the probability of our being wrong, under Indian conditions of state capacity, is higher.

Do fewer things

We in India are late industrializers. We built a democracy at an early stage of development. Democracy has brought a large number of demands upon the state. It is difficult for elected leaders to ignore these demands. Too often, we have succumbed to mission creep. We tend to go after too many policy problems, and end up with inadequate resourcing on each of them. We are weak in public policy and public administration—across all areas—so the cost of undertaking any one of those activities is high.

There is a lot to gain by paring down to a smaller set of priorities, focusing upon them, and making genuine progress. If the scarce resources—of money and man-hours of key persons—could *focus* on a small set of important problems, we would get a lot more done. Along the way, we would learn how to own and operate a state.

This can be seen as one more message in sequencing. The correct sequence is to first focus on a few problems, learn how to do politics and public management, and then scale out into a larger number of problems.

Economist Joseph Stiglitz has argued that in developing countries, there are rampant market failures, and this calls for a larger scale of state intervention. While we agree on the presence of many market failures, our proposal would run in the opposite direction. We would argue in favour of the largest possible state that is feasible while achieving competence, and this is likely to be a very small state.

The virtue of simplicity

When state capacity is high, a government can embark on more complex plans. When state capacity is low, the only things that will work correctly are simple plans.

This was a major theme in the evolution of tax policy in India in recent decades. Reduce the number of rates, reduce exemptions, reduce complexity—these were the themes around which major progress was made.[2]

As an example, consider the prospect of a subsidy, implemented through the tax system, for things that involve positive externalities. In theory, this can be a good thing. There *is* market failure when there are positive externalities, and there *is* a case for a subsidy, and sometimes that subsidy can be delivered through the tax system.

Suppose highway construction is to be financed by tax-exempt bonds. The policy analysis of tax-exempt bonds is, however, a very complicated affair. When we confront a positive externality, and think of a public subsidy, we must have numerical estimates of how large the externality is, which guides the design of the subsidy. Giving an entity or a class of entities the ability to issue tax-exempt bonds constitutes a certain magnitude of subsidy, which may or may not be commensurate with the magnitude of the positive externality.

Once the precedent is set, that highway developers are able to issue tax-exempt bonds, there will be a clamour for other kinds of tax-exempt bonds. Should this be given to airports also? What about irrigation? Is the positive externality associated with all kinds of infrastructure the same? Why stop at infrastructure? What about a firm that gives loans to poor people? Why not have tax-exempt bonds for hospitals?

Under conditions of low state capacity, the only safe place to be is to have no tax-exempt bonds. If a subsidy has to be paid, it is best to do this through the expenditure programmes of government, where there will be better scrutiny of the relative magnitudes of expenditures.

Example 50: Information utilities

There is an emerging field in India, of 'information utilities' that perform commercial functions. There are two ways in which this industry can come about. One pathway is to have multiple competing private firms, with a layer of consumer protection and checks on market power such as interoperability regulation. This is the approach taken in the construction of NSDL, CDSL, etc. There is an alternative approach: to build a government monopoly. RBI is in the process of building such a monopoly, which is called the Public Credit Registry (PCR).

This is an inferior path for three reasons. First, concentrating information about private persons in the hands of government is harmful for society. We are generally better off with a government that knows less about us, and this is even more important at the early stages of building a republic, where there are few checks on the abuse of information. Second, monopolies generally fare worse than competitive industries at fostering innovation and cost reduction. Third, RBI has quite a challenge on its hands, of learning how to achieve state capacity on its core functions of inflation targeting and regulating banks. The pathway for RBI lies in focusing on its main tasks, and learning to do them well, rather than building a sprawling empire.[3]

Example 51: Competition between exchanges

Financial exchanges can compete, offering diverse products for trading, methods of trading, etc. There is a normal market process of listening to what users want, investing in innovations, learning from mistakes, changing course, etc., all playing out at exchanges with rapid feedback from successful adoption (or not) by financial market participants.

The government is involved in the working of financial markets in the form of addressing market failures. While exchanges innovate, the role of the government is to ensure that there is no collapse of the system of financial trading, and to enforce against market abuse. Apart from this, there is no role for the government.

In India, however, we have evolved a remarkable central planning system where every detail about the design of the exchange is controlled by SEBI. Every exchange in India looks the same to the user, and the features and capabilities of the exchange are controlled by SEBI.

This has generated a remarkable shadow-boxing where the process of competition between exchanges is played out as rival influences upon SEBI. Each exchange lobbies in favour of changes in the SEBI-specified product design that will increase its own market share. The only competition between exchanges is for influence at SEBI.

Under Indian conditions of state capacity, SEBI fares poorly when the competitive energy between exchanges is played out at the arena of SEBI. Under Indian conditions of state capacity, the power of central planning placed at SEBI—unmoored of market feedback—yields a poor design of the trading system.

In recent years, this has given a stream of actions by SEBI that have a negative impact upon market quality. At first blush, we may think that the answer lies in improved state capacity at SEBI. However, the real issue is that comprehensive central planning systems work particularly badly when there is low state capacity. The deeper solution is to remove SEBI from the crossfire of competition between exchanges.

Example 52: Industrial policy

We frequently hear demands for a government to 'pick winners' such as an industry (e.g., making wall clocks) and/or a location (e.g., Morbi, Gujarat), and push the private sector in this direction either through tax incentives or subsidies or coercion.

The experience of mature economies such as Japan or the US shows us that industrial policy works badly, even under those conditions of state capacity. Under Indian conditions of state capacity, industrial policy is best avoided. There is a large chance of mistakes by the state, and there is a large opportunity cost of the human and financial resources that are put into these battles.

We should get uncomfortable when any Indian government agency encourages or discourages any industry or location. As an example, RBI has capital control restrictions that favour nine industries, including nanotechnology and poultry. No economist knows enough about the structure of the Indian economy to make such a decision.

In the 1970s, the Santacruz Electronic Export Processing Zone (SEEPZ) was built by policymakers based on the idea that the electronics industry needed encouragement, and this encouragement was given in the form of zero customs duties. The elimination of customs duties is always a good policy, and this gave gains. The industries that came out of SEEPZ, however, were not what policymakers visualized. India did not start exporting electronics owing to the SEEPZ experiment. SEEPZ instead gave birth to the Indian software and diamond industries. The elixir that worked was not the ability of a policymaker to pick winners; it was the removal of trade barriers.

Example 53: Leadership in technological standards

The US government built the Global Positioning System (GPS) and the European public sector telecom companies built the Global System for Mobile communication (GSM). This makes us wonder whether the Indian state can play a role in developing and pushing technological standards.

As an example, consider the GPS. The GPS project was begun by the US Department of Defense in 1973, aiming for military applications. In 1983, when flight no. KAL 007 was shot down by the USSR after straying into USSR airspace, Ronald Reagan released GPS access for civilians as a global public good. Initially, the information available for civilian use was deliberately degraded. In 2000, Bill Clinton released full access to GPS information into the global public domain.

Would the Indian military leadership have had the ability to get a system like GPS to work in about a decade? Would they have had the public policy capabilities to release it into the public domain as a global public good? There is a greater chance of mistakes, in such efforts in India. Hence, we should be more sceptical about such efforts taking place in an environment of low state capacity.

Learning the meta technology of how to run the state

In the early history of many successful states, the leadership focused primarily on two problems: raising taxes and waging wars.

Learning-by-doing took place through the pursuit of these two activities. State capacity in the early days in the UK and in Sweden was learned by building large, complex organizations which raised taxes and waged wars.

The learning-by-doing that took place was not just about the narrow problems of raising taxes and waging wars. The learning-by-doing that took place was about larger ideas about how to organize the state. The general capability of public policy and public administration was learned in these two areas, which was then transplanted into other areas.

This ladder of capability is useful when thinking about the problem of state capacity in India. The strategy for public policy in India should be to pare down the number of objectives to a few core public goods such as the criminal justice system. Our task for a few decades is to learn how to build state capacity in those areas. The problem is not just the narrow question of learning how to run the criminal justice system, but the larger lessons of how to achieve state capacity.

Once we have these capabilities in the country, there would be the possibility of broadening out to a more expansive set of market failures. That would be a political choice for future generations.

Summing up

If we were in Sweden, we would do normal public economics: We would identify market failure and address it. If we live in a country with low state capacity, how does this change our thinking?

In the international experience, waging war was an important pathway to developing state capacity. That pathway is not open to India, given the nuclear deterrent.

When there is low state capacity, there is a bigger chance of state power being used in wrong ways. Therefore, it is wise to use coercion mildly. When state capacity is low, tax rates should be low, expenditures on public programmes should be low, the investigative powers of the agencies should be low and the punishments that are encoded into laws should be low.

When state capacity is low, we should design simple interventions that are easy to implement. A single-rate GST makes lower demands of state capacity, in the annual process of making the budget and in the everyday process of tax administration.

The weak state has highly limited resources of money, of the time of capable staff, and the management time of the leadership. Rather than spread this widely, it makes more sense, under conditions of low state capacity, to attempt doing fewer things.

How to choose these fewer things? One useful test is whether there is a market failure. Many things should not be done, as they do not address market failure. The core of any state is four elements: the criminal justice system, the judiciary, tax collection and financial regulation. Without these, there can be no economy. Hence, these four areas should be the limited areas of focus. We should learn how to run a state by building capability in these four areas.

31

Rolling up your sleeves
to build state capacity

Don't fix the pipes; fix the institutions that fix the pipes.

Old saying in the field of drinking water

The defining challenge in India is the construction of state capacity. At present, we are limited in our management capabilities in public policy. This imposes important restrictions upon what the state may attempt. We must focus, we must go after important market failures and avoid diffusing effort across a large number of areas. The primal functions of the state are issues like safety, which calls for building armed forces and a criminal justice system. The primal functions of the state are pure public goods like clean air. We should focus on these areas and learn how to do public administration.

There are two temptations that need to be avoided. The first is the pleasure of solving one small problem. A senior policymaker may discern a problem in an action by (say) Food Safety and

Standards Authority of India (FSSAI) and may expend a great deal of time and trouble in solving it. This may be satisfying, but this is a poor use of top management time. Top management must delve deeper: Why is it that intelligent and well meaning personnel at FSSAI came up with a poor outcome? This takes us to deeper questions about incentives and processes at FSSAI.

The second temptation that should be avoided is the great man theory of history. It is all too easy to personalize the poor outcomes at an agency and look for a staffing change. Conversely, we tend to look for heroes when undertaking recruitment decisions, lionize the hero, and expect all problems to be solved once a great man has been appointed. This line of thought is doomed to failure. The primary determinant of policy outcomes is the organization design and not the personnel. Great men also respond to incentives, and pursue their own self-interest: hence, we have repeatedly been disappointed when great men exited a position and we looked back at their report card.

Dispersion of power

Public choice theory and political science emphasize the dangers of concentration of power. Concentrated power will generally be abused for personal gains by the persons wielding the power. This encourages us to disperse power. Mature democracies work by limiting the power of every player in public life. As an example, the United States president has a narrow ('enumerated') list of powers under the US Constitution. Unlike the Indian arrangement, the US president does not even control the annual budget, nor does he control the draft legislation that is tabled for discussion by legislators.

It is better to have power dispersed between the three wings of government—the legislative, executive and judicial branches. In this, public choice theory takes us to the same argument as the traditional wisdom of liberal democracy on the value of separation of powers. It is better to organize the state around three branches: the legislature (which enacts the Indian Penal Code), the executive (which investigates crimes and prosecutes some) and the judiciary (which conducts hearings and awards punishments, and is immune to the displeasure of the executive).

It is better to have a bicameral legislature, and different clocks for the selection of representatives in the Lok Sabha and the Rajya Sabha, in order to avoid the possibility of a momentary infatuation of voters inducing concentration of power. In the design of the Constitution of India, voters have to be infatuated on a sustained basis for many years for one party to gain control of the Lok Sabha and the Rajya Sabha.

It is better to have power dispersed vertically between the Union government, state governments and local governments. In this, public choice theory takes us to the same argument as traditional wisdom of liberal democracy on the value of decentralization.

It is better for any one industry to be answerable to many masters ranging from income tax law to competition law to sectoral regulation. If an industry is excessively dominated by one regulatory agency, this generally yields poor outcomes owing to the concentration of power.

It is better for power to be dispersed between the ruling party and the opposition. The standing committees of Parliament are an example of establishing institutions that foster negotiation, and the dispersion of power. Bills are processed by standing committees, and in every case that we have been personally involved, we have seen that standing committees have improved bills. Standing committees, which are Shivraj Patil's contribution to the Indian institutional infrastructure, have become a forum for negotiation between gentlemen in private, as opposed to the grandstanding and hostility that tends to be on display. This gives us greater power sharing.

Politicians should go out of office but not out of power.[1] All lawmakers should have a continuous engagement with the legislative process, and perform the oversight role of the legislature, whether in or out of power. This helps create a repeated game and an environment of reciprocity. This takes the system closer to a cooperative equilibrium.

What goes into the law

Public choice theory helps us to think about the drafting of law. In the framework of liberal democracy, we normally think that parliamentary authorization is required, through law, for all coercion of free persons by the state. Hence, our traditional concept has been that the text of the law must authorize the coercion of private persons, and that no coercion should take place unless approved by lawmakers.

Public choice theory gives us a new insight into the drafting of a law. It calls for a second element in every law: the checks and balances that are required to make the state behave well. We in India have traditionally been over-optimistic about a benevolent state, and have skimped on the checks and balances that create accountability and performance. We need to take public choice theory to heart, and thereby bring sound procedures into law where agencies and personnel are mistrusted with power, so as to produce better performance by the state apparatus.

As an example, consider the law that creates UIDAI. It has to contain two parts. The first part involves coercing private persons, to say that if they wish to be part of a government welfare programme, they have no choice but to submit to intrusive biometric requirements. The second part involves coercing the officials in UIDAI, and all public and private persons who utilize the UIDAI data, to engage in fair play towards the people. The need for this second part flows from public choice theory, the scepticism about the benevolence of the state.

Looking deeper into organization design

The policy community should focus on the medium-term agenda of building state capacity rather than the short-term agenda of fixing one small policy problem at a time. Our prime focus should thus be the subject of organization design. Good policy outcomes come from a sound organization design, and vice versa.

Organization design comprises the specification of objectives, the design of the organogram (the organization diagram), and the process manuals.

Clarity of purpose of the agent

A central feature of the road ahead is the concept of *agencification*: the establishment of focused agencies that perform clearly specified public policy objectives. High-performance agencies are those with clear objectives, sound design of the organogram and sound processes.

Departments of governments are political creatures, and are led by a minister who is a career politician. They are part of the turbulent world of politics. Agencies are technical organizations, outside departments that perform a well-specified task. Some agencies in India like to see themselves as political players, rivalling the importance of departments of government. However, agencies should be set up with narrow, technical and non-political functions.

These agencies can be public or private. In a PPP contract, a private agent may build a road. This requires drafting a complex contract, and then engaging in contract management around this complex contract. In a canteen contract, a private agent may run a canteen in a government organization. This also requires drafting a complex contract, and then engaging in contract management around this complex contract.

Alternatively, a parliamentary law may create a regulator like FSSAI or a financial agency such as the RBI. This requires drafting a complex contract—the law—and then engaging in contract management around this complex contract. This is the day-to-day functioning of the government department that deals with FSSAI or the RBI.

Delegate whatever you can

Managers of a government department must identify as many clear sub-problems as possible, and kick off a set of agencies (either private or public) thus creating focused teams which pursue well specified objectives. If the agent is a government agency, the relationship is defined in a law or an executive order. If the agent is a private person, the relationship is defined in a contract. This rearrangement is termed 'agencification' in the field of new public management. The principal should contract out everything that can be contracted out, in this fashion.

After this is done, the work of the department splits into two tracks:

1. Contract management for each of these relationships; and
2. Performing, within the department, all the difficult functions which are not easy to specify, where there are political complexities, which are not mere technical problems.

The maximal delegation of technical problems into a group of agencies is valuable as it frees up capacity in the department for the political problems that cannot be delegated.

We should not think that once something has been delegated, the principal can drop down to zero engagement. The principal–agent relationship will only work correctly when the principal stays engaged in the work of the agent and engages in contract management as specified in the relevant legal instrument. This will require capacity and resourcing at the principal.

Example 54: A Ministry of Finance for the twenty-first century

As an example, in 2004, we worked on a Ministry of Finance committee report, 'Ministry of Finance for the 21st Century'.[2] This was an attempt at rethinking the organization design of the Ministry of Finance, which comprises organization structure and processes. A key part of this work was carving out sub-problems from the overall tasks of the Ministry of Finance, and assigning these to a constellation of agencies.

This involves clarifying the role of RBI, setting up the Public Debt Management Agency (PDMA), etc. The separation between policy formulation and policy implementation yields clean thinking in policy formulation. This requires moving towards a unified Internal Revenue Service which fuses the Central Board of Direct Taxes (CBDT) and the Central Board of Excise and Customs (CBEC), and delivers a professional tax administration with political independence, while the formulation of tax policy (leading up to the drafting of the Finance Act) takes place in the Ministry of Finance.

Hygiene in constructing agencies

The rule of law is the most important infrastructure of all.

Three elements of wisdom are useful in designing sound agency arrangements. The separation of powers doctrine argues that it is better to separate legislative, executive and judicial powers across three distinct organizations. To the extent that more than one of these is brought into a single organization, there is concentration of power, which inevitably leads to abuse of power.

We in India are at the early stages of learning how to construct state capacity. We should systematically use separation of powers as a tool for inducing greater performance. Conversely, where separation of powers is absent (e.g., at a regulator like SEBI), we should recognize that it will now be *more difficult* to achieve state capacity, and greater effort will need to be made on other accountability mechanisms, in order to obtain performance.

The second element of wisdom is about the rule of law. Fair play by the state and its agents is a moral and political objective. However, the rule of law is also a tool for achieving state capacity. When there are failures on the rule of law, this places arbitrary power in the hands of officials and politicians. This leads to abuse of power and low state capacity.

The third element of wisdom is about the powers of an agency. At the outset, it is important to give low powers to an agency. Government agencies should have low levels of direct and indirect coercive power. This includes the power to raid a person, the power to tap phone conversations, the power to spend money, the power to punish a person, etc. Power corrupts, and the greater the power of the personnel of an agency, the harder it will be for that agency to achieve state capacity.

Swedish or UK levels of coercive power should only be given to an agency when it has Swedish or UK levels of capability. Conversely, Swedish or UK levels of investigative powers or punishments are always inappropriate in India. The daily expansion of criminal offences increases the likelihood of state failure.

Six components of the law that creates an agency

The law that establishes an agency requires six key elements:

1. *Clarity of objective:* Accountability can only come about when there is clarity of purpose. Vague, multiple or conflicting objectives cater to corruption and incompetence.
2. *Formal processes for legislative functions:* The law must write the due process through which the agency wields the power to write law.
3. *Formal processes for executive functions:* The law must write the due process through which the agency performs executive functions like licensing and investigation. This is analogous to the role of the Criminal Procedure Code in binding the police to how they function.
4. *Formal processes for judicial functions:* The law must write the due process through which the judicial functions are performed. There must be a hearing, the person conducting the proceedings must be unconflicted, orders and penalties must be reasoned, and an efficacious appeal must be possible.
5. *Reporting and accountability:* The agency must release enough information about its own functioning so as to be held accountable for its use of public resources and wielding the coercive power of the state.
6. *Board:* The law must write the role and structure of the board. The board must have a majority of non-government members, who must hold the management accountable; and the board must control the design of the organization. A majority of outside directors is essential in switching the strategic conversations from loyalty to voice.[3]

These six elements are well understood in mature democracies and are the foundation of high-performance government organizations, worldwide, but these are missing in Indian laws that create agencies. These six elements are worked out thoroughly in the draft Indian Financial Code (IFC), that was drafted by the Financial Sector Legislative Reforms Commission (FSLRC).

It is commonly argued that in India, we have fine laws which are badly implemented. We would argue the reverse: the bad outcomes that we see in India flow from badly drafted laws. When laws encode these six elements, we will obtain superior performance from agencies.

If these six elements are not encoded in the law that governs an agency, there is an intermediate stage where the board of an agency adopts these rules with the legal status of board resolutions. As an example, the IBBI has adopted a board regulation that establishes a legislative process in the absence of these elements in the IBC. This can get an agency on the path to high performance while a sound law has not yet been drafted.

Establish a leadership

There are many elements of the Indian state where the leadership has atrophied. Examples of these include most government hospitals, police stations, colleges, etc. At organizations without a leadership, we have a large number of functionaries operating in fixed process manuals, living each day exactly like they had lived previous days.

The role of the leadership is to have a situational awareness of *the organization*. What is the role of the organization? How are we faring today? What new information has come in? How should we respond to this information? The leadership knows the mandate of the organization, looks at the daily flow of information, and continually takes management decisions that reshape the organization so as to better respond to events in a way that ultimately delivers better on the mandate.

We have low state capacity when there is no leadership that thinks in this fashion, when the organization has a fixed budget year after year, and the organization is impervious to information. There are no feedback loops, and the organization has stopped thinking.

The law that establishes an agency should clearly establish its leadership and governance. There must be strong MIS, which feed information to the board, which must have a majority of independent directors, and also control the organization design. This will help prevent the organization from collapsing into slumber.

Containing discretion

In India, we have swung between extremes of executive discretion and executive paralysis. On one hand, in many parts of the Indian state, there is remarkable and excessive executive discretion. At the same time, in many parts of the Indian state, there is now a fear of making decisions which has slowed down routine work. Government museums are unable to acquire works of art as they fear the use of discretion in their purchases.

These two phenomena are closely interconnected. In any liberal democracy, there is a fundamental lack of legitimacy of an executive that possesses extreme discretion. When the basic rules of the game support extreme executive discretion, in time, a backlash develops and then we get snarled in CAG, Central Bureau of Investigation (CBI), Central Vigilance Commission (CVC) or Central Information Commission (CIC). It is ironic to see that some of the difficulties now visible in the working of (say) the CBI are also grounded in the same problem of extreme executive discretion.

When we think about 'what is hard' in state building, it is clear that high-quality discretionary decisions are difficult. To the extent that processes can eliminate discretion, that makes things easier. But there is no avoiding discretion in the working of any state. Some of the most important things that states do involve seeing the world, forming a judgement and making a discretionary decision. This is a recurring theme across the criminal justice system, the judiciary, the tax system and financial regulation. State building requires achieving good discretionary decisions. A state that cannot exercise discretion is an ineffectual one.

In the Indian debate, incumbent officials who are used to high discretion are vocal in criticizing reforms proposals which establish due process, and simultaneously complain about the death of discretion. We must see that the old ways are untenable: India has reached a point in its trajectory where the executive discretion that was normal and acceptable from the 1970s to the 1990s is now seen as illegitimate and will run into trouble.

For example, the TRAI regulation on dropped calls was struck down by the Supreme Court in 2016 on the grounds that TRAI's process for regulation-making was not adequately transparent.[4] Such a decision would probably not have emanated from the Supreme Court in previous decades.

The way forward is to find the middle road, of well-defined processes that govern the legislative, executive and judicial functions in all elements of the state. It is only when these processes are sound that officials will be able to have a certain kind of controlled discretion, which is simultaneously surrounded by checks and balances so as to achieve legitimacy and auditability. Formal processes, embedded in the law, are the prerequisites for wielding discretion, which is the prerequisite for state capacity.

Example 55: Reducing arbitrary power in tax administration

Tax officials obtained draconian powers under the excuse that these were essential for increasing the tax/GDP ratio. Tax officials draft their own procedural law, and thus have excessive control of the steady process through which greater powers are appropriated. Alongside this, tax rates have generally crept up; they are seldom reduced.

Greater coercive power and higher tax rates give us higher stakes: this makes it harder to achieve state capacity. The importance of tax officials has gone up, but the tax/GDP ratio has not.

If there is a proposal to reform the tax system, where reduced powers and greater checks and balances are a central issue, the incumbent tax officials will promise the decision makers that this will result in reduced tax revenues.

Time and money in building state capacity

The conventional Indian way of starting a new agency, e.g., a regulator, consists of enacting a law, hiring a few people, getting some temporary office space, and declaring the agency open for business. This is certain to yield operational rout. The agency drowns under the load that is placed upon it in the early days. It gets consumed in firefighting and never recovers.

We do differently, in India, on hard infrastructure. We know that an expressway costs Rs 150 million per kilometre. We know that in order to build an expressway, we must do systematic project management, enumerate all the sub-tasks that are required, and coordinate them in an overall project plan. Only after all elements are completed do we inaugurate the expressway. This same approach is required for building state capacity!

When a new government agency has to be built, or an old government agency has to be fixed, this will require time and money. For instance, building a regulator of doctors and hospitals is an expensive project. We should be willing to commit adequate resourcing to it. We should build this organization in much the systematic way that private equity funds build private organizations:

writing process manuals, building IT systems, setting up office facilities, recruiting and training staff, and only then doing the ribbon cutting.

In the development of the capability of the criminal justice system, it makes sense to start with a narrow set of crimes (for instance, riot, murder) and focus only on these. This will involve writing a manual for investigation, a manual for prosecution, working out the required resourcing, training the staff in working within the manuals, establishing feedback loops for continuous improvement as well as a dashboard of performance metrics. We have to establish capabilities in the executive, get judges used to how this will work and establish a jurisprudence—for one offence at a time. Once this is done, the next crime can be taken up. This constitutes a sequential process of building state capacity.

Similarly, for SEBI to learn how to enforce against market abuse, the logical place to start is with exactly one specific offence, for instance, 'price manipulation through a short squeeze'. For this one offence, the correct regulation has to be drafted replacing the vagueness and low evidentiary standards of the present market-abuse regulation, the manual for investigation has to be drafted, the manual for prosecution has to be drafted, white papers have to be released into the public domain, the internal staff have to be trained in living by these manuals, and MIS has to be built to watch over the enforcement process. The market and the judges have to understand the law, and the jurisprudence has to build up illuminating the borderline cases. In about two years, it should be possible to get SEBI up to the ability to detect and enforce against one tangible element of market abuse. Only after this is mastered can the management then start on a second element of market abuse.

The armed forces have the luxury of not fighting wars on most days, and have developed a sound culture of enormous training schedules that run all through the year. In other parts of government, training tends to be short-changed in an environment of crisis management. This is a vicious cycle: weak institutions are engulfed in crisis management, and cut corners in training, which engenders institutional weakness.

Once a policymaker decides that an expressway must be built, everyone is comfortable that it will take n number of years before the expressway is inaugurated. In similar fashion, once it has been decided that a new organization like the Insolvency and Bankruptcy Board of India (IBBI) will be built, everyone should be comfortable that this will take two years before it can be inaugurated.[5]

Administrative law to the fore

In Indian public policy, it is exciting to work on inflation targeting or net neutrality or Nifty futures trading in Singapore. A great fraction of conference time is devoted to political economy, to painting the map of interests and envisaging grand bargains.

Administrative law is considered the dull backwater, that should concern junior bureaucrats only. However, we think that the cutting edge of building state capacity lies in the dry detail of formal processes, rules, and checks and balances, in the subject of administrative law.

Clean slate versus reforming an existing organization

The material of this chapter readily fits into the challenge of building a brand-new organization. But most of the machinery of the Indian state is already in place. A great deal of bad decisions and the wrong political economy are now in play.

Public choice theory helps us see the difficulties that we are up against. Incumbents value arbitrary power and do not share the goals of the organization. There will be resistance against the reforms effort. It should not be surprising when (for instance) CCI employees are hostile to CCI reforms.

Summing up

When there is one practical error that has taken place in one government organization, we should generally resist the impulse of solving it. We should go deeper. Why did intelligent and well-meaning people make such a mistake? What was the structure of incentives that led them to this mistake? This leads us to the question of organization design.

Recruiting famous people or skilled people will not change the organization design. Building state capacity will not come out of hiring Indian Administrative Service (IAS) or non-IAS or private people.

Government works better when there is dispersion of power. A great deal of failure comes from a few individuals controlling excessive power. Checks and balances are key.

The drafting of law involves two key elements. First, law authorizes the coercion of private people. Second, the law must address the principal–agent problem between the citizen and the state. An array of checks and balances must be built in, when drafting the law, in order to address public choice concerns, to create accountability mechanisms.

Government departments in India are overloaded with many tasks and it is hard to reform this. 'Agencification' will help. Establish an organization outside the department, give it a clear objective, and hold it accountable. Departments must contract out, to such agencies, all technical functions which can be contracted out through well-specified laws. Once this process is complete, the work inside the department will consist of (a) participating in the governance of the external agencies, and solving the principal–agent problem between department and agency, and (b) all the unexpected things and political problems, which could not be contracted out.

'Agencification' will work better when there is a great focus upon rule of law, separation of powers, and low coercion. Agencies must have low powers of investigation, punishment, spending, etc. Only after an agency is proven as having high levels of state capacity can a slow process of giving more power be evaluated. We should only get up to UK-style or Swedish-style powers and punishments when we get up to UK-style or Swedish-style state capacity.

The law that sets up an agency must have clarity of purpose, formal processes for legislative-executive-judicial functions, reporting and accountability, and correct design of the composition and functions of the board. About 140 sections of law, which set up this machinery, is found in the draft Indian Financial Code, version 1.1.

Agencies can sometimes collapse into everyday practical activities, and a loss of strategic thinking. Functionaries would show up to work every day and do the same work that they did the previous day. The board and the top management of the agency have to provide leadership. This involves a feedback loop of taking in information, developing a situational awareness, and undertaking actions that deliver the mandate of the agency. This is related to the teeth-to-tail ratio problem: if an agency is only paying salaries of front-line field operatives, it is all teeth and no tail, it has lost the ability to think.

Discretionary power is routinely abused in the Indian state. The answer is not to remove all discretion. If there is no ability to see the world, and choose the right response, there can be no state capacity. The answer lies in establishing formal procedures with the rule of law, so that discretion is contained in checks and balances.

Administrative law is thus at the heart of the Indian journey.

Building a bridge requires money and time. From the decision to build the bridge to the inauguration, it takes a long time. In similar fashion, building an agency requires money and time. Merely hiring a few people and renting an office do not give a working agency. When a fledgling agency is asked to do work, this is premature load bearing and it generates an organizational collapse.

When reforms have to be brought to existing agencies, the incumbent officials resent reductions in their arbitrary power. They argue that if a policeman has to go to a judge and get a warrant before entering a home, we will fail to catch criminals. But *it is only in a police state that a policeman's job is easy.*

32

Dealing with constraints in information

Earlier in this book, we showed the lack of information about the economy as a root cause of why public policy fails. What is a policymaker to do, when faced with these constraints?

Scepticism on public data

In India, we cannot assume that when data is released by a government agency, it is sound. The uncritical use of data is a major flaw that is hampering numerous research papers that study Indian economics, and policymakers have been often misled when they have relied on public statistics.[1]

We must then evaluate the soundness of each public data source before commencing to use it. Each of us needs to commit considerable resources to *evaluating* the soundness of various kinds of statistics that are available in our field.

Better use of private data sources and anecdata

Policymakers must rely more on market-based sources of information that help the policy correct itself. In most sectors of the economy, market participants are producing information that they mostly keep to themselves because it is proprietary. Policymakers can help discover relevant parts of that information by creating incentives for market participants.

For instance, when there is not enough information to price a public service based on a ground-up costing, they can use reverse auctions to discover a reasonable price. Similarly, policymakers may also rely more on competitive market structures to reduce the need for information and analysis. For instance, for setting tariff in infrastructure sectors, instead of relying on ground-up costing, regulators could set the tariffs based on benchmarks of the industry, so that those performing worse than the average get a disincentive.

In India, our public policy capabilities are highly circumscribed by the unavailability of data. This creates the need for informal information channels. In an ideal world, we would like to have statistics and analytical models. In our reality in India, our ability to undertake formal economic analysis on many problems is limited.

When quantitative analysis is infeasible, we should do more qualitative research. Every policy thinker in India must thus have a strong emphasis on a human network in the real world, on going out on field trips, on looking at our world, listening to people, and trying to assimilate what they are saying. We do not have the luxury of reading papers and looking at data; we have to look directly at the world.

If a field is well instrumented, with high-quality data, a new person can come into it and rapidly pick up the ropes. The information set in India, in most fields, is composed of soft information that is picked up over the years from a human network in an environment of trust. For this reason, successful work in public policy in a given field in India requires long years of experience in the field. It is hard for a person to learn a new field rapidly.

Kicking off improvements in measurement

I must study politics and war that my sons may have liberty to study mathematics and philosophy.

John Adams

We must also prioritize time and resources for improvements of the statistics. Every policymaker should kick off long-range initiatives to improve statistics in her area. Economic statistics is not just the work of the CSO—it is the work of myriad persons all across the economy. We must prioritize the capture of information and the release of information.

When sound new statistical measures come about, at first they will have inadequate and short time series for a long time. Often, we will not be the beneficiaries of the statistical system improvements that we initiate. Just as *a country becomes great when men plant trees that they will not live to enjoy the shade of*, a country becomes great when men and women initiate data-gathering efforts that they will not live to enjoy the fruits of.

Example 56: Outcomes measurement in education

The most famous episode in India of outcomes measurement was the work by Pratham, to measure what schoolchildren know, through their Annual Status of Education Report (ASER) survey. ASER measurement has two great strengths. First, ASER measures outcomes (what children know) as opposed to the traditional measurement of inputs (school buildings built, teachers hired, etc.) or outputs (kids enrolled). Further, ASER is not part of the government, and it is hence more immune to pressures to distort the data or block the release of data when the data is painting an unflattering picture.

ASER surveys began in 2005, and have been extremely influential in showing the lack of learning achievements by schoolchildren in India. When you compare this data against the launch of Sarva Shiksha Abhiyaan (2000–01) and further back to the launch of the District Primary Education Programme (1993), there is a sense that we would have fared much better if an ASER-style measurement had begun much earlier. This would have created feedback loops and helped rapidly improve the design decisions from 1993 to 2003, which have proved much harder to reverse when the bad news started coming in from ASER surveys in 2005 onward.

Example 57: Outcomes measurement in the criminal justice system

In each area, it would be wise to start the process of state building with outcomes measurement. The entire enterprise of the criminal justice system should lead to one outcome: young women feeling safe when walking alone in public places at night. This can be directly measured using surveys, where we ask parents the time in the evening when they feel teenage daughters should be back at home. The establishment of crime victimization surveys should be the first milestone in reforms of the criminal justice system.

Episodic versus long-term measurement

Many academic economists initiate a project, gather custom data for that project, and stop measuring when the project is finished. This data is kept confidential by the researcher. While all knowledge is useful, this approach to measurement is less effective from the viewpoint of society.

What is more valuable are methods for measurement which run all the time and which are widely available. When measurement is done all the time, it becomes possible to assess the consequences of an event.

As an example, Andhra Pradesh banned microfinance in 2010. This called for research on understanding the impact of the ban. The Centre for Monitoring Indian Economy (CMIE) had been surveying 11,000 households in Andhra Pradesh, three times a year, all the time. Households in regions of other states were also observed, where there was no ban on microfinance. This made possible a comparison of regions within Andhra Pradesh which were hit by the ban against matched regions elsewhere in India which were not hit by the ban.[2]

It takes time to develop sound measurement systems

Tiger conservation leaped into prominence with the establishment of Project Tiger in 1972. It took about thirty years to lay the foundations of measurement.

Important new developments took place in this field from 2002 to 2006. Every four years since 2006, the Indian government conducts a national census of tigers and other wildlife. The 'All-India Tiger Estimation Report 2018' was prepared by the National Tiger Conservation Authority (NTCA) in collaboration with the Wildlife Institute of India (WII), the World Wide Fund-India (WWF-I), state forest departments and many volunteers and non-profit organizations.

The most recent survey deployed 44,000 field staff who conducted habitat surveys across the twenty tiger–occupied states of India, checking some 381,400 sq. km for tigers and their prey. The team placed paired camera traps at 26,838 locations across 139 study sites, which collected 34.8 million photos. The WII and NCTA developed the methodology for conducting the tiger survey after extensive consultations with experts and through a rigorous peer-review process. The methodology combines field combing to record carnivore tracks, remote sensing data, hidden cameras, four indigenously developed software systems, including one that tracks tiger flank stripe patterns, and DNA profiling.

None of this is cast in stone. An active debate continues to take place, in the intellectual community, about the strengths and weaknesses of the measurement programme. Iterative refinement is taking place based on these debates. The only trusted measurement system is one that is continuously scrutinized, criticized and refined.

This work is an example of the long and slow process required in laying the foundations of measurement, of deep collaboration between the state and civil society and of the use of old knowledge and new research methods.

For every economic policy researcher or practitioner who feels exhausted at the thought of measurement in the problem before her—whether it is crime, courts, capital controls or air quality— the scale of work on the measurement of tigers is an inspiring story.

Principles for data release by the government

In previous years, the statistical system run by the government involved organizations which utilized a great deal of microeconomic data, that was kept secret, and released useful aggregate data. In the modern world, this can be reimagined. The most important role that the government can now play is to obtain and release micro data. The private sector will find diverse ways to utilize this as well.

As an example, in the old world, the Survey of India produced maps. The Survey of India conducted surveys, created internal data sets, and used these to create maps. In the modern world, the scarce resource is those large-scale survey data sets. The private sector is quite able to construct a variety of maps on its own. The role of the Survey of India thus needs to shift to building the public goods of maps data and releasing this database. Similar concepts apply for the Census of India.

Similarly, the government can release GDP data. It would be better to release all the underlying micro data that is used to compute GDP. After that, different users will process this data in different ways and form their own picture about what is going on in the economy.

Two useful principles to think about data release are:

1. If something can be obtained using the Right to Information (RTI) Act, it should be released pre-emptively. We should progressively expand the scope of items under 'duty to publish' of the RTI Act.
2. If a data set was created using public funding, it should be released into the public domain in machine-readable form, while taking care to mask identifying information that would harm the privacy of private persons.

Summing up

A great deal of data in India is of low quality. This includes data that is produced by government agencies and the official statistical system. All official data cannot be trusted. We must take great interest in the methods and administrative difficulties, of each data source, before deciding to use it.

There are many coping mechanisms. Policy design can plan to discover prices through auctions, rather than assume that adequate information is available up front. There is a greater role for qualitative research, given the weaknesses of quantitative research.

Every policymaker must kick off long-range improvements in measurement. The most valuable thing, for the Indian policy process, is sustained measurement, and not one-off measurement.

When a phenomenon is measured, again and again, we develop the long-term time series, and the observation of many units and many geographical locations. These are the most useful data sets of the country.

Government needs to release much more information in the public domain, particularly record-level anonymized micro data. What can be obtained through the RTI Act should be published. Data that is made using public money should always be released to the public. The private sector and the research community will do good things with data files, the only thing required of the government is to release the micro data.

33

Investing in knowledge institutions

The safe strategy in public policy is to incrementally evolve—making small moves, obtaining feedback from the empirical evidence, and refining policy work in response to evidence. This process requires the construction of trusted data sets. It also requires intellectual capabilities in analysing this information and feeding knowledge back into the policy process.

It is generally difficult to recruit these analytical capabilities into the Indian state. The two worlds—main-line civil servant vs intellectual capabilities—are far apart in terms of organizational culture and recruitment profile. In the long run, this should change. The ultimate aim of a knowledge society is an arrangement where all government intervention is grounded in a research process.

But for many years, we may expect that the organizational DNA in the state is not conducive to recruiting researchers or to creating the conditions in which they can be productive. Under these conditions, it is particularly important for Indian government organizations to develop deep partnerships with knowledge institutions.

Policymakers in government tend to be in the din and noise of the day-to-day policy process. The departments of government suffer from a high pace of staffing changes. Government organizations tend to defend the prevailing policy positions, which is not conducive to the intellectual process of understanding many points of view and analysing them dispassionately.

Knowledge institutions have the luxury of not answering Parliament questions, or getting hijacked by the newspaper headlines. This gives an opportunity for sustained focus, over long years, that is required to think properly on a given question. Knowledge institutions are not bound by the prevailing policy positions of the government, and are thus able to exercise pure rational thinking on the questions of the age.

Knowledge partnerships that play in the market for ideas

Policy institutions need to establish long-term relationships with multiple research institutions. This is not easily done. Just as government suffers from capacity constraints in India, there is limited capacity in academic institutions in India also. However, capacity at research institutions evolves in response to greater engagement with policy institutions.

In a knowledge partnership, the role of government institutions is to foster the supply side of research (by resourcing it with an environment of long-term stability) and the demand side (by asking questions of researchers).

The first priority of research institutions must be to build new knowledge and participate in the public discourse. This involves understanding what is going wrong in the country and criticizing it. Research capabilities must first be proven in the public domain landscape of the research community. The privilege of giving policy advice, and being part of the policy process, should be limited to the persons who achieve the status of public intellectuals, through writing and speaking in the public domain, and earning respect for honesty and knowledge.

A well-functioning policy process involves systematically identifying problems, enumerating rival solutions, choosing the least-intrusive solution, implementing it, and measuring the extent to which the problem is solved. There is a natural role for knowledge institutions in assessing the extent to which market failure is indeed present, in inventing new solutions, in cost–benefit analysis, and in concurrent evaluation through which measurement is done about the extent to which the problem is solved. There is value in bringing academic institutions into such roles on the grounds of better abilities in working with evidence and concepts of public economics, and on the grounds of a more dispassionate and evidence-based approach.

Increasing analytical capability in government

Level I: At its best, an Indian government organization should be imbued with analytical capabilities. It should be able to utilize evidence to conduct research and utilize this for the policy process. This would then be comparable to the best-policy organizations seen in mature market economies, where the internal staff have research capabilities and are able to produce high-quality work. Once research capabilities inside the government organization are adequate, the knowledge institutions of society contribute to the policy process through research products that they release into the public domain (which are utilized by government employees), through criticism of the status quo, and through participation in the public debate about reforms. This is the destination that we should aspire for in India, which is many years away.

Level II: The second best path is one where the Indian government organization lacks these capabilities, but is able to forge deep partnerships with research institutions. Through this, evidence and research would be brought into the innermost discussions about policymaking.

Level III: The weakest path is that of a conventional Indian policy institution, which lacks a research culture, and lacks deep partnerships with research institutions. The lack of knowledge partnerships comes about either owing to lack of interest in ideas, or from the insistence that academic institutions must be subservient to government officials. Such policy institutions produce the lowest-quality work in the policy process.

What knowledge partnerships are not

A knowledge partnership contract has the basic rhythm of building knowledge in the public domain, passing the market test in the market for ideas, criticizing the status quo and participating in the public debate, and then being available to render policy advice to a government institution. In conventional government contracting, there are three kinds of relationships which are confused as being knowledge partnership contracts.

Governments regularly give out specific assignments to consulting firms or law firms, to deliver a tangible work product. These tangible work products are important, but they come late in the policy pipeline. They do not substitute for intellectual capabilities at a much earlier stage, where more basic questions are being asked. Knowledge institutions are valuable at a more basic level: *What is the problem that we see? Is it a market failure? What is the lowest cost intervention? Do the benefits outweigh the costs? How do we build state capacity for achieving this intervention?* Knowledge institutions should invent the New Pension System; a law firm would draft the contract with a pension fund manager much later in the process of policy implementation.

Governments also regularly contract with manpower firms, who supply junior staff who take instructions and perform tasks. Such staffing contracts are also not knowledge partnership contracts.

Governments also have communications specialists who do public relations. Crafting and sending out a message, sending out messages into the social media, supporting the government in public debates, this is not the work of knowledge partners. Government organizations need to understand that the freedom of mind in academic institutions is the key to obtaining high-quality advice. When you ask a researcher to be a spokesman, you get neither spokesman nor researcher.

The healthy functioning of knowledge partnership contracts requires effort and capability on both sides. Government organizations need to be patient, knowing that capacity creation takes time. Government organizations need to avoid falling into the three stereotypes of the contracts with consulting firms, manpower firms and PR firms.

On their side, knowledge institutions also need to change gears in order to be useful partners. The ultimate purpose of an academic institution in India is to acquire metis, create authentic knowledge about India, to diffuse knowledge into India, and to be part of the process of changing India. Academic institutions need to shift gears away from a focus on publishing in international journals, which goes with catering to the interests and priorities of editors and referees who are far away.

The long-term foundations for policy research

In the short term, the Indian policy community has to make do with the academic institutions and researchers which are available.

We must, however, recognize that these individuals and institutions are part of the fuller research ecosystem, where the key element is the universities.

Research and capability in the humanities and social sciences, all across the country, is what lays the foundations for policy-oriented research. The universities build the foundational papers and also build the people. The policy community reaps the fruits of the labours of the universities.

At a deeper level, a great deal of the difficulties that we have seen in India in recent decades are related to the atrophying of capability in the universities in the humanities and social sciences. India has invested in building science and technology at universities. In these fields, research done overseas is directly applicable in India, and India can actually free-ride on knowledge production overseas, but we build human capital by having universities in India.

We have cut corners on building humanities and social sciences at universities, and these are fields where knowledge on India can only be produced in India. Through this, we have hampered *knowledge* on India, and also the human capital in the country. Building the republic will require strong capabilities in the humanities and social sciences in Indian universities.

Summing up

Knowledge institutions shape the discourse. Complex reforms, such as the GST or inflation targeting, cannot be achieved as a palace coup; they require a shift in the entire discourse. Sustained work by large numbers of intellectuals in knowledge institutions is essential to achieving the new level of thinking.

Every policymaker will benefit by setting up a few knowledge partnership contracts, and take effort to make them work. In the short term, they are low-cost initiatives. In the long run, these will yield a qualitatively superior trajectory of the policy process.

This approach needs to be applied in all parts of government. Whether it is in Karnataka or in Shimoga, policymakers require capable knowledge institutions, which are steeped in the local context, and develop metis.

The intelligentsia in public policy is derived from the broad foundations of the humanities and social science knowledge that is made in the universities. In India, public investments in the universities have emphasized science and engineering and neglected the humanities and social sciences. Building the republic requires capabilities in the universities—in the humanities and the social sciences.

Part VI

Applying these ideas: some examples

34

Building the perfect GST
in a low-capacity state

Many of the themes of this book come together in the GST reform. What is the best path to the GST?

From the viewpoint of state capacity, it makes sense to start with a low single rate. This is the easiest GST to implement, as it is administratively simple and the incentives for evasion are lowest. To make this concrete, consider the possibility of a single flat rate of 10 per cent GST with a comprehensive base. This draws on the global wisdom that the right way to do a GST is to have a single rate. A single 10 per cent rate applied on 70 per cent of the economy yields 7 per cent of GDP as tax revenue, and even if we actually obtain a part of this, we are broadly okay. At this low rate, it would have been possible to avoid all exclusions. Petroleum products could have gone in, real estate could have gone in.

To many of us in India, a single rate appears sharply different from the present arrangements. It is always possible to layer non-VATable sin taxes on top of the basic GST, which would serve as Pigouvian taxes. Individual state governments can choose how they wish to think about alcohol taxation. A carbon tax can potentially be layered on top of the GST. A state like Sikkim, which prizes environmental protection, may impose a sin tax on plastic consumption. We should decouple our thinking between two distinct problems: a single-rate GST and a collection of non-VATable sin taxes.

The distortion associated with a tax rate goes up in proportion to the rate squared. Hence, the low value (10 per cent) would have gone with a reduced distortion, and thus enabled a higher level of GDP. The marginal cost of public funds would have come down. Government (at all levels) is an important buyer of goods and services, and the low 10 per cent rate would have generated a beneficial impact upon the expenditure side also, thus reducing the net impact on the budget. This is related to the mistaken focus on short-term revenue neutrality, when the right objective should have been long-term budget neutrality.

The human energy that was spent on negotiations about thousands of products could instead have been devoted to getting a simple administrative process done. The very simplicity of this tax policy would have made it easier to build the IT system, get payments done on time, match invoices as was done in the TIN in 2004, and integrate with GST-on-imports and zero-rated exports. Simplicity of tax policy would have created feasibility of sound tax administration, even at low levels of state capacity.

The leadership could have clearly said: *This is an experiment.* We are going to learn how to make this work, and we are here to discover how much this self-enforcing tax is going to yield in terms of tax revenues for the first two years. The leadership could have said to taxpayers: Comply with this 10 per cent rate and the rate will not go up, and all of us will be the beneficiaries.

The 10 per cent rate would have induced optimism on the part of the domestic and global private sector. India would have earned respect worldwide for having capabilities in policymaking. This would have fostered investment and thus GDP growth.

In the first two years, significant resource reallocation would have started taking place, with firms discovering more efficient ways of working. This would have fed back into higher GDP growth and thus tax revenues.

If these first two years had worked out well, that would be a triumph. If tax revenues were stubbornly low, the rate could have been raised from 10 per cent to 12 per cent. The right sequencing is to take on a harder problem (a higher tax rate) later in the game, as this requires greater state capacity.

There is an interesting and self-stabilizing phenomenon associated with a large tax shortfall at the 10 per cent rate. Suppose it became clear that 10 per cent was not going to work, that the rate was likely to go up to (say) 12 per cent next year. Households would see this and increase their consumption, knowing that prices would go up in the future. This would give buoyant business-cycle conditions, and enlarged consumption, which would partly offset the difficulties.[1]

Summing up

The principles of this book suggest that the right way to design the GST is a single rate, a low rate, a comprehensive base, with an elegantly simple administrative system.

35

Health policy

Prevention versus cure

The founding intuition of the field of health policy is the tension between prevention and cure. Policymakers always face two rival pathways in health policy: of utilizing incremental expenditure or coercion for the purpose of preventing ill health versus utilizing incremental expenditure or coercion for the purpose of healthcare. In India, too little has been done by way of prevention, so the gains from incremental effort in prevention are substantial.

Consider road safety. When a person suffers from a road accident that is not fatal, there are three consequences: (a) Pain and unhappiness; (b) If the affected person is a worker, there is the loss of output and possibly income on account of reduced days of work; and (c) Expenditures on healthcare. Given that India has some of the highest rates of road accidents in the world, on the margin, prevention seems better than cure. We are better off with fewer road accidents, rather than having casualties and then supplying the commensurate healthcare services.

A little general equilibrium intuition is useful in thinking about a world where fewer people require healthcare. If road safety in India was improved, there would be fewer jobs in trauma centres. The resources which go into producing healthcare, for a preventable accident, are reallocated by society when accidents are prevented. Healthcare production requires labour and capital in order to produce ambulance services, trauma centres, medical supplies, etc. In a world with fewer accidents, these resources get reallocated into producing goods and services that people actually like, such as movies and clothes. When accidents are prevented, not only does society reduce expenditure on healthcare, we become better off because those same resources are shifted to producing things that people actually want.

A world with fewer road accidents is thus one where some individuals experience less pain and suffering, there is less lost output, and society gains happiness as some resources switch from producing healthcare services to producing things that people actually like. At Indian levels of road safety, this is better than producing healthcare services to address the problem of road accidents.

There is something awkward in counting the production of healthcare services, associated with preventable problems, as part of GDP. When air quality in India gets worse, there is greater purchase of healthcare services, and GDP as conventionally counted goes up. This detracts from the notion of higher GDP as synonymous with higher consumption and choice in the hands of the people. In a good country, we would spend *less* on healthcare as fewer people would get sick. We suspect that GDP will become a better measure of consumption and welfare if the healthcare expenditures, associated with preventable events, are *subtracted* from GDP.

The case for state intervention in health

The standard recipe of public economics is to start from conditions with no state, and identify the market failures. What goes wrong when we have pure laissez faire, when the government does nothing about health? There is a neat split between two classes of market failure.

> **Public health:** Consider the eradication of smallpox in India in 1975.[1] Once smallpox was eliminated, everyone gained welfare: this joy is non-rival and non-excludable. Controlling communicable diseases, and controlling sources of ill health such as road safety or natural disasters—these are public goods.
>
> The second class of market failure in the field of health concerns externalities. Pollution of water or air, and the impact of one infected person upon another, involve negative externalities. Here also, there is market failure and thus a case for state intervention.
>
> 'Public health' is defined as the population-scale initiatives that address externalities and provide public goods. Public health mostly involves prevention and not cure: it obtains a healthier population through reduction in sickness. In contrast, most healthcare involves private goods and not public goods.
>
> There is a great deal of confusion around terminology in this field. There is a need for a sharp delineation between four phrases: 'public good', 'market failure', 'public health' and 'healthcare'. The phrase 'public health' is often misunderstood to mean 'healthcare'. Many think that 'public health' is the health of the public. Conversely, it is often incorrectly assumed that 'healthcare' is a 'public good'. The phrase 'public health expenditure' is often applied for government expenditures on healthcare, and it is particularly confusing because it contains the

phrase 'public health' which is the antonym of 'healthcare'. The phrase 'government healthcare expenditure' is unambiguous and thus preferable.

Many of the advanced economies of today have been engaged in public health for a very long time. As an example, the UK began work on clean water in 1858 and on clean air in 1952.[2] In many aspects, the public policy initiatives that address externalities and public goods in health are in place, in advanced economies.[3] As a consequence, there is limited interest in public health in the contemporary policy debates of advanced economies.

But in countries such as India, public health is not a solved problem. There is often an inappropriate transfer of concepts and priorities, from the health policy debates of advanced economies, into Indian thinking about health policy. This has given a certain loss of focus upon public health in India.

In 2018, the World Health Organization began a 'Common Goods in Health' (CGH) initiative.[4] The attempt here is to bring back a focus upon the population-scale policy actions, i.e., addressing externalities and providing public goods, in health policy. The phrase 'Common Goods in Health' is unambiguous, and may help reduce the confusion associated with the phrases 'public health', 'public goods', 'healthcare' and 'market failure'.

Healthcare: India has drifted into a largely unregulated private healthcare market. Most healthcare services are purchased from private doctors and hospitals. The private healthcare market suffers from the other two kinds of market failure: asymmetric information and market power.

People respond to incentives.
Doctors are people.
Doctors respond to incentives.

The economic analysis of the behaviour of doctors and hospitals yields great insights. In some ideal world, doctors are altruistic. However, in the real world, the behaviour of doctors is shaped by their self-interest and the objective of revenue maximization.

There is extreme asymmetric information between a doctor and a patient. When a doctor says that a magnetic resonance imaging (MRI) is required, the patient is likely to comply. When the MRI laboratory pays a kickback to the doctor, as is common in India, medical malpractice arises. Prices of healthcare tend to skyrocket when individuals are unable to engage in comparison shopping for healthcare services with predictability of expenditures.

In a simple for-profit setting, the incentive of the doctor is not to heal the patient. The incentive of the doctor is to extract maximal revenue. Alongside this, it is efficient to make the patient feel subjectively better. This is done by over-prescribing antibiotics, by prescribing steroids (that briefly make a person feel better), by having a good bedside manner, by earning likes on social media, etc. Such strategies do not heal, but they generate more referrals. In a simple for-profit setting, there is no incentive for the doctor to guide the patient into pathways that prevent future requirements of healthcare.

Public policy initiatives are required to address these market failures in healthcare.

The Indian journey

Under colonial rule, there was an emphasis on the public goods of sanitation and communicable disease. A government committee, led by Sir Joseph Bhore from 1943 to 1946, envisaged a shift in focus from public health to healthcare, and advocated a government-run healthcare system. This was an extremely influential report, and shaped a large reorientation of health policy in the following decades.[5]

By the 1980s, it was clear that these modifications were working poorly. The disease burden was high, owing to weaknesses in public health. The government-dominated healthcare system was working poorly.[6] Individuals were increasingly resorting to private healthcare. Politicians became increasingly aware of the unhappiness of individuals.

Ideally, these difficulties should have generated a fresh focus upon public health. However, building capabilities in public health is difficult. To have tens of thousands of health workers, all over India, who fight mosquitoes, is a difficult problem in public administration.

Health policy in recent decades has instead taken the path of least resistance—to use public money to buy insurance (often from private health insurance companies) for individuals who would obtain healthcare services from private healthcare providers.[7] This is an inefficient path in three ways: Weak public health gives a high disease burden, there is market failure in the private healthcare industry, and there is market failure in the health insurance industry.[8]

Policy pathways in public health

It is striking to see that there was greater capability in India, in the 1970s, on fighting mosquitoes than is the case today. We have regressed from preventing malaria by fighting mosquitoes in the 1970s, to treating patients who have malaria, dengue or Zika. Problems such as air quality and road safety have become worse in India today than these were many decades ago. There is a need to revive public health, and reduce the extent to which persons require healthcare. Ironically, the weaker the healthcare system, the greater the gains from prevention.

The focus of health policy in India must be upon prevention, i.e., upon public health. This includes immunization, disease vectors such as mosquitoes, monitoring of disease outbreaks and fighting epidemics, drug safety, food safety, air quality, water quality, waste management, disaster risk resilience, disaster response, etc. These areas require prioritization and the development of state capacity.

A lot of public health lies outside the administrative boundaries of the Ministry of Health. As an example, air quality is a key public health crisis that afflicts north India. However, the problem of air quality lies in the Ministry of Environment and not the Ministry of Health. Public health considerations need to shape the working of many ministries. As an example, the Indian road safety crisis is a first-order challenge for public health. The agencies building and operating roads should carry targets for accident rates and not just targets for kilometres of highways built.

Policy pathways in healthcare

At present, we face a difficult situation in healthcare. The public sector is not effective at translating expenditures into healthcare services. Privately produced healthcare is afflicted with market failure. Health insurance companies suffer from poor financial regulation (of insurance) and from dealing with a malfunctioning healthcare system.

Greater government spending on healthcare is popular. At present, there are two pathways for this increased expenditure. More money can be put into government healthcare facilities such as primary health centres (PHCs) or government hospitals. Alternatively, more money can be put into health insurance companies who intermediate between individuals and private healthcare providers. Both these pathways work poorly. As a consequence, the welfare gains from increased government expenditure on healthcare, under the present paradigm of healthcare, are likely to be low.

The key insight lies in system thinking, in re-imagining the contractual relationships to achieve incentive compatibility. Imagine a contract between a network of healthcare providers and the patient which underwrites all healthcare for the patient for life, in exchange for fixed monthly payments. This must be not just one doctor, but a network of providers that covers all aspects of healthcare. When you get sick, you would go to your healthcare network, and they would render you healthcare services, at no additional cost. Such networks are called 'Health Maintenance Organizations' (HMOs).

Once this style of contracting is done, the incentives of the healthcare producer change. Now, the HMO is paid by you every month, and these payments are clean profit for them, *until you get sick*. When you get sick, you impose costs upon them. They have no incentive to over-prescribe procedures, and their incentive is to keep you healthy.

Now the HMO has the incentive to ask you to come in for regular check-ups, so that problems are caught early. At all ages, immunization will be pushed by the HMO, so as to avoid the costs associated with illness. The choice of treatments will be done with a view to keeping you healthy.

At present, the conversation between a doctor and a patient in India is a transactional one, where symptoms are described and treatments are explained. The time in that room is a powerful opportunity to change behaviour. A few minutes spent by the doctor evangelizing better behaviour tends to have a significant impact on behaviour and health. As an example, a doctor might say: 'I'm prescribing a programme of exercise for you, and I want you to come back to me in three months and we will look at the improvements in your cholesterol numbers.' This would be quite motivating for most patients. Such practices that result in improved health are incentive-compatible for the HMO, as they yield reduced costs and higher profit.

A doctor in an HMO who sees a surge of an infectious disease in her neighbourhood would have the incentive to talk with public health officials, and initiate public health responses which address the epidemic at the root cause. This is incentive-compatible as the HMO makes more money when fewer people get sick.

In the UK, the government runs such a system, and it is called the National Health Service (NHS). Under this, there is one general practitioner (GP) tied to each person.[9] On average, there are 0.58 GPs per 1000 persons. The GP is a civil servant who is paid a salary, and charges nothing to the patient. The GP's incentive is to keep the person healthy, so that the person comes back to her fewer times per year.

This is a logical and simple design that generates the correct incentives for the GP. However, the sound operation of the UK NHS requires UK-style state capacity. The UK government is able to make sure that GPs show up to work, and are conscientious about their work even though this is a transaction-intensive, discretion-intensive service. Under present Indian conditions of state capacity, this is infeasible, outside of islands of state capacity such as AIIMS.

Addressing these difficulties of healthcare requires system thinking. It is hard to see how the self-organizing system of the market economy will find the HMO solution. The present structure of incentives encourages doctors to earn super normal incomes by over-prescribing procedures and thus earning revenues and kickbacks. This is analogous to the emergence of the New Pension System in the context of money management. Left to itself, the private sector finds it hard to break away from the toxic sales practices of insurance companies and mutual funds, and the supernormal fees charged by fund managers who do not add value.

At the same time, system thinking is a highly difficult problem in public policy; at low levels of state capacity it is too easy for central planning to emerge with the wrong answers. A tremendous amount of work is now required, in policy thinking on healthcare in India, to find the right pathways for system design, while recognizing that system thinking is a difficult problem in public policy.

The correlation between GDP and health

In the international experience, when a country gets richer, the health of the population improves. This is a strong correlation.

However, like all correlations, we should not jump to the conclusion that there is a causal relationship between the two. In some respects, we can see how becoming richer enables better health in India. As an example, a richer family would have better nutrition, and be able to spend more on private healthcare. A richer family would generally have higher education, and better knowledge feeds into better health. However, there are also many elements in India, where increased prosperity has harmed the disease burden. As an example, we now have the new challenges of air quality and road safety, which are harming people today, which were not present a few decades ago.

We should not assume that higher GDP growth will always give us improvements in the health of the population, in line with what has happened on average in the international experience. That average international experience is predicated on sophisticated health policy thinking, that has come about in each country as the country achieved a greater intellectual capacity in public policy. We in India will need to achieve an improved intellectual capacity, in public policy work on public health and on healthcare, in order to obtain the full translation of higher GDP into improved health.

Summing up

Health policy is one of the hardest parts of public policy. The toolkit of market failure and state capacity gives us important insights into the field. There is a neat and vertical split between two classes of market failure (public goods and externalities) that shape the field of 'public health' or 'common goods for health' and the other two classes of market failure (asymmetric information and market power) that shape healthcare.

We in India need to change course. Under the present trajectory, GDP growth is inducing greater ill health through problems such as pollution, natural disasters and road safety. In the government, public health capabilities have atrophied: we do worse on critical problems like vector control when compared with many decades ago. Voters are unhappy, and the government is trying to subsidize their purchase of private healthcare services from a private healthcare system that suffers from extensive market failure. Thinking about market failure and state capacity from first principles is required in public health and in healthcare.

As in many other fields, there is a lot of interest in technological fixes for health policy. There is undoubtedly great opportunity in using better technology, ranging from mundane process automation using better data handling, all the way to artificial intelligence (AI) systems that will replace doctors. However, the foundation of beneficial technology adoption lies in incentives. Our first priority has to be to address the foundations: to reorganize health policy around the problems of market failure and state capacity.

Under each of the two wings—public health and healthcare—a research community is required and the full policy pipeline is required. We need to establish data sets, develop a research literature, incubate diverse policy proposals, debate them, develop a mature point of view on how the problems will be solved, present these choices to legislators, enact new laws, and then build the state capacity to enforce these laws. Health policy is a less mature field in India, in the development of the policy pipeline, when compared with two other examples shown in companion chapters: GST and financial economic policy.

36

Financial economic policy

Financial economic policy is about the things that the government does in financial markets, financial intermediaries, the creation of money, and the mechanics of government borrowing. While it stands alongside fiscal policy, there is a clear distinction between the two. Fiscal policy decides how much to borrow, and financial economic policy decides how to borrow.

The case for state intervention in finance

As with all other questions in public policy, the point of departure is the working of a pure free market. If the government did nothing in this field, what would go wrong? We can identify four main issues:

- There is a market failure in the form of *externalities* when there is a crisis on the financial markets. When private persons maximize their own interests, they sometimes do things which impose harm upon others by destabilizing the financial system.

Government intervention helps increase the probability of consistent working of the financial system.

Government intervention helps a lay participant feel certain that when securities are bought on the exchange, there will be no glitch in the payment of money and receipt of securities. Similarly, when a financial firm has made promises to lay persons, and comes to bankruptcy, the government helps clean up the mess and reduce the negative externalities imposed upon others.

- There is a problem of *asymmetric information* with both financial markets and financial intermediaries.

Government intervention on financial markets, to improve disclosure and combat market abuse, improves the confidence with which individuals participate in financial markets.

Similarly, an individual will find it difficult to know when the promises of a bank or an insurance company can be trusted. This is analogous to the problem of drug safety: an individual buying medicines is not able to put in the effort required to test the purity of the drug. The government helps by running a regulatory system through which the promises of financial firms are upheld with a high probability.

- The creation of money, which can be done by a state, facilitates transactions in the local economy. The creation of money has features of a public good that facilitates transactions, and a public good of reduced macroeconomic volatility through the working of monetary policy.[1]

- An institutional arrangement is required to perform the investment banking function for the government. This would represent the government in the financial markets, and represent the financial markets in the budget process. This is a utility that is required for the fiscal system to borrow.

Financial economic policy is about addressing these four objectives: combat negative externalities, combat asymmetric information, invent money, and establish an investment banker for the government.

The market failure in finance

> *It is essential to place the function of consumer protection at the heart of financial regulation.*

> FSLRC report, Vol. 1, page 45[2]

When a household deals with a financial firm such as a bank, the household does not have a reasonable ability to understand the soundness of a bank. Financial firms are often unfair in their dealings with households.[3] When a bank does fail, the household does not have a reasonable ability to participate in the conventional bankruptcy process. If we insist upon *caveat emptor*, i.e., 'buyer beware', in the relationship between unsophisticated households and financial firms, this would greatly narrow household participation in finance. Government intervention is required from the viewpoint of consumer protection to address these three problems. This is done through three paths:

1. A financial regulator looks at the relationship between financial firms and consumers, and coerces financial firms to engage in greater fair play. This includes truthful disclosure, fair contract terms, etc.
2. A financial regulator engages in 'micro-prudential regulation', where financial firms that make promises (such as banks and insurance companies) are coerced into low levels of risk. This caps their probability of failure and ensures that the promises

that they have made are upheld with a high probability. This is analogous to drug safety regulation which ensures that with a high probability, the drug purchased by a consumer in a shop is efficacious.

3. Sometimes, financial firms have made intense promises to households and they go bankrupt. At this time, a 'resolution corporation' is required, which is a specialized bankruptcy process. This pays out some money to households in the form of deposit insurance and runs a swift resolution process which minimizes the negative externalities upon the economy as a consequence of firm failure.

Financial markets are the vast impersonal systems for organized trading in securities. Government intervention combats externalities, asymmetric information and market power in the working of financial markets through three pathways.

1. A buyer of securities requires a high level of assurance that after the transaction, money will be paid and securities will be received. This requires micro-prudential regulation of exchange infrastructure.

2. Ample disclosures need to be made available by all issuers of securities, so that financial market speculators are well informed. This requires regulation of disclosures by issuers of securities.

3. Participants in the securities markets require a high level of assurance that market abuse is absent. This requires that the regulator must enforce against market abuse. Market abuse comes in two kinds: market-based abuse, which is about exploiting market power on financial markets, and information-based abuse, which is about falsifying the information seen by speculators about firms.

A plausible financial regulatory architecture

To perform these functions, we require a group of four government agencies:

1. A *central bank*, which creates the Indian rupee.
2. A *financial regulator*, which does consumer protection in the sense described above.
3. A *resolution corporation*, a specialized bankruptcy process for the class of financial firms which make intense promises to households, such as banks and insurance companies. All other financial firms—namely those which make no promises to unsophisticated households—should utilize the ordinary bankruptcy process of the Insolvency and Bankruptcy Code (IBC).
4. A *public debt management agency*, the investment banker for the government.

Public choice theory comes in the way of the sound working of each of these four organizations. The officials that man these organizations are likely to favour arbitrary power and low accountability. Officials may be overeager to ban certain kinds of business activity, so as to obtain peace of mind from not having to take responsibility for regulatory functions. Officials may cross the line from regulation into central planning, and micromanage private persons in their quest for personal power. Regulators can deploy their powers to investigate, prosecute and punish in a selective way.

In each of these four organizations, we must worry about the puzzle of creating the checks and balances which are conducive to good outcomes.

Achieving state capacity for the central bank

When a central bank creates money, there is the possibility of excessive money creation. The creation of money needs to be anchored into the real economy. In addition, the entire work process of creating money—i.e., monetary policy—requires an accountability mechanism. These problems are solved by requiring that the central bank deliver on an inflation target. The 4 per cent CPI inflation target achieves two things. First, it holds RBI accountable. Second, it establishes a self-adjusting system for the production of money which creates the public good of macroeconomic stabilization. When the engine of creating money is placed under the control of an inflation target, this becomes a tool for macroeconomic stabilization. When times are tough, inflation will tend to be low, and the central bank will cut rates, and vice versa.

There is a long lag between changes in monetary policy and their impact upon the economy. There is a danger that monetary policy can be used to influence elections. In the year prior to elections, interest rates will be cut by a supportive central bank to help the incumbent government win elections, and the resulting inflation surge will take place after elections are complete. In order to address this, there is a need for central bank independence in the narrow function of setting the short-term policy interest rate.

This is achieved by shifting the power of monetary policy away from one person (the RBI governor, who can be pressured by the ruling party) to a committee that is dominated by non-RBI employees.[4] For an analogy, if there is one judge, there is a greater risk of political pressure upon the judge, but if there is a bench of judges and power is dispersed, it is harder to bring pressure upon all of them.

In the class of public policy problems, monetary policy is a relatively easy problem. It involves a small number of transactions: about four to six meetings of the Monetary Policy Committee every year. It involves low stakes: these are not decisions which induce a very large impact upon any private person. It involves relatively low discretion: The actions of the MPC are anchored to forecasted CPI, and it is easy to look at the headline CPI and know how well the decisions of the MPC have worked out. Finally, it requires less secrecy. There are no state secrets of note, and the entire process can be swathed in transparency. To make a central bank work, we only require a small number of people who understand macroeconomics in the country, and we require that they are appointed upon the MPC.

Achieving state capacity for the regulator

In contrast with monetary policy, financial regulation is hard. There are a large number of transactions: roughly speaking, there are about 1000 supervisors at financial regulators interacting continuously with about 2000 significant financial firms. The stakes are very high: huge profit and loss flow from the decisions of financial regulators; the powers to license, raid, investigate and punish can destroy careers and firms. There is extreme discretion in how a certain situation is treated. There is a need for secrecy in the enforcement function. For these reasons, while monetary policy is easy, financial regulation is hard.[5]

In the international experience, regulators fuse legislative and executive functions. The parliamentary law that establishes a regulator carefully defines the spots where the regulator has the authority to write law in the form of 'regulations'. In addition, regulators have executive functions of licensing, investigation and prosecution.

In the concept of liberal democracy, regulators are in an unusual situation in that *law* is written by officials. There is a lack of democratic legitimacy when unelected officials are given the power to write law. Similarly, regulators exercise state power, in licensing and enforcement, without the oversight of elected representatives. Many elements of institutional design are required in order to address the dangers associated with this 'democratic deficit'.

The first element of this is governance of the organization by a board which has a majority of independent directors. The officials who run the organization must be accountable to this board, where a majority of persons are external experts and stakeholders. The board must control the internal processes, organization diagram and budget of the regulator. With a majority of independent members, the board should police the management of the regulator, watching for violations of the rule of law.

For the purpose of writing law (i.e., regulations), a formal process must be followed. Regulation-making projects must emanate from a decision of the board, taken under conditions of transparency (release of board agenda papers and minutes).

Once a regulation-making project is initiated, the staff must be required to build a documentation packet, articulating the problem that is sought to be solved, demonstrating that it is a market failure, and demonstrating that the proposed intervention is the least intrusive alternative available. This documentation packet must be put into public consultation, in order to solicit the views of affected persons and intellectuals. This packet, and the responses from the public, should lead up to a discussion, refinement and decision at the board of the agency. Only the board should be able to release a new regulation.

Public choice theory predicts that the staff of a regulator will favour arbitrary power in the legislative and executive functions.

Hence, the parliamentary law which defines the regulator must write down the processes of regulation-making, licensing, investigation and prosecution in considerable detail. At an early stage of state capacity, the regulator must be given low powers of investigation and punishment, so as to protect the feedback loops of the push-back against regulatory actions from the economy. Where regulators are powerful, private persons are meek, and fail to criticize the work of regulators, which ensures low-quality work by regulators.

Difficulties of the Indian experience

The Indian experience with financial economic policy features many important deviations from this normative depiction.

Prior to 2015, RBI had no objective, and as public choice theory would predict, many infirmities were observed. The prime function of the central bank is to deliver low and stable inflation. However, India has a long history of high and unstable inflation. From 2015 onward, a formal objective—an inflation target—was placed upon the RBI. This has helped anchor the Indian rupee and has created an accountability mechanism for RBI.[6]

RBI independence has, however, not been achieved, as the RBI governor effectively controls the Monetary Policy Committee. There is thus the possibility of pressure upon this one person (the governor) to cut interest rates, by the ruling party, in the year leading up to the elections. In addition, the Ministry of Finance has the power to give directions to RBI on any subject, without any transparency.

The work of financial regulation is spread across RBI, SEBI, Insurance Regulatory and Development Authority of India (IRDAI) and PFRDA. All these agencies feature important deviations from good governance principles for regulators.[7] There is arbitrary power in regulation-making, licensing, investigation, and prosecution. At an early stage of development of state capacity, substantial powers of investigation and punishment have been placed at regulators, which has hampered the emergence of state capacity.

The regulation-making and licensing powers have been used, in India, to create a comprehensive central planning system, where every product and process of the private sector is controlled by the financial agencies. These interventions often have no foundation in terms of market failure. As an example, SEBI controls the time of day at which exchanges start and stop their operations. Similarly, SEBI now has de facto control of the names of the board of directors and the management team of exchange institutions. This is a level of central planning that was not found with industrial firms in India in 1991.

An unusual feature of regulators in India, which is not seen elsewhere in the world, is that the judicial function has also been placed at regulators. When this is done, regulators fuse the legislative, executive and judicial branches of the state. There is no separation of powers, and conventional civil servants, who lack judicial independence, are playing the role of a judge. This is an unusual arrangement, given that separation of powers is part of the 'basic structure' doctrine of Indian constitutional law.[8]

As a consequence of these infirmities in the foundations of public administration of financial regulators, the state capacity in financial regulation which has come about is limited. We have a crisis-ridden financial system that does a poor job of raising financial resources and allocating them into the real economy.

While RBI does monetary policy, it also does many other things. As an example, it does financial regulation and runs exchange infrastructure for the bond market and the currency market. This sprawling agenda has hindered focus and accountability, and engendered low performance.

There are four clear tasks in financial economic policy: monetary policy, financial regulation, resolution, and public debt management. Many other things are done in Indian financial economic policy, going beyond these four tasks, which are deficient in rationale. These include capital controls, government-owned financial institutions to address perceived failures of the financial system (e.g., National Bank for Agriculture and Rural Development [NABARD] or Mudra Bank), government-owned banks, directed lending, the system of 'financial repression' through which financial firms are forced to lend to the government, etc.

The process of financial reform

At the outset, equity market trading took place by open outcry at the BSE, which was controlled by its members. Settlement took place through physical share certificates, and there was a chronic problem with counterfeit share certificates. The BSE closed down many times, out of its inability to manage payments efficiently.

The first phase of financial reform in India was triggered by the requirement for foreign capital inflows after 1991 and the Harshad Mehta scandal in 1992. This led to a remarkable phase of change, led by a remarkable community of public-minded people. SEBI was established as a new regulator. Modern exchange infrastructure was established in the form of the National Stock Exchange (NSE), the National Securities Clearing Corporation (NSCC) and the National Stock Depository Limited (NSDL). Electronic trading and derivatives trading were introduced. These were transformative reforms. One of the pioneers of this work, Ravi Narain, said that when satellite trading through NSE reached a remote town in India, it was transformative on the scale of the first railway line reaching the town. The improvements of the equity market of that period were an important part of the enabling environment for the high growth of the 1991–2011 period.[9]

This was followed by a series of government committee reports, which mapped out the journey of financial economic policy. These included a report on capital controls led by U.K. Sinha, one on consumer protection led by Dhirendra Swarup, one on public debt management led by Jahangir Aziz, one on international finance led by Percy Mistry, and one on domestic finance led by Raghuram Rajan.[10] These five reports worked out a broadly coherent vision for the next stage of the reforms. The changes that were called for required large-scale changes in the laws that created agencies and controlled government intervention in finance.

These ideas were brought together by the Financial Sector Legislative Reforms Commission (FSLRC), which worked from 2011 to 2015. FSLRC drafted a single law, the Indian Financial Code which replaces sixty-one existing laws.[11] A few elements of this work have been translated into implementation, such as inflation targeting, but most have not. The Indian Financial Code, version 1.1, is the pending agenda for financial reforms.

In this period, the policy pipeline was fully working, from data to research to creative policy proposals, to government committee reports to the drafting of law and the construction of state capacity to enforce new laws. These successes were grounded in a financial reforms community. A coherent set of persons played various roles through this period, and brought a consistent intellectual framework into all this work. The reforms process was led by the Ministry of Finance, SEBI and NSE. A large number of individuals across government, academics and financial firms participated in the work. As an example, 146 individuals were involved in FSLRC in various capacities.[12] For the next phase of the financial reforms, a comparable community will need to be recreated.

Summing up

Financial economic policy is about the working of financial intermediaries, financial markets, money creation and government borrowing.

Market failure in the form of externalities and asymmetric information is present in the working of financial markets, and in the engagement of unsophisticated households with financial intermediaries. Government intervention is required to address this. At the same time, 'consumer protection' in finance does not mean that unsophisticated households earn risk-less profits. All users of financial products should face the usual risk/reward trade-offs.

An unsophisticated household dealing with a bank is much like an unsophisticated household buying medicines. Regulation is required to ensure that promises are upheld with a reasonably high probability. In the case of financial markets, regulators push for better disclosure, the reliable working of financial markets and enforcement against market abuse.

The tasks of government in financial economic policy can be achieved using four agencies: a financial regulator, a central bank, a resolution corporation (which is a specialized bankruptcy process for certain financial firms) and a public debt management agency.

The usual public choice problems come in the way of the working of these organizations. There is a principal–agent problem; the staff of the agencies resists accountability and performance.

Inflation targeting is an accountability mechanism that puts a check upon printed money. The central bank is held accountable for running the printing presses at a rate that generates 4 per cent CPI inflation. This is a big step forward for obtaining state capacity at the central bank.

There is a problem of political independence of monetary policy, which can be resolved by shifting the power to set the short-term rate from one individual to the MPC. If the MPC is dominated by one person, e.g., if the persons who vote are the employees of the RBI governor, these gains are not obtained.

Achieving state capacity in financial regulation is extremely difficult. It involves a large number of transactions, high discretion, high stakes and high secrecy.

Indian finance has worked reasonably poorly on all four aspects of state intervention, as these are difficult problems, and as there have been many mistakes in the policy pathways that have been chosen.

The full policy pipeline worked in the equity market reforms starting with the G.S. Patel Committee in 1984. The early years of SEBI and NSE gave a quantum leap in the working of the equity market in the 1992–2001 period. After this, the committee process, and a strong community, gave the drafting of the Indian Financial Code, version 1.1, in 2015. The next phase of financial reform will require constructing a comparable community as the first phase.

37

Dealing with macroeconomic and financial crises

States face political crises, constitutional crises, national security crises, and economic crises. In this chapter, we look closely at economic crises. The Indian economy, more than mature market economies, has periods of growth punctuated by periods of macroeconomic/financial crises. Dealing with crises is hence more important in the Indian setting than is the case in advanced economies.

This is a place where some elements of the orthodoxy—of the main arguments of the preceding chapters—have to be temporarily jettisoned. This is a field which is more art than science. This field is thus interesting from two points of view: because macroeconomic/financial crises are important, and because they yield fresh insights into the principles of public policy.

Defining a crisis

Some people see crises as dramatic events that take place in a short time. A big crash in stock prices, or the default of a large firm like Lehman Brothers—these are treated as the required markers for declaring a financial crisis. This is, however, not a useful definition. The key thing to watch for is an adverse impact upon the functioning of the real economy.

The defining feature, when the word 'crisis' must be used, is when the difficulties of the financial system have an adverse impact upon the working of the real economy. If a few financial firms fail, and (say) the overall car loan business works out okay (albeit with some shifts in market share), it is not a crisis. But if stress in the financial system generates an adverse impact upon quantities and prices in that market for car loans, it is a financial crisis.

By this definition, a sharp decline in stock prices does not (in and of itself) constitute a crisis, as long as the institutional apparatus surrounding the exchange is working properly. Asset prices are made by speculators peering into the future, and it is perfectly normal for those views to change every now and then, resulting in large changes in asset prices. Similarly, the ups and downs of the business cycle are part of the routine process of the market economy. Each downturn is not a crisis.

In the best of times, the Indian financial system works poorly. Its components are closer to malfunction, when compared with the financial system of advanced economies. As an example, whether in good times or bad, many firms in India with a balance sheet of Rs 1 billion find it difficult to access credit. Fairly modest shocks are able to disrupt the normal flow of economic activity. The treatment of financial crisis that is seen in advanced economies needs to be adapted significantly to make it useful under Indian conditions.

The ebb and flow of fear

Finance is the brain of the economy.

Joseph Stiglitz

This 'brain of the economy' is distributed across the senior decision makers of about 2000 financial firms and the individual investors that they serve. Booms are enabled by these decision makers feeling safe, and thus taking greater risk. This enables greater financing of risky projects, and triggers off an investment boom. Conversely, downturns are associated with fear. The decision makers become sceptical and retreat into safety. This generates reduced availability of risk capital. This hampers investment and yields a business cycle downturn.

The fear that is on the minds of decision makers comes in two kinds. A person may feel sceptical about the future of the economy. Or, a person may feel fear at a personal level, and consequently resort to risk-averse strategies. Such fears at a personal level include possibilities of job loss, firm closure, and investigations.

In addressing a macroeconomic/financial crisis, the main objective of policymakers is to address and reverse this contagious fear.

The three big downturns of recent decades

In the Indian experience of recent decades, we see three big downturns.

The late 1980s. Difficulties from the late 1980s onward led up to a balance of payments crisis, and an IMF programme, in 1991. Alongside this, we got a collapse of the BSE in 1992.

The late 1990s. The investment boom of the mid-1990s petered out with a succession of shocks: the 1997 Asian crisis, RBI's 200 basis points interest rate hike in 1998, India's nuclear tests in May 1998, the dot-com crash in the US in March 2000, and then the 9/11 attacks. Alongside this, we got the Ketan Parekh scandal, the collapse of the Calcutta Stock Exchange, the UTI crisis (July 2001) and distress at the development finance institutions (Industrial Development Bank of India [IDBI] and Industrial Finance Corporation of India [IFCI]).

From 2008 onward. The investment boom of the early years of the twenty-first century petered out with the 2008 crisis in the US, and the Mumbai attacks. Alongside this, we got the Satyam scandal (January 2009). From 2011 onward, this morphed into a problem of credit quality in a significant proportion of financial and non-financial firms. Loose fiscal policy was used to combat the problems of 2008–09, but turned into a fiscal/currency crisis in 2012–13. The data shows a turning point in 2011.

Another way to think about this experience is to focus on the two big booms. There was an investment boom in the 1990s which led up to a credit crisis in the late 1990s. And, there was an investment boom during 2003–08. India of the recent decades is a tale of two booms and three downturns. This chapter is about doing public policy in the depth of these downturns.

The problem of administrative boundaries

Ordinarily, financial regulators think about one financial firm at a time, focusing on consumer protection and micro-prudential regulation of this firm. In the present Indian financial regulatory architecture, this involves RBI looking at banks, SEBI looking at mutual funds, etc.

The essence of macroeconomic/financial crises is complex interactions running across the entire financial system. As an example, a critical feature of the 2008 crisis was the interplay between mutual funds, NBFCs and the real estate business. Relationships between markets and firms, that cut across administrative boundaries, are often not understood by sectoral regulators. Understanding and defusing financial crises requires an ability to understand the whole financial system—seeing the woods for the trees.

The FSLRC proposal involves the establishment of a 'Council of Regulators', the Financial Stability and Development Council (FSDC), which would work on systemic risk regulation and crisis management. FSDC would have board members who are the chairpersons of financial agencies (thus bringing all the knowledge and decision-making capacity into the room), and a technical secretariat which develops data sets and skill in thinking about systemic risk. In the absence of the FSDC technical secretariat, the task of systemic risk analysis and crisis management takes place at the Department of Economic Affairs, supported by its associated research institutions.

The problem of feedback loops

The market economy is ordinarily a resilient creature that recovers from shocks. The process of firm failure is good for surviving competitors, as they gain pricing power and are able to access resources at lower prices. Firm failure is a problem for the affected firm, but not of the economy.

This is not the case with macroeconomic/financial crises. Financial crises lack ready pathways for exit; in fact, there are positive feedback loops. As an example, consider a country in a fiscal crisis, where the government is finding it difficult to borrow on the scale required to finance the deficit. The fiscal crisis adversely affects GDP growth. When GDP growth is lower, tax revenues go down and generally expenditure goes up. This worsens the fiscal crisis.

In every crisis, it is important for policymakers to understand the positive feedback loops which are in operation, and try to disrupt some of the positive feedback loops. The word 'pro-cyclicality' is also used for 'positive feedback loops'.

Examples of these positive feedback loops abound in crises in India. The classic interplay between macroeconomics and finance in a credit crisis runs as follows. The banks get into trouble, and pull back from lending. This hampers the working of real sector firms, and more of them get into trouble. This worsens the credit quality of banks.

Fire sales are a source of feedback loops. As an example, suppose the firms/individuals who are in trouble are overexposed to real estate. Distressed persons sell real estate in order to obtain cash which they badly require. Large and urgent sales have an adverse impact upon real estate prices. This worsens the position of the firms/individuals who are exposed to real estate.

When a downturn begins, forecasted inflation goes down. This makes previously negotiated nominal debt contracts more expensive. Suppose there is a loan at a nominal interest rate of 8 per cent. Suppose a downturn begins, and forecasted inflation goes down from 4 per cent to 2 per cent. Now the real interest rate associated with the loan goes *up* from 4 per cent to 6 per cent, which makes things worse. When things are bad, higher real interest rates make it worse. When the central bank correctly runs an inflation-targeting system, this positive feedback loop is defused, because a decline in forecasted inflation will induce the central bank to cut interest rates.[1]

Risk-averse bureaucrats in India often react to revelations of difficulty by enacting new regulations which restrict private persons more. The greater the extent to which a regulator was responsible for the difficulties, the greater is their virtue signalling. At a time when the system is stressed and risk capital is scarce, greater restrictions upon private persons further hamper risk-taking. This is another positive feedback loop.

India's journey in financial regulation from the late 1980s has a steady layering of reduced economic freedom after each crisis, because these crisis-response measures are seldom reversed. Policymakers should be cautious about hawkish measures that are implemented in a crisis for two reasons: first, to avoid positive feedback loops, and second, owing to the possibility that these 'tough' crisis responses will have adverse consequences for the economy over a sustained period.

Recessions uncover what auditors do not

> *Only when the tide goes out do you discover who's been swimming naked.*

Warren Buffett

In a crisis, it does not rain, it pours. When times are difficult, some unexpected things break down. As an example, after the Lehman collapse in September 2008 and the Mumbai attacks in November 2008, we got the Satyam collapse in January 2009.[2]

This is not accidental. In every boom, there are some organizations which are over-exuberant, and are propelled into exceptional growth by the times and by dubious tactics. They juggle many balls and manage to keep up a facade of success, as long as the times are good. They tend to be relatively young and flashy firms, and spend on press relations, lobby with bureaucrats and politicians, that put in more effort on image and influencing policy rather than the substance of innovation and cost-cutting. They are the darlings of the stock market in their moment of glory.

There is an element of a Ponzi scheme here: the early investors are given fabulous returns using capital brought in by the next wave of investors. The consolidated financial statements show poor profits: the firm runs a lavish expenditure programme by using money belonging to lenders or shareholders, and not operating profit.

When the tide turns, it becomes impossible to keep up the show, and bad news tumbles out. This bad news ranges from mundane business failure to lurid revelations of fraud and violations of law.

These revelations tend to emerge when the times are bad. This is one element of the feedback loops that are operating in a crisis.

Should budgetary resources be used for a bailout?

In this book, we have emphasized that public expenditure is a precious resource. Obtaining public funds is not easy: Each rupee of public spending imposes a cost of about Rs 3 upon society.

In a financial crisis, when there is a discussion about the use of public money, such a high bar should be applied. We should estimate projected GDP under two scenarios: if Rs X of fiscal resources are used versus if they are not used. The decision to use fiscal resources should require a high bar: an impact upon GDP of five or ten times the proposed spending.

For some people, all use of fiscal resources in a macroeconomic/ financial crisis is abhorrent. The question should instead be viewed in a pragmatic and not ideological way. The use of public money to help resolve a crisis is no different from any other use of public money. Public money should be used when, and only when, the value for money is very high. The gains to society from using public money should be well above the 3X test.

The use of public money in resolving a financial crisis runs the risk of moral hazard. Private persons may take bigger risks in the future, if they know that they will be bailed out by the exchequer. The intervention should involve features that are fairly painful to the shareholders and decision makers of a failed institution, to contain such moral hazard. As an example, the US Federal government's involvement in AIG was extremely painful, financially, for the erstwhile shareholders and managers of AIG.[3]

The word 'bailout' suggests that a favour is being done to the shareholders and managers of a failed financial firm. As emphasized above, the terms of the intervention can be structured in a way that imposes extreme financial pain upon the erstwhile shareholders and managers. The focus of the policy action should be to improve the results for the economy, and not to bail out one financial firm.

The urge to hit back

When financial stress unfolds, there is unhappiness in the air. The public is keen to ascribe blame upon some people, particularly when there are revelations of fraud, and when fiscal resources are spent. The phrase *privatization of profit and socialization of loss* gains much currency.

In one recent failed firm in India, six elements of government action were initiated—from the Serious Fraud Investigation Office (SFIO), the Ministry of Corporate Affairs, the National Financial Regulatory Authority (NFRA), the Institute of Chartered Accountants of India (ICAI), the Securities and Exchange Board of India (SEBI) and the Enforcement Directorate (ED).

My administration is the only thing between you and the pitchforks.

Barack Obama to bankers on 27 March 2009[4]

Much as it may be satisfying to hit back, this may not be the best path from the viewpoint of the economy. The essence of a financial crisis is a surge in fear on the part of the decision makers of 2000 financial firms. Particularly in India, where investigation capabilities are poor, there is the risk that a careful investigation into a narrow violation morphs into a fishing inquiry that expands to many more individuals and entities. Investigations can turn into witch-hunts, with motivations such as extortion, personal vendetta, and settling scores. Each person drawn into the investigation, and a few dozen close friends, will experience enhanced fear owing to the investigation and thus pull back from risk-taking.

A certain subset of financial decisions (to lend or to invest) will always go bad. When investigations are in the air, financial firms will become more risk averse, at a time when stressed firms require equity and debt capital. This constitutes one more element of positive feedback loops.

Policymaking in normal times versus a crisis

Under normal circumstances, we aim for the development of institutional capacity. This involves clarity of objectives, development of process manuals, and skills in the humans to operate those manuals. As an example, banking supervision can be refined over the years into a process-driven activity. Over the years, institutional capacity for banking supervision can develop.

Macroeconomic/financial crises resist the development of such manuals for two reasons. The first problem is that these are not activities which take place every day. The economic policy community must perhaps learn from the defence community, about how the FSDC staff can continuously train, in peacetime, for the next war. At present, the staff of policy organizations like the Ministry of Finance are not training in peacetime for the next crisis; they are fully taken doing other things.[5]

All happy families are alike; each unhappy family is unhappy in its own way.

Anna Karenina by Leo Tolstoy

The second problem is that each crisis is different. All bank failure is alike, which enables process manuals for banking supervision. But each macroeconomic/financial crisis is different.[6] This hampers the development of manuals. The long and slow process of refinement of institutional capacity does not come about when dealing with crises. The policymakers can have some concepts and principles, but no tangible recipe for action.

> *Events, dear boy, events.*
>
> Response by UK prime minister Harold Macmillan
> when a journalist asked what is most
> likely to blow governments off course

At the same time, mere tactical, day-to-day responses do not suffice in crisis management. A coherent intellectual framework of economic policy is required, through which facts are parsed, a strategy is established, and day-to-day decisions are made. Only when such a coherent framework is present can a large number of practical decisions—spread across time and across individuals—be rendered coherent. If policymaking degenerates into a series of tactical battles, there is no strategy, and this will work poorly.[7]

Given the weakness of institutions in India, the response to a macroeconomic/financial crisis is primarily about the key individuals who are in place and their intellectual framework. Economic policy at such times requires people who have been carved by institutions and experience for such a moment. A coalition of persons at the key policymaking institutions needs to come together. This requires a combination of intellectual capacity, a culture of brain-storming and problem solving, and trust.[8]

Knowledge institutions are particularly valuable in a crisis environment. Under normal circumstances, if the task at hand is supervising a bank, this fits in fine with the process manual, and the role of knowledge institutions is limited to reviewing the process manual and helping to strengthen it. In crisis management, in contrast, conceptual knowledge about the working of the system is required. In India, this generally resides at knowledge institutions.

Predictability of policymaking in a crisis environment

In peacetime, government operates off process manuals, and the private sector can predict how government will behave because the process manuals are in the public domain. In a crisis, however, there are no manuals.

As has been emphasized earlier, the key feature of crises is the fear in the minds of decision makers in financial firms. If the behaviour of government is unpredictable, this (in and of itself) is an additional source of risk.

While the private sector will always praise policymakers in public, there is a lack of trust in policy capacity in their eyes. Private persons keenly watch policymakers in a crisis, and wonder: *Does this person get what is going on? What does her self-interest lead her to do?* Policymakers often try to be positive, and say that things will be fine. They then run the risk of losing respect in the eyes of private persons. When there is mistrust of the policymakers, this generates greater fear.

This is where a coherent intellectual framework of policy becomes particularly important. As an example, the 'Committee to save the world' of 1997 (comprising Larry Summers, Ben Bernanke and Robert Rubin) had a shared philosophy that was widely understood by private persons. This induced predictability in crisis response. Even though we were on a journey without maps, with no clear process manuals that defined what should be done in the crisis, the private sector had a fair sense about how these policymakers would behave.

For this reason, it is not enough for policymakers to know what is going on. It is essential for policymakers to *display* that expertise, and communicate their intellectual framework, through white papers, speeches and committee reports. There is a long tradition in the Ministry of Finance, of the top twenty persons going out into conferences and seminars every week, to engage in a two-way street: To hear from experts about what is going on, and to earn the trust of private persons by displaying knowledge and an intellectual framework.

How much time do we have?

A useful insight from global history is that macroeconomic/ financial crises play out reasonably slowly. They are not like wars, which play out rapidly. As an example, the Indo-Pakistan war of 1971 ran from 3 December to 16 December. Macroeconomic/ financial crises play out over longer time periods. As an example, the East Asian Crisis ran from 1997 to 1999.[9]

Ordinarily, the policy process in a liberal democracy must be slow and deliberative. Ideas need to be discussed, consensus needs to be achieved, political compromises need to be negotiated, and each announcement must come with a future date on which it becomes effective. Policymaking in a crisis needs to be a bit faster than this.

A crisis is, at heart, an outbreak of fear in the minds of private decision makers. The objective of policymakers should be to show a complete understanding of the situation, and multiple initiatives that address problems in the main, so that the fear can subside. The sooner the fear subsides, the sooner the macroeconomy will heal. Through every day of delay, the positive feedback loops induce greater damage.

This objective of speed in a crisis involves two capacity constraints. The first is the capacity constraint of the leadership: how quickly can the leadership understand the crisis, and do a high-level design of the responses? The second capacity constraint is that of execution. There is a shortage of staffers in the Ministry of Finance, the RBI and SEBI who can lead sub-components of the overall crisis management. Can multiple initiatives be run in parallel, without loss of fidelity to the original objective?

The fog of war

While macroeconomic/financial crises are not two-week affairs, they unfold at a rapid pace when compared with the delays of the statistical system. As an example, through calendar year 2008, when the world economy and the Indian economy were losing momentum, policymakers had relatively little information about the state of the economy in calendar year 2008 itself.

In a crisis, the noise in the media is deafening. Many policy initiatives are taken, which will impact upon the system, but in ways that are not yet fully known. These three factors—the noise in the media, the policy actions that have yet to play out, and the delays in data release—come together to induce a 'fog of war'. In the midst of a crisis, it is difficult to know what is going on.

Financial markets are a key source of *information* in a crisis. Asset prices are forward-looking and suffer from no delay in data release. Financial markets produce important derived information systems such as the implied volatility. To the extent that deep and liquid markets continue to function efficiently, in the storm, this is a valuable tool for information gathering by policymakers.

Alongside this, financial market *participants* have a great deal of knowledge. The precise difficulties in various financial markets and instruments, the sites in the system of asset pricing where arbitrage and liquidity are breaking down—these are pregnant with insights into understanding and solving the crisis. Policymakers should exploit the rich information that comes out of modern financial markets, and have deep human connections into financial market participants so as to generate the level of trust required for candid conversations. These benefits, however, only accrue when there have been years of development of liquidity and market efficiency in the financial markets. In India, we have seen a stream of regulatory actions that retard market quality, and thus reduce the usefulness of information derived from financial markets.

The need for closure

In normal times, the instinct of the policy process is to not solve a problem, but to kick the can down the road. In a macroeconomic/ financial crisis, however, the critical building blocks of the crisis cannot be deferred into the future. Once the private sector has formed a picture of the key elements of the crisis, its fear will not subside until they are solved. It is worth remembering the two key ideas in firm failure.

When a firm goes bust, the loss has already taken place, all that remains is the question of who bears the loss. The bankruptcy process controls the allocation of the loss. Legal certainty is created by a well-functioning bankruptcy process (i.e., IBC for most firms and the resolution corporation for certain financial firms). Most of the time, in a crisis, there are elements of the landscape where such certainty is lacking. As an example, in the US in 2008, it was not clear how the endgame for Lehman Brothers or AIG would work out, or how the loss would be allocated. This uncertainty generated fear.

In normal times, policymakers should strengthen the institutional framework so that a bankruptcy process is in place, which covers all firms, and works well. Once a crisis starts, the limitations of the bankruptcy framework will come to the fore. At that time, bankruptcy process reforms are not an alternative. Exceptional solutions will need to be devised, and postponing the bad news will not be accepted by the private sector.

A bankrupt firm is a melting ice cube. Every delay in resolution increases the cost of resolution. Particularly when there is a combination of fiscal stress and potential fiscal expenses for resolution, delaying things makes it worse as the price tag will go up.

Example 58: The UTI crisis

There were two root cause problems in the UTI in 2001:

- Some schemes were 'assured return schemes': they made promises about the returns that would be obtained, but lacked the financial engineering backing up these assurances. The sustained difficulties of the macroeconomy from July 1997 (the Thai crisis) onward led to weak asset prices, and put these assurances under threat.
- In a scheme named 'US-64', the claimed 'net asset value (NAV)' was overstated. Unsophisticated households discovered that they had actually made losses, when the true NAV was revealed.

When these problems were revealed, this induced a crisis. This was solved through a three-pronged strategy.

Finance Minister Yashwant Sinha decided that fiscal resources would be used to bear half the losses experienced by unsophisticated households. This struck a balance between the unhappiness of households, who felt betrayed by a government organization, versus the fiscal dangers of taking on unlimited liability associated with public sector financial firms.

Finance Secretary S. Narayan and governor of the RBI Bimal Jalan designed the resolution strategy for UTI. This is the work which would ordinarily have been done by the resolution corporation, but this institution did not exist. The NAV-based schemes of UTI were placed in a 'good UTI', and the remainder were placed in a 'bad UTI' which was gradually wound down.

To preserve credibility in the eyes of the market, every use of public money must be accompanied by structural reform. The commitment to building a mature market economy was underlined by repealing the erstwhile UTI Act, converting the 'good UTI' into an ordinary company under the Companies Act, partially privatizing it, and placing it unambiguously under the normal regulatory regime of SEBI for mutual funds.

When the crisis started, traditional thinkers in the Indian policy process were asking for a complete fiscal bailout for unsophisticated households, and a continuation of UTI in its old ways, with incremental reforms (shift US-64 to a true NAV-based system, use financial derivatives for implementing returns assurances). If that path had been taken, the private sector would have been less impressed.

From the viewpoint of moral hazard, and the concern about bailouts, the arithmetic worked out well for the government. It took a long time for the assets in 'bad UTI' to be sold, but when these were finally liquidated, the government actually turned a profit.

Macro policy in a crisis

In an ideal world, macroeconomic policy should respond to a downturn with expansionary monetary and fiscal policy. As an example, the US and the UK had very large enlargements of the deficit, and cut interest rates to 0, in response to the crisis of 2008–09.

The ability to enlarge borrowing when faced with a crisis is, however, the luxury of a country that has invested in normal times in building up sound fiscal institutions. Many pieces are required, that make up sound fiscal institutions. In normal times, the country must run small primary surpluses. There must be a public debt management agency which engages with non-coerced lenders to the government. There must be a long history of trust in the release of sound data, of a government that behaves in a responsible way, and repays on debt. Once these foundations are in place, it becomes possible to vastly increase borrowing when faced with a crisis.

In contrast, some crises are *fiscal*, and the market feels that the path of sovereign borrowing is unsustainable. At this time, there is no alternative in crisis response but to sharply reduce government borrowing. This hurts the economy at a difficult time, but there is no alternative. This was the path taken in India in 2012–13.[10] In normal times, deficit reduction is contractionary. But in a fiscal crisis, deficit reduction reduces fear in financial markets, thus giving an 'expansionary fiscal consolidation'.

In similar fashion, monetary policy should swing into action when there is a crisis. Macroeconomic difficulties would result in forecasted inflation going below the target. The MPC would see this, and cut rates. The market would not be concerned about the possibility of an inflationary surge in the future, as the central bank is bound to deliver on the stated inflation target. Here also, the long years of establishing a sound institutional apparatus of inflation targeting can pay off nicely at a time of crisis, where it becomes possible to sharply cut rates without triggering fears of an inflation crisis.

The shock absorbers in a crisis

Stock prices, real estate prices and the rupee are key shock absorbers in a crisis. When the times become difficult, these prices should go down. This should make the assets more attractive from the viewpoint of domestic and foreign investors.

If, on the other hand, there are artificial attempts at distorting these prices, this can be harmful. As an example, consider a government that defends the exchange rate in a time of crisis. As economist Jayanth Varma has emphasized, this makes it *more* attractive for foreign investors to leave, as they are getting a better deal with a distorted exchange rate that might not last into the future. The enhanced exit of foreign investors, owing to exchange rate policy, generates *increased* stress in the economy.[11]

Example 59: Financial markets that stay open

On 17 May 2004, the UPA unexpectedly won the general elections, and Nifty crashed. There were concerns about whether the exchanges and clearing houses would survive this. This was particularly problematic at a time when the previous cabinet had exited but the new cabinet had not yet been formed, so there was no minister of finance. Some policymakers felt that the exchanges should be closed down. But the exchanges worked through the storm. While the new government had not yet settled in, Manmohan Singh (who was then a former finance minister) came out with a statement which helped reduce the fear.

After the Lehman default, the UK regulator banned short selling on the stock market for twenty-nine financial firms.[12] After this, there were demands in India that short selling and possibly derivatives trading for some financial firm equities should be banned. But policymakers rode through the storm without introducing such bans.

The terrorist attack in Mumbai started on Wednesday, 26 November 2008. There was a debate among policymakers about financial trading on 27 November (Thursday). Some argued that traders would panic and markets would crash, given that the gun battle was in progress at the Taj hotel, within earshot of some financial firms. The exchanges worked through the storm.

In each of these episodes, the right thing to do was to let the market process work out. The essence of a crisis is fear. There is no greater fear, for private persons, than not being able to see asset prices that are discovered on a fair marketplace, and not having the option value of being able to sell assets on the market if desired. If the marketplace is shut down, or if certain kinds of traders are banned, trust in the price is lost, and fear is exacerbated.

Prevention is better than cure

The time to fix the roof is when the sun is shining.

John F. Kennedy

The task of a policymaker grappling with a macroeconomic/ financial crisis is an unpleasant one. We should distil the misery of all previous crises, and find the energy to do the things that will head off crises.

How do we achieve macroeconomic/financial stability? By pursuing four objectives:

- Fiscal policy must be sound. Running small primary surpluses in most years and thereby paying down debt, thus having fiscal space for occasional large borrowing when disaster strikes.
- Inflation targeting anchors money, it stabilizes the macroeconomy and the exchange rate.

- Financial regulation must be sound, protecting the vitality of free men and women that do financial activities but addressing the market failure.
- Deep and liquid financial markets, that are allowed to adjust, are the shock absorbers. We must do everything possible to foster greater market quality, i.e., liquidity, resiliency and market efficiency.

In peacetime, we must nurture these foundations. In India, we have made some progress towards these goals.

The Fiscal Responsibility and Budget Management (FRBM) Act gave fiscal prudence for some years, but that has run into many difficulties. The formal objective of the RBI is now the delivery of 4 per cent CPI inflation. Some items of the FSLRC vision have been implemented, but most have not, and many financial intermediaries are beset with concerns about solvency. We made some progress on deep and liquid markets in the 1992–2001 period, but things have deteriorated in the following years. We moved up to a flexible exchange rate from 1993 till 2014, but exchange rate flexibility declined thereafter.

Even at the incipient stage of a crisis, sharp actions on these four fronts can stave off greater difficulties. It is the responsibility of public intellectuals and policymakers to speak truth to power at such times. As an example, in 2012, a sharp fiscal correction was initiated, and helped reduce the downstream difficulties.[13] It was a difficult message to give the political leadership of the time, to undertake a fiscal correction when the general election was nearing.

Summing up

A macroeconomic/financial crisis is defined as a time when the normal functioning of the real economy is impaired. The Indian experience contains three important downturns: late 1980s, late 1990s and from 2008 onward. At the root of the crises is an upsurge of fear in the minds of the key decision makers of 2000 financial firms.

Understanding and defusing crises require a view of the entire financial system. The administrative boundaries of existing financial agencies generally limit their information and world view. Systemic risk regulation requires system-wide data and the FSDC technical secretariat that will use this data for policy formulation.

There are positive feedback loops in every crisis. When things get bad, they get worse. These need to be understood and defused. Recessions uncover what auditors do not: In each crisis, some skeletons come out of the closet, and exacerbate the fear. A greater awareness of these dubious firms in peacetime will help reduce the damage caused by their unveiling in a crisis.

When there is an evaluation of the use of fiscal resources to help resolve a crisis, the usual test should apply. The marginal cost of public funds is about three times the apparent cost, so public money should be used when the value for money safely becomes more than threefold. The way in which public money is used should be designed to contain moral hazard.

Investigations and witch-hunts will generally exacerbate the fear, particularly given low state capacity at the agencies in India.

Financial agencies (central bank, regulator, resolution corporation, debt management agency) normally work on well-defined process manuals. Crisis management has to go off the manual. At the same time, mere day-to-day tactical actions do not suffice. An intellectual framework, an understanding of the crisis, and a strategy of response are required. This is efficient in and of itself, and is also essential in earning the respect of the private sector. If government actions are all tactics and no strategy, the government will drive up the uncertainty.

When institutional quality is weak, this task—of understanding the crisis and developing a strategy to respond to it—requires individuals who have been carved by experience and institutions for this moment. These capabilities are required all across the policy institutions, and there is a need for intellectual coherence, mutual respect and trust between the leadership of all the key policy institutions. The intellectual framework of the team, communicated to the private sector, will create predictability about how the government will respond to future scenarios.

Macroeconomic/financial crises are not like wars, they do not start and end in two weeks. They generally last for over two years. Policymakers face a 'fog of war' in this period, where events are moving fast but the standard statistics are quite dated.

For fear to subside, the key building blocks of the crisis have to be comprehensively addressed. The option of letting problems simmer for some time longer, on the critical parts of the problem, is not there in a crisis.

If fiscal policy has been sound, a large expansion of the fiscal deficit can help support demand in a crisis. But if fiscal stress is at the heart of a crisis, this possibility is ruled out.

A formal inflation targeting system reassures the market that monetary policy will not go out of control. This gives greater space for cutting rates when faced with a crisis.

Free movement of asset prices is a shock absorber. A big depreciation of the exchange rate, for example, makes local assets more attractive and bolsters exports.

Prevention is better than cure. The long-term nurturing of inflation targeting, small primary surpluses, sound financial regulation, and deep and liquid financial markets—these make the country less crisis-prone.

Part VII

Parting words

38

Do no harm

Set a high bar for coercion

> *Dullness in matters of government is a good sign and not a bad one. In particular, dullness in parliamentary government is a test of its excellence, an indication of its success.*

Walter Bagehot

We do not understand the world enough, and every intervention will work out poorly compared with what was originally envisaged. Hence, we should be very cautious before we set out to coerce private persons.

There is now an increasing recognition in India of the need to be cautious about spending public money. It is now well understood that the public expenditure process results in the wastage of most of the resources that go in. It makes more sense to first demand that an expenditure programme successfully addresses market failure, before committing large sums of money into it. In similar fashion, we should become stingy in the use of coercion. Before a government official or agency is given powers to investigate or punish, there must be a high assurance that there are checks and balances, rule of law, and state capacity. More intrusive powers of investigations, and larger punishments, should be written into laws only after ascertaining that less intrusive powers and smaller punishments are being wielded well.

In India, too many people are ready to propose that the state mandate something. One part of the excessive willingness to coerce comes from the public policy establishment. For example, we are not able to get business into Gujarat International Finance Tec-City (GIFT-City), so the proposed solution is to force overseas Nifty derivatives activity to go into GIFT-City.

Demands for state coercion come from the private sector also. The private sector is comfortable with a government that interferes. The standard procedure for gaining competitive advantage is to try to obtain government coercion against rivals. This perhaps reflects the long history of Indian socialism. Firms have developed capabilities in competing through manipulation of the policy process, instead of developing superior products.

The trigger-happy approach to coercing private persons needs to change, for India to develop a healthy state. The bar of evidence and argument that is required before the state coerces a private person should be set very high. This reflects a Hippocratic oath of public policy: We should have strong foundations of evidence and analysis before we harm certain persons.

A key element of doing better, when compared with gratuitous state intervention, is to require demonstration of harm. In our policy discourse, we should demand proof of harm before state intervention is contemplated. When a government intervenes in the absence of demonstrated harm, this is likely to reflect mere political lobbying by one special interest group or another.

Our weary belief is that the outcome of every policy intervention will surprise us. We should be mindful of our limitations in re-engineering society, and crossing the river by feeling the stones.[1]

'Make haste slowly' is thus a good rule when thinking about structural change in the economy.

Respecting individuals and avoiding social engineering have value in and of themselves. No one person should impose a value system upon other persons. In addition, social engineering is fraught with difficulty. We do not know enough to be successful social engineers. If we bumble about, interfering in a machinery that we only dimly understand, we will often make things worse. The Hippocratic oath, when applied into the world of public policy, translates into eschewing social engineering.

We should move fairly briskly on modifications *of the state apparatus*, engaged in the routine management process of understanding areas of failure and undertaking reorganization. But we should be wary of policy plans that aim to remake society.

The optimist in her labyrinth

Policy analysts generally mean well, and are able to see things that a government is doing wrong. It is important to look deeper, and understand *why* the government is making mistakes. Politicians and officials sometimes lack a technical understanding, but most of the time, the mistakes are emerging out of faulty *incentives*. It does not suffice to (say) have domain knowledge on drug safety, and criticize what the Indian state does wrong on drug safety. We have to learn to step into the shoes of the establishment, and understand why it fails. The change that matters is the deeper change, of the incentives of politicians and officials.

The optimist proposing a new regulator often slips into the illusion that she, or people like her, will man the new regulator and will make decisions for the good of the people. But in reality, each new regulator will have processes, incentives and staffing much like the existing regulators. Unless deeper changes are made to the incentives of the politicians and officials, we should expect that a new regulator will be a disappointment like the others that came before it.

The only grounds for optimism when establishing a new regulator is when there is a deeper change in the working of the regulator, with about 140 sections of law that set it going on a better foundation. If these 140 sections of law are not done correctly, each new regulator will become one more element of the apparatus of central planning, raids and investigations.

Heed the law of unintended consequences

I beseech you, in the bowels of Christ, think it possible that you may be mistaken.

Oliver Cromwell, 5 August 1650

Intervening in social systems is a messy business, and very often, things go wrong. The Indian landscape is littered with outcomes that were the opposite of what was intended. APMCs were not intended to create entrenched power in the hands of traders. Land ceiling acts were not intended to create shortages of real estate and high prices for real estate. Bank nationalization was not intended to hamper growth, stability and inclusion.

Why do these things go wrong? Why do we joke about the 'law of unintended consequences'? Many things are simultaneously going on, which work against us.[2]

Error: Our facts and our analytical models are incomplete; there is a 'knowledge constraint'. We know less than we think. Hence, we make errors.

Wishful thinking: We suffer from 'confirmation bias'; we tend to look for the facts that support our positions. Once a tentative position is taken, we lose objectivity. This has become a bigger issue in the world of electronic and social media, where it has become harder for a policymaker to change positions.

Political economy dominates: The ideal technocratic plan is never implemented in the real world. What will be put to field will always be tugged at by various political considerations, it will always be a suboptimal version of the starting point of the discussion. The best laid plans of well meaning intellectuals turn into a mess on the way to execution.

Limitations of execution: There is an administrative constraint holding up the translation of idea into execution. The frail management systems through which policy initiatives are implemented result in an intervention which diverges substantially from what was originally intended. Innovators in policy thinking often find themselves saying, some years later: *I did not mislead, you mis-followed.* To the extent that we take implementation constraints seriously in policy design, we will fare better.

The plan gets derailed: As the boxer Mike Tyson said, 'Everybody has a plan until they get punched in the mouth.' We start doing something, but unexpected events show up, and we are forced to respond.

Time horizons: A policy strategy may work as intended in the long term, but it can yield unpleasant side effects in the short term.

People respond to incentives: Individuals, officials and politicians, all respond to incentives. The Lucas critique is at work; behaviour changes once a new policy is introduced. This often changes the world when compared with what was understood at the time the policy analysis was undertaken. This is completely unlike physical systems. The behaviour of air molecules does not change when we use them to put planes aloft. But in social science settings, the empirical regularities which were present in the data are modified when policymakers change incentives and thus behaviour.

Non-linearities: Unintended consequences flow from non-linear science. Non-linearities, and the interactions of a large number of moving parts, are notorious for potentially inducing chaos in physical systems. Social systems suffer from the even greater problem that the moving parts are not fixed creatures but optimizing persons. It would be hard enough to analyse non-linear interactions between 1.3 billion people; it is even harder to do this as each one is a sentient being in the quest for life, liberty and happiness.

Consider it possible you may be mistaken

By default, the public policy process is loath to admit failure and change course. Bureaucracies prefer to stay in their comfort zone, they tend to favour intensification of existing programmes as opposed to deeper reform.

Politicians and officials are loath to admit there was a mistake.

The outcomes will be improved if there are formal processes that encourage questioning. Every intervention into society should be subject to ex post review, to ask the question: Did this deliver on its objectives? Does the ex post cost–benefit analysis line up with the ex ante cost–benefit analysis? Did the benefits, as revealed in operation, actually outweigh the costs as revealed in operation?

Public policy is a process of hypothesis testing, of forming a theory about the world, and experimenting with interventions that are thought to help. This process takes place under conditions of poor knowledge and hostile political economy. Formal rules that shift the process towards greater cogitation and rational analysis will produce better outcomes.

Pathways to less government intervention

The field of public policy has a tension at its core. We are exhilarated at understanding market failures, and setting up state machinery that makes everyone better off by addressing market failures. But we understand how badly the state works, under real-world conditions. We roll out state interventions with a heavy heart.

The state is an engine which is supposed to convert coercive power into human welfare. At its best, this results in the blossoming of poetry and science. But coercive power is all too easily abused, and the state is then an engine through which coercive power is used by a few to inflict harm.

A young soldier glorifies warfare, while a wise general knows that war is hell. We feel similarly about public policy. A young person who is not excited about doing good by addressing market failures has no heart. A grown-up who is not afraid of state intervention going horribly wrong has no brain. We should know how to set up the machinery of bureaucratic intervention into the economy, but we should always dread rolling this out.

The single-window chimera

Every now and then, we hear proposals in India to hold state coercion intact, and make life easier for private persons by setting up 'single-window approval'. There are two problems with this approach.

First, we do not make the Gestapo nicer by setting up a pleasant front desk. Single-window systems do not solve the problem of state coercion, and the threat of raids and punishments including possibly criminal sanctions. Second, in the absence of deeper reform, it is hard to build single-window systems that overcome a maze of restrictions. Many or most enthusiastic announcements of single-window systems fail to work out in practice.

We must go deeper. We reform by whittling down and correcting state intervention, not putting a user interface on it. The reform required in the early 1990s was not a single-window system governing IPO approvals, it was the abolition of the office of the controller of capital issues. The reform required in trade liberalization was not a single-window system for import approvals, it was the removal of trade barriers. Our problem in India is inappropriate state coercion that limits cross-border activities, and this is not solved by a single-window system governing approvals for cross-border activities.

Elements of reduced scope for state intervention

There are many elements through which the scope of state intervention can be reduced.

Is there a market failure? Market failure is the technical core of public policy. There is great value in systematically using the toolkit of public goods, externalities, asymmetric information and market power.

Is a Coasean solution feasible? Many times, the correct way forward lies in establishing property rights and judicial infrastructure. Once this is done, Coasean negotiation will find the optimum answer without requiring the bureaucratic machinery.

Do traditional community solutions work well? Elinor Ostrom has reminded us of the remarkable outcomes through some traditional community arrangements. Those wielding state power should respect the possibilities for purely decentralized solutions to spring up, that allocate common goods without requiring a bureaucratic apparatus.

Can we free-ride on state capacity outside India? There is a class of problems where India can free-ride on the policy institutions of advanced economies. These should be utilized to the extent possible, while having a full understanding of the limitations of international experience.

Can some of the work of regulation be pushed down to private firms? Consider the problem of regulating taxis. One possibility lies in setting up a bureaucratic machinery that engages with each taxi driver. Another pathway lies in contracting out this regulation to private taxi companies. Aggregation business models, such as AirBnB, have an incentive to utilize customer feedback and supervisory staff to improve the quality of their customer experience.[3]

In general, this is an easier path for the construction of state capacity as the number of transactions is reduced.

This approach has been particularly successful with 'financial market infrastructure institutions' (FMIIs) such as stock exchanges. Exchanges work as the front line of regulation, and engage in detail with hundreds of financial firms performing a large number of transactions. This reduces the demand for state capacity at the regulator. The problem that flows from this approach is the tension between the profit motive of an exchange and this regulatory function.

Does modern technology make it possible to remove the market failure? Sometimes, there are clever solutions through which a market failure can be eliminated. Consider the electromagnetic spectrum. At first blush, we think that the use of spectrum is rival: one person communicating at a certain frequency precludes others from using it. The state is then needed in establishing property rights to spectrum. This requires creating a bureaucratic machinery which auctions spectrum, and polices for violations.

However, there is an alternative methodology, which is used in cordless phones or WiFi, where intelligent devices establish a self-organizing system through which spectrum is shared. Intelligence at each device coupled with healthy protocols makes sharing of spectrum possible. Such technologies convert spectrum from rival to non-rival.

Once this is feasible, the need for government control of spectrum allocation is removed. This is an attractive path, particularly under conditions of low state capacity. All that the state needs to do is to say that certain frequencies are available for unlicensed use, and back this up with rules for fair play by devices as has been done by the US FCC.

In recent years, there has been a debate in India about the V-band and the E-band, where the Department of Telecommunications has a choice between making it unlicensed spectrum or auctioning it off to private persons.[4] We would favour the former: a non-state solution is generally superior, particularly under conditions of low state capacity.

Do we have the state capacity? There are many elements of market failure which are legitimate areas for state intervention, and such state intervention is being done in mature market economies. But in India, we have much less state capacity, so certain areas of work are outside our budget constraint and should be dropped.

Intellectual capacity and its limitations

Social systems are complex creatures, and it requires a great deal of intellectual capacity to devise the right interventions. In this book, we repeatedly argue in favour of crossing the river by feeling the stones, an empirical process of introducing small interventions and watching the empirical evidence. We should know that most of the time we are wrong, so we should always be willing to backtrack based on the empirical evidence.

The design of interventions and the slow careful process of rolling out (and backtracking) are a research process. We should measure the economy well. We start with a theory about the world, introduce an intervention, find out whether it worked, and then make the next move. The development of this kind of intellectual capability is integral to developing state capacity, and it is hard to obtain this.

39

Prioritize institution building over just GDP growth

The dominant imperative for India is to increase GDP, so as to bring prosperity to over a billion people. There are few things more important than our challenge of becoming rich before we become old. We know, from the historical experience, that the only way out of mass poverty is to obtain modest rates of growth of per capita GDP that are sustained for many decades. As an example, if per capita GDP grows at 4 per cent per year, there is one doubling every eighteen years. Per capita GDP would go up by eight times in fifty years, and at the end of this, we would have graduated beyond middle income.

The problem with focusing on GDP growth as the immediate determinant of policy decisions is that there are many pathways to obtaining short spurts of GDP growth. GDP growth can be obtained through a great surge of debt, through a boom in government investment, by destroying the environment, by distorting the exchange rate, by establishing central planning structures that use coercion to mobilize and deploy resources, etc. Each of these pathways gives a short spurt of growth, but does not last in the long run.

The experiences of the USSR and Japan are salutary reminders of the ability of states to set up short bursts of growth through methods that lack sustainability. For each USSR or Japan that actually managed to obtain state-led growth for a few decades, the historical experience contains many countries that failed to do even this much when opting for a state-led model of growth.

In a simplistic notion of development, we have to combine capital and modern technology in order to achieve high productivity. This can readily lead to notions of high modernism. In the extreme, we may think of placing modern technology into government-owned monopolies, and using state coercion to force everyone to work with these monopolies. In the short run, this does give capital deepening and technical change. But this works out poorly in the medium term. We cannot be assured of benevolent and competent leaders in the public sector. We lose out on the energy of private innovation and competition. The economy loses flexibility and continuous adaptation when it is trapped by dominant state-controlled monopolies. And when we go down this route, we tend to revere and prioritize the big-prestige projects over the subtlety of institutions.

Many technologists slip into a different strain of high modernism, with an enthusiasm for designing state-run or state-imposed monopolies upon the economy. Deep knowledge of the humanities and social sciences is an antidote for this optimism. We are generally better off with multiple competing efforts, organic evolution of standards and technologies, and the minimal involvement of the state. A good model to look back upon is the rise of the Internet. While there was public funding in the research that built the Internet, there was no state coercion to encourage or force the use of Internet standards. If anything, the global telecom giants—many of whom were public sector companies—had put their shoulders behind a different standard (X.25), and they were wrong in their key design ideas.

A complex modern economy only works when it is a self-organizing system. It has to have the creative efforts of a large number of individuals, all working in their own self-interest. Central planning and a leadership role for the state do not work for a modern complex economy.

Building the republic, then, is about the policy institutions which shape the incentives of each person and help intermediate the interactions between individuals. Building these institutions is a slow and complex problem. In the short run, it is always possible to obtain GDP growth without solving these deeper problems. We would all do well to shift focus from the numbers for GDP growth, to focusing on the state of health of state institutions.

In the short run, central planning and state-led development can yield GDP growth. But as the economy becomes more complex, the need for state institutions that reshape incentives becomes even greater. Spurts in growth that are state-led tend to peter out. The only way to run the fifty-year marathon is through building institutions. We should pursue institution building rather than GDP growth. Sustained improvement in institutional quality is hard, but it is the only way to obtain sustained GDP growth.

Success is not assured

The early rhetoric about economic development viewed an underdeveloped country as a child. Growth was inevitable, it was only a matter of putting in a few auxiliary actions that helped and enabled that process. In this worldview, we run the risk of thinking that progress is inevitable, that progress involves steel mills, and we can save everyone the time and trouble by having state-run steel mills.

We now know that there is no inevitability about the rise of a country into the ranks of a prosperous democracy. There are only four countries which were poor in 1945, that are now prosperous democracies: South Korea, Taiwan, Chile and Israel.

A prominent measure of state capability in a globally comparable data set is available, for the 1996–2012 period.[1] By this measure, state capability has risen in only a few countries over this period, and state capability in India *declined* in this period. Our institutional capacity got worse in a period of strong GDP growth. We do wrong in equating GDP growth with improvement in the foundations for GDP growth.[2]

Turning to the Indian experience, we can conjecture a mechanism through which higher GDP growth *caused* reduced state capacity. When bigger rupee values are at stake, private persons have more to gain by undermining state institutions. The resources that are brought to bear, to attack the working of state institutions, are larger when GDP is higher.

We vividly saw this in India, in the period after 2005, when India was starting to reap remarkable success by private firms. The prospective gains from subverting state institutions were suddenly larger, and we got bigger investments into attacks on institutions. State apparatus that used to work when million-rupee bribes were offered broke down when the offers went to billions of rupees.

Perhaps India's growth of 1979–2011 was not adequately grounded in the required institutional capacity to be a prosperous liberal democracy, and perhaps this has something to do with the difficulties that have been seen after 2011.

Keeping score

The advantage of a well-measured GDP is that it can become a report card for the government. However, as argued above, it is possible to get GDP growth for a short time through all sorts of bad policies. The path to becoming an advanced country lies in many generations of sustained improvement in institutions. If we are not to keep score using GDP growth, what measures could be useful?

There is no one measure of institutional quality, but we can think of a few measures that are useful in thinking about how we are faring in building a republic.

Safety: The number of young women walking alone on a street, at night, shows the extent of perceived safety and the functioning of the criminal justice system. This is a good measure of Indian institutional quality.

Flight of millionaires: The number of millionaires who emigrate out of India, per year, is an important measure. Millionaires in India are not ordinary people. They have acquired deep locale-specific knowledge, have achieved economic success and have roots in India. They do not leave the country looking for better economic opportunities. They are buying homes and citizenship in a mature liberal democracy owing to the fear of expropriation at home. Their departure suggests there are concerns about safety and the rule of law in India. Similar problems are being seen in China also. Our progress towards the rule of law is measured by the extent to which millionaires do not seek to leave the country.

Flight of India-centric firms: The phenomenon of India-centric firms that do not organize themselves as an Indian company is quite revealing. These firms go through considerable expense to set up a Singapore-based or a London-based entity, so as to avoid the legal and political risk associated with being an Indian company. This is a telling sign of institutional failure in India.

Flight of India-centric trading: Trading activity in the Indian rupee and the Nifty should, by rights, be located in India. However, from 2007 onward, over half of this activity has shifted to overseas locations. This reflects the failure of Indian institutions. Every year, we get new repressive measures in financial regulation, tax policy and capital controls, which pushes a greater proportion of activity overseas. This market share is a revealing indicator of Indian institutional quality.

Flight of India-centric contract enforcement: The extent to which private contracts in India rely on arbitration outside India is a comment on the quality of the Indian legal system. If India's courts, judges, lawyers and laws worked better, it would be much cheaper to settle disputes in India. The fact that vastly greater legal costs are incurred outside India is a demonstration of Indian institutional weakness.

Mocking the powerful: The extent to which comedy shows torment the present leadership is a measure of the de facto freedom of speech present in the country. Under the rule of law, a Donald Trump is unable to inflict harm upon all persons who build these shows. The extent to which comedy shows take on the most powerful figures is a measure of institutional quality in India.

40

Conclusion

At Independence, the conceptual framework of policy was developed by Jawaharlal Nehru, B.R. Ambedkar, P.C. Mahalanobis, Pitambar Pant, Sukhamoy Chakravarty and others. This involved a developmental state, and a lead role for the state in the evolution of the country. At the time, it was felt that there was a shortage of capital in India. They also felt that a sophisticated financial system could not be achieved in India, and envisioned a significant role for the state in *supplanting* the private financial system in order to address the problem of missing markets.[1]

We call this the 'Mark 1 strategy'. It induced an early growth acceleration compared with the pre-war data, and then ran into many difficulties. By the 1970s, it was clear that the licence–permit raj was not working well. Central planning induces stagnation.

The conceptual framework of the next phase was developed by Jagdish Bhagwati, T.N. Srinivasan, Manmohan Singh, D.T. Lakdawala, Ashok Desai, Arun Shourie, Montek Ahluwalia, M. Narasimham, Padma Desai, Anne Krueger, I.G. Patel, Raja Chelliah and others.[2] The change in course began with the Janata Party in 1977, and rapidly yielded results in the form of higher growth from 1979 onward. Through the 1980s, there was a gradual process of domestic liberalization, while preserving autarky when it came to the international engagement. The reforms of 1991–2004 gave a big step forward in domestic liberalization of the real economy, in financial reforms and in scaling down autarky.[3]

By this time, a sophisticated financial system started emerging, and the appropriate role of the state shifted from *producing* financial services to *regulating* private financial service providers. In addition, opening up to the global financial system eased resource constraints. The gap between investment and savings is financed by capital inflows. This changed the notion in the minds of Indian policymakers that capital is in short supply. The bottlenecks now lay not in capital, but in economic freedom and in institutional quality.

This 'Mark 2 strategy' unfolded from 1977 onward, and yielded a great outburst of growth during 1991–2011. These two decades stand out as the best growth experience in India's history. For the first time, the growth pessimists were proven wrong, and India got strong growth. This impacted upon all quartiles of the income distribution. For the rich, there was wealth creation of a kind that had never been seen before. The middle class graduated to being able to afford appliances, devices and plane tickets. The poor got poverty reduction on a massive scale. For the first time in India's history, the headcount of the poor shrank.

There was an optimism in this period of a kind that was perhaps last seen immediately after Independence. Finally, to many of us, India was getting on its feet.

The growth model of 1991–2011 has not carried forward into the following years. Private 'under implementation' investment projects rose from Rs 10 trillion in 2006 to Rs 50 trillion in 2011. After that, there has been a decline in *nominal* terms, to Rs 40 trillion in mid-2019. The share of non-workers, in the working-age population, stands at 60.43 per cent, in April–June 2019.[4] These statistics illustrate the difficulties that have arisen in the post-2011 period.[5]

In many other countries, the phenomenon of a 'middle income trap' has been observed. At the early stages of development, the simple mobilization of labour and capital suffices to escape from abject poverty. But once the minimal market economy is in place, a different level of institutional quality is required. The maturation of firms and the government creates the need for complex contracts, contract enforcement, economic regulation, and institutions that intermediate and channel the conflicts between social groups. When a middle-income country seeks to rise to a mature market economy, and institutional capacity is weak, growth stalls.

Long years ago, we made a tryst with destiny, and we must find our way out of these dark woods. The most important question in Indian economics and policymaking today is that of diagnosing and addressing the sources of underperformance that have arisen from 2011 onward. A phenomenon of this size cannot just come about owing to some events. There is a need for a conceptual framework, in understanding what happened, and then in changing it.

This book constitutes our attempt in this direction, to finding the Mark 3 framework. In this, we build on the work of Abhijit Banerjee, Avinash Dixit, Bibek Debroy, Devesh Kapur, Esther Duflo, Jeff Hammer, Kaushik Basu, Lant Pritchett, Nandan Nilekani, Pratap Bhanu Mehta and others.

Our key idea is that a lot of government intervention, and the licence-permit-inspector raj, remains in place. The early dawn of economic freedom, that was promised in 1991, has not evolved into a mature market economy. Private persons are beset with government intervention. The instincts of central planning are alive and well among policymakers. There is a great deal of arbitrary power in the hands of government. Extensive interference in the economy by the government, the policy risk associated with future interventions, and the fear of how arbitrary power in the hands of the government will be used have led to a loss of confidence in the private sector.

When India was a small economy, the GDP was small, and the gains from violating rules were relatively small. The tenfold growth in the size of the economy created new opportunities to obtain wealth. The gains from violating rules went up sharply. Large resources were brought to bear upon subverting state institutions. The foundations of state institutions, in terms of the rule of law and checks and balances were always weak. This combination of an amplified effort by private persons to subvert institutions, coupled with low state capacity, has resulted in a decline of institutional quality.

On the policy side, there was a rough idea that there should be less state intervention, and that light-touch economic regulation should be done by a new breed of economic regulators. This has worked out unsatisfactorily. The executive powers of regulators, in licensing and enforcement, constitute a new level of intrusive control, of a kind which was not present before 1991. The new regulators are often the new central planners. As was seen prior to 1991, central planning has induced stagnation.

Addressing these problems requires going to the foundations. Why do we require state intervention? Why is state capacity low? How should state organizations be constructed so as to cater to a gradual improvement of state capacity? What is the right approach to public policy when state capacity is low? These are the most important questions of Indian economics today.

Economic thinkers of the previous decades tended to focus on economics more narrowly, on issues such as the green revolution or heavy industry or trade liberalization. In finding the Mark 3 framework, we need to more explicitly locate ourselves in the intersection of politics and the economy. To make sustained economic growth possible, we require the republic.

The founding energy of liberal democracy is the pursuit of freedom, of people being masters of their own fate. There is a need to recognize how well many things work without government intervention. We need to shift away from notions of a developmental state, where big initiatives originate from the government, towards a philosophy of respect for the self-organizing system that is a free society. We need to rely far more on private negotiations, private contracts, and civil society solutions, rather than turning to the government to solve problems. The state should be the last resort in resolving difficulties, not the first.

The toolkit of four kinds of market failure, drawn from public economics, helps identify the areas where there is a case for state intervention. Public choice theory steers us away from optimism about the state, and shows us the root cause of low state capacity. The state is not a benevolent actor, it is formed of self-interested persons. Individuals and state agencies crave arbitrary power. The path to state capacity lies in checks and balances, and dispersed power.

The laws that define government intervention need to be written with a focus on removing arbitrary power, controlling the ways in which officials engage with private persons, and establishing the rule of law. This new approach to writing law is of essence in building the republic.

Our traditional notion of political economy is about competing coalition of *voters*, where special interests mobilize to block reforms. A remarkable feature of India is the role of established bureaucratic formations as the constituency in favour of arbitrary power of the administrative state, and as the opponents of reform. The officials like the rule of officials. The central planners and the agencies are arrayed against rule of law and a market economy.

There is a capability trap when coercive power is given to weak organizations. Once an organization has the power to coerce, and the checks and balances are weak, there will be a steady slide into abuse of coercive power. The private sector is fearful of the arbitrary power wielded by officials, and does not speak up. There is no voice, but there is an exit in the form of reduced investment. There is a lack of a feedback loop where difficulties kick off improvements. Too often, in fact, we are seeing the opposite kind of feedback loop, where agencies fail in their work, but the political system responds by giving them greater arbitrary power to investigate and punish, which induces a further reduction in their capabilities.

The path to state capacity lies in being stingy with public expenditure and with coercive power. Government organizations should have to prove themselves, before significant money or coercive power is placed in their hands. UK levels of coercive power in a tax administration can only be justified when the tax administration rises to UK levels of rule of law.

The policy landscape in India today is a sprawling scene where a large number of state interventions are in place, and most of them work poorly. The path to progress lies in narrowing the scope of the state, picking fewer battles, and first learning how to run the government at high levels of state capacity. The four primal requirements of a state are the criminal justice system, the judiciary, the tax system and financial regulation. Our prime objective should be to learn how to be a capable state in these four areas.

We share the objectives of people working in numerous fields—total factor productivity, infrastructure, better design of poverty programmes, urbanization, sustainability, etc. There is intricate domain knowledge in each field such as agriculture. Each of these is a compelling area, where there are great possibilities, and where the impact will be enormous. The public economics and public administration of this book are a general toolkit that can be applied in diverse settings, that can set off virtuous cycles of progress in all these areas.

Acknowledgements

One owes an intellectual debt to so many people. Some of them are no more. With every formal and informal interaction with our fellow economists and thinkers, we chip away at understanding the art and science of economic policy. I particularly wish to thank Abhay Pethe, Arbind Modi, Arjun Sengupta, Arun Shourie, Arvind Panagariya, Arvind Subramaniam, Arvind Virmani, Ashok Desai, Avinash Dixit, Bhanoji Rao, Bimal Jalan, C. Rangarajan, D.K. Shrivastava, Daniel McFadden, Daniel Yergin, Devesh Kapur, George Kopits, Harsh Vardhan Singh, Horst Kohler, I.G. Patel, Indira Rajaraman, Jagdish Bhagwati, Jayanta Roy, M. Govinda Rao, Michael Mussa, Montek Ahluwalia, Morris Adelman, Murillo Portugal, Narendra Jadhav, Nitin Desai, Partho Shome, Patricia Annez-Clarke, Pratap Bhanu Mehta, Raja Chelliah, Rajiv Kumar, Rakesh Mohan, Rathin Roy, Roberto Zagha, Satya Poddar, Shankar Acharya, Sharad Desai, Shubhashis Gangopadhyay, Stan Fischer, Sukhamoy Chakravarty, Surjit Bhalla, Thomas Marschak, Urjit Patel and Yoginder Alagh.

To achieve successful policy outcomes in India, we need the deft hands of accomplished mandarins, and I was fortunate to observe some truly outstanding ones at close quarters. They are a major inspiration for this book. Towards this, I am greatly indebted to Abid Hussain, Amarnath Verma, B.K. Zutshi, B.L. Das, C.R.K. Rao Sahib, Gopi Arora, G.V. Ramakrishna, Lavraj Kumar, Nandan Nilekani, Naresh Chandra, N.K. Singh, P.N. Haksar, R. Vasudevan, S.P. Shukla, S. Venkitaraman and Y. Venugopal Reddy.

In the difficult challenges of the coming years, we require the combination of economic knowledge and the gift for statecraft that they have.

The political leadership, at its best, is able to see opportunities for progress in a difficult situation, and seize opportunities for game-changing reforms. This requires strength of character, an entrepreneurial sense of timing and a commitment to progress in the long run. Arun Jaitley, Atal Bihari Vajpayee, Capt. Satish Sharma, D.P. Dhar, George Fernandes, Jaswant Singh, J. Vengal Rao, Dr Manmohan Singh, Mohan Dharia, P. Chidambaram, Pranab Mukherjee and Yashwant Sinha were the political leaders who gave me the opportunity to experience the highs and lows in some the great 'policy yagnas' of the past forty years. For this, I am deeply grateful to them. Lessons from these experiences form the core of many sections of this book.

I want to express deep gratitude to my life partner Lata Kelkar, without whose selfless support this exciting journey of policymaking would not even have been possible. Finally, continuous inspiration for this project came from our daughter Sujata, her husband Nitesh, and our grandchildren Akash and Aarav, who have been a boundless source of love and joy.

—Vijay Kelkar

All of us are a linear combination of our influences. At an early stage, at IIT Bombay, I was inspired by Gopal Shevare, K. Sudhakar, D.B. Phatak and Ira Bidkar. At graduate school at the University of Southern California, I was privileged to get an insight into the worldviews and analytical frameworks of Lee Lillard, Andy Weiss, Yoram Weiss, Jeff Nugent, Cheng Hsiao and Richard Easterlin.

I am grateful to all my colleagues from CMIE, IGIDR, the Ministry of Finance and NIPFP who disagreed with me, criticized me and made me see things in new ways. I thank Yashwant Sinha, Rakesh Mohan and Jaimini Bhagwati for my induction into the UTI crisis at the Ministry of Finance. I was blessed to have observed the work of three great finance ministers leading up to 2005, and to have worked closely with Arbind Modi, Ashok Lahiri, S. Narayan, U.K. Sinha and Vijay Kelkar.

My thinking on public economics and public administration draws from the worldview and wisdom of Ashok Desai, Jeff Hammer, Junaid Ahmad, Kirit Parikh, Lant Pritchett, Percy Mistry, Rajiv Mehrishi and Shekhar Shah.

My work in macroeconomics and finance was a partnership with K.P. Krishnan, Ila Patnaik, Josh Felman and Susan Thomas. The founders of the modern Indian equity market—R.H. Patil, C.B. Bhave and Ravi Narain—were a source of inspiration for what economic reforms can be.

I learnt enormously from the community that engineered the financial reforms of the 1990s and the first decade of the new millennium: Ashish Chauhan, Chitra Ramakrishna, C.M. Vasudev, Jaimini Bhagwati, Jayanth Varma, L.C. Gupta, Percy Mistry, P.J. Nayak, Raghavan Putran, Rajesh Doshi, Raju Chitale, Rakesh Mohan, Shashank Saksena, S. Narayan, Surendra Dave, U.K. Sinha and Usha Thorat.

Ashish Chauhan, V. Balasubramaniam, Ratna Madeka, Lakshmi Patel, G.M. Shenoy and Shuvam Misra were co-creators, with Susan Thomas and me, in Nifty, PRISM and many other innovations of the early years of the equity market.

My work on pensions was a collaboration with Anand Bordia, A.P. Singh, Dhirendra Swarup, Gautam Bhardwaj, John Piggott, Renuka Sane, Robert Palacios and Surendra Dave.

My work in public finance draws on Vijay Kelkar, Arbind Modi, Ashok Lahiri, M. Govinda Rao, Amaresh Bagchi and Rathin Roy.

My thinking on the statistical system is formed of many decades of watching CMIE build organizational capability in the field, and the perfectionism of Mahesh Vyas.

Discussions with Y. Venugopal Reddy, M. Govinda Rao and Junaid Ahmad shaped my thinking on decentralization.

I learnt about firms and the pathways to transforming firm productivity from Mahesh Vyas, Vishal Nevatia, Pramod Kabra, Harsh Vardhan, T. Koshy, Sanjiv Shah and Deep Narayan.

The cast of 146 persons in FSLRC, particularly B.N. Srikrishna, Dhirendra Swarup, C.K. Gopal Nair, M. Sahoo, Somasekhar Sundaresan, A.P. Singh and Harsh Vardhan, influenced my thinking on financial economic policy, writing laws and building state capacity.

Susan Thomas, Rajeswari Sengupta, Anjali Sharma, Bhargavi Zaveri, T.K. Vishwanathan, M. Sahoo and K.P. Krishnan shaped my thinking in bankruptcy, after the handoff from FSLRC to BLRC.

Watching Montek Ahluwalia, D. Subbarao, C.B. Bhave, Ashok Chawla, U.K. Sinha, K.P. Krishnan and Jahangir Aziz, and the sprawling cast of the Indian crisis response in 2008, shaped my understanding of macroeconomic and financial crises.

Jeff Hammer, Nachiket Mor, Sandhya Venkateswaran, Amrita Agarwal and Shubho Roy have shaped my thinking on public health and healthcare.

Technology policy now cuts across a broad array of issues in public policy, and my thinking on this was shaped by Nandan Nilekani, R.S. Sharma, A.P. Singh, Sanjay Jain, Sunil Abraham, Vijay Madan, C.B. Bhave, Viral Shah and Smriti Parsheera.

From 2007, Ila Patnaik and I had the exhilarating experience of building a small research group at NIPFP. We were blessed by a procession of young geniuses who came into this work, challenged our assumptions and improved our thinking. In particular, we thank Anirudh Burman, Apoorva Gupta, Bhargavi Zaveri, Bhavyaa Sharma, Chirag Anand, Pramod Sinha, Pratik Datta, Radhika Pandey, Shekhar Hari Kumar, Shubho Roy, Smriti Parsheera, Suyash Rai and Vimal Balasubramaniam for these experiences.

—Ajay Shah

Gurcharan Das, Pratap Bhanu Mehta, Ram Guha and Jerry Rao encouraged us at the early stages of this project, and helped us to follow in their footsteps of writing important books.

Suyash Rai, Renuka Sane and Bhuvana Anand helped us in finding the statue in the marble, going from the early-stage draft to the linear flow of the table of contents.

Rajeev Kapoor, Subhashis Gangopadhyay, Shubho Roy, Anirudh Burman, Sanjeev Ahluwalia, Satya Poddar, Sumit Bose, Rajeswari Sengupta, Kaushik Krishnan and Surbhi Bhatia read early drafts and induced numerous improvements. Ayush Patnaik forced us to up our game on numerous weak arguments. Kusan Biswas helped us stay organized by setting up elegant Latex solutions for the writing process.

The team at Penguin was a delight to work with. They warmed to the concept of the book early, and steadfastly helped in carrying it through into the form in your hands. We thank Tarini Uppal and Shantanu Ray Chaudhuri for their skill, enthusiasm and support.

—Vijay Kelkar and Ajay Shah

Notes

Part I: Foundations

Chapter 1: The purpose of government

1. The mainstream strategy among Indian policymakers, on crypto-currency, is articulated in Subhash Chandra Garg, '*Report of the Committee to propose specific actions to be taken in relation to Virtual Currencies*', technical report (Ministry of Finance, July 2019), http://bit.ly/2MagIwi.
2. Andrew L. Russell, 'OSI: The Internet that wasn't', *IEEE Spectrum*, July 2013, https://spectrum.ieee.org/tech-history/cyberspace/osi-the-internet-that-wasnt.
3. Ana Swanson, 'Meet the Four-Eyed, Eight-Tentacled Monopoly That Is Making Your Glasses So Expensive', *Forbes*, September 2014, https://www.forbes.com/sites/anaswanson/2014/09/10/meet-the-four-eyed-eight-tentacled-monopoly-that-is-making-your-glasses-so-expensive/#6d0fa3486b66.

Chapter 3: A long history of failure

1. This evidence is from the IDFC Institute's 'SATARC' Crime Victimization Surveys. IDFC Institute, '*Safety trends and reporting of crime (SATARC)*', technical report (IDFC Institute, 2017), http://www.idfcinstitute.org/site/assets/files/12318/satarc_april272017.pdf.
2. Karthik Muralidharan et al., '*The fiscal cost of weak governance: Evidence from teacher absence in India*', technical report (The World Bank, 2016).
3. Angela N. Kisakye et al., 'Regulatory mechanisms for absenteeism in the health sector: A systematic review of strategies and their implementation', *Journal of Healthcare Leadership*, 2016, https://www.dovepress.com/regulatory-

mechanisms-for-absenteeism-in-the-health-sector-a-systemati-peer-reviewed-article-JHL.

4.   Shalini Rudra, 'Immunization coverage: India far away from meeting targets', *Observer Research Foundation,* 2017, https://www.orfonline.org/expert-speak/immunization-coverage-india-far-away-from-meeting-targets/.

5.   These facts are drawn from: Avani Kapur, Mridusmita Bordoloi, and Ritwik Shukla, 'Sarva Shiksha Abhiyan', *Accountability Initiative,* 2018, https://accountabilityindia.in/publication/sarva-shiksha-abhiyan-ssa/; ASER Centre, 'Annual School Education Report 2016', 2017; Geeta Gandhi Kingdon, 'The private schooling phenomenon in India: A review', 2017.

Part II: Diagnosing the Indian experience

Chapter 5: Why do things go wrong?

1.   Robert E. Lucas, 'Econometric Policy Evaluation: A Critique', in *The Phillips Curve and Labour Markets,* ed. Karl Brunner and Allan H. Meltzer, Vol. 1, Carnegie-Rochester Conference Series on Public Policy (Amsterdam: North-Holland Publishing Company, 1976), pp. 19–46.

2.   This broad result recurs in various parts of the economics literature, e.g., see Martin Feldstein, 'Tax avoidance and the deadweight loss of the income tax', *The Review of Economics and Statistics, Vol.* 81, No. 4, November 1999, pp. 674–80, https://www.nber.org/papers/w5055.pdf; John Creedy, *'The excess burden of taxation and why it (approximately) quadruples when the tax rate doubles',* technical report (New Zealand Treasury, December 2003), https://treasury.govt.nz/sites/default/files/2007-10/twp03-29.pdf.

3.   C. Rajagopalachari, *'Why Swatantra?',* technical report (Swatantra Party, April 1973), https://www.livemint.com/Sundayapp/XlvTGlfJcdJu9mQGZcksTI/C-Rajagopalachari--Why-Swatantra.html.

4.   James M. Buchanan and Gordon Tullock, *The Calculus of Consent: Logical Foundations of Constitutional Democracy (Ann Arbor: University of Michigan Press, 1962).*

5.   Kenneth J. Arrow, 'A Difficulty in the Concept of Social Welfare', *Journal of Political Economy, Vol.* 58, No. 4, 1950, pp. 328–46, issn:00223808, 1537534X, http://www.jstor.org/stable/1828886.

Part III: The science

Chapter 6: People respond to incentives

1.   Alexander Hamer, 'The Curious Case of the Great Hanoi Rat Hunt', *Real History,* October 2018, https://realhistory.co/2018/10/11/great-hanoi-rat-hunt/.

2.   Xue Yujie, 'The Gadget That Boosts Your Step Count While You Nap', *Sixth Tone,* 28 June 2018, https://www.sixthtone.com/news/1002530/the-gadget-that-boosts-your-step-count-while-you-nap.

3. Matthew Wright, 'Amsterdam's taxing narrow houses', *Science, writing, reason and stuff,* 28 October 2012, https://mjwrightnz.wordpress.com/2012/10/28/amsterdams-taxing-narrow-houses/.

4. This was done through: Vijay Kelkar, 'Report of the Committee on Category-II Drugs', technical report (Ministry of Industry, August 1987).

5. Isaac Frazier and Zachary Frazier, 'Rewarding Bad Behavior,' *UN.A.BRIDGED,* February 2017, http://www.un-a-bridged.com/rewarding-bad-behavior/.

6. Daniel Kahneman, *Thinking, fast and slow* (New York: Farrar, Straus and Giroux, 2011).

Chapter 7: Going with the grain of the price system

1. As an example of this phenomenon, see Ajit Kanitkar, 'Case of tur dal farmers shows that hiking minimum support price won't help if implementation is poor', *Scroll.in,* February 2018, https://scroll.in/article/869545/case-of-tur-dal-farmers-shows-that-hiking-minimum-support-price-wont-help-if-implementation-is-poor.

2. Susan Thomas, 'Agricultural commodity markets in India: Policy issues for growth', in *Derivatives Markets in India,* ed. Susan Thomas (Tata Mcgraw Hill, 2003), http://citeseerx.ist.psu.edu/viewdoc/download?doi=10.1.1.197.6692&rep=rep1&type=pdf.

3. Anirudh Burman et al., *'Diagnosing and overcoming sustained food price volatility: Enabling a National Market for Food',* technical report 236 (NIPFP, July 2018), https://macrofinance.nipfp.org.in/releases/BPRS_national-market-for-food.html.

4. Ashok Gulati and Anil Sharma, 'Freeing trade in agriculture: Implications for resource use efficiency and cropping pattern changes', *Economic and Political Weekly,* Vol. 32, No. 52, 1997, https://www.jstor.org/stable/4406230; Kirit S. Parikh et al., *Towards Free Trade in Agriculture* (Springer, 2013); Kirit S. Parikh et al., 'Agricultural trade liberalization: growth, welfare and large country effects', *Agricultural Economics,* Vol. 17, No. 1, 1997, https://www.sciencedirect.com/science/article/pii/S0169515097000170.

5. Garry Pursell and Ashok Gulati, *Liberalising Indian agriculture: an agenda for reform* (Washington DC: World Bank Publications, 1993); Anirudh Burman et al., *'Diagnosing and overcoming sustained food price volatility'.*

6. This section builds on Ajay Shah, 'Prices, fast and slow,' *Business Standard,* July 2018, http://www.mayin.org/ajayshah/MEDIA/2018/prices_fast_and_slow.html.

Chapter 8: More competition, always

1. Smriti Parsheera, Ajay Shah and Avirup Bose, *'Competition issues in India's online economy',* technical report 194 (NIPFP, April 2017), https://macrofinance.nipfp.org.in/releases/ ParsheeraShahBose2017_onlineBusinesses.html.

2. For the Indian bankruptcy reform, see, T. K. Viswanathan, *Bankruptcy Law Reforms Committee: Rationale and Design*' (Ministry of Finance, November 2015), https://goo.gl/W4KLXc; Ajay Shah and Susan Thomas, 'The Indian bankruptcy reform: The state of the art, 2018,' *The Leap Blog*, December 2018, https:// blog.theleapjournal.org/2018/12/the- indian- bankruptcy- reform-state-of.html.

3. Megha Patnaik, '*Tax, lies and red tape*', technical report (ISI Delhi, 2019).

4. Ajay Shah, 'Indian capitalism is not doomed', *The Leap Blog*, September 2012, https://blog.theleapjournal.org/2012/09/indian-capitalism-is-not-doomed.html.

5. For a story about how firm exit took place in India in the absence of the bankruptcy code, see Ashish K. Mishra, 'Indiaplaza.com: How an Indian e-commerce firm ran out of cash', *Mint*, 21 July 2015, https://www.livemint.com/Companies/fuuj34vscVDBRjwrBld7sJ/Indiaplazacom-How-an-Indian-ecommerce-ran-out-of-cash.html.

6. This example is from Ila Patnaik, 'Creative destruction', *Business Standard*, 16 July 2003, http://openlib.org/home/ila/MEDIA/2003/stdbooths.html.

Chapter 9: Trace out the general equilibrium effects

1. For an example, see N.S.S. Narayana, Kirit S. Parikh and T.N. Srinivasan, 'Rural works programs in India: costs and benefits', *Journal of Development Economics*, Vol. 29, No. 2, 1988. This paper analyses a rural works programme in general equilibrium. https://www.sciencedirect.com/science/ article/ pii/0304387888900326.

Chapter 10: Go to the root cause, use the smallest possible force

1. Wikipedia, 'List of countries by traffic-related death rate', *Wikipedia.com*, 2019, https://en.wikipedia.org/wiki/List_of_countries_by_traffic-related_death_rate.

2. This section builds on Ajay Shah, 'Occam's razor of public policy', *The Leap Blog*, January 2016, https://blog.theleapjournal.org/2016/01/occams-razor-of-public-policy.html.

3. J.N. Bhagwati and V.K. Ramaswami, 'Domestic distortions, tariffs and the theory of optimum subsidy', *Journal of Political Economy, Vol*, 71, No. 1, 1963, pp. 44–50.

4. PRS Legislative Research, '*The Companies (Amendment) Bill, 2019*', technical report (PRS, 2019), https://www.prsindia.org/billtrack/companies-amendment-bill-2019.

Chapter 11: Redistribution is fraught with trouble

1. S. Mahendra Dev and Ajit K. Ranade, 'Employment Guarantee Scheme and Employment Security', in *Social and Economic Security in India*, ed. S. Mahendra Dev et al. (New Delhi: Institute for Human Development, 2001).

Chapter 12: Private solutions for market failure

1. Ronald H. Coase, 'The problem of social cost', *Journal of Law and Economics* III, Vol. 3, pp. 1–44, October 1960.
2. Partha Sarathi Biswas, 'Pollination opportunity: Money beyond honey', *The Indian Express*, 9 March 2017, https://indianexpress.com/article/india/pollination-opportunity-money-beyond-honey-4560991/.
3. G. Hardin, 'The tragedy of the commons', *Science, Vol.* 162, No. 3859, December 1968. Pp. 1243–48, https://science.sciencemag.org/content/162/3859/1243.
4. For an Indian view of these ideas see, Parth J. Shah and Vidisha Maitra, eds., *Terracotta Reader: A Market Approach to the Environment* (New Delhi: Academic Foundation in association with Centre for Civil Society, 2005).

Chapter 13: Bring cold calculations into the policy process

1. For a less optimistic view of cost–benefit analysis, see John H. Cochrane, 'Challenges for Cost–Benefit Analysis of Financial Regulation', *Journal of Legal Studies, Vol.* 43, June 2014, https://faculty.chicagobooth.edu/john.cochrane/research/papers/cochrane_benefits_costs_JLS.pdf.
2. The draft Indian Financial code, FSLRC, *Indian Financial Code*, Version 1.1 (Ministry of Finance, July 2015), places such requirements upon the regulation-making process. https://goo.gl/hdAQoW.

Chapter 14: Ask the right question

1. Vijay Kelkar and Ajay Shah, 'Six battlegrounds for the war on corruption', *Mint*, 21 November 2016, http://www. mayin.org/ajayshah/MEDIA/2016/six_battlegrounds.html.
2. Vijay Kelkar, Vikash Yadav and Praveen Chaudhry, 'Reforming the Governance of the International Monetary Fund', *World Economy, Vol.* 27, No. 5, May 2004, pp. 727–43.

Chapter 15: Taking decentralization seriously

1. Montek S. Ahluwalia, 'State Level Performance Under Economic Reforms in India', in *Economic Policy Reforms and the Indian Economy*, ed. Anne O. Krueger (Chicago: University of Chicago Press, 2002), pp. 91–125; Vivek Dehejia and Praveen Chakravarty, *'India's Curious Case of Economic Divergence',* technical report (IDFC Institute, November 2016), http://www.idfcinstitute.org/knowledge/publications/working-and-briefing-papers/indias-curious-case-of-economic-divergence/; Praveen Chakravarty and Vivek Dehejia, *'India's Income Divergence: Governance or Development Model?',* technical report

(IDFC Institute, March 2017), http://www.idfcinstitute.org/knowledge/publications/working-and-briefing-papers/indias-income-divergence-governance-or-development-model/.

2. James C. Scott, *Seeing Like a State: How Certain Schemes to Improve the Human Condition Have Failed* (New Haven: Yale University Press, 1998).

3. Jairam Ramesh, '*Lessons from reorganizing India's states: and why Uttar Pradesh needs to be divided*', technical report (C.D. Deshmukh Memorial Lecture, January 2019), https://scroll. in/article/909436/jairam-ramesh-a-potted-history-of-reorganizing-indias-states-and-why-uttar-pradesh-should-be-next.

4. Vijay Kelkar, 'Towards India's new fiscal federalism', *Journal of Quantitative Economics, Vol.* 17, No. 1, March 2019, works out the legal aspects of sharing GST with sub-national governments, which involves the establishment of a consolidated fund at the level of governments of the third tier. https://ideas.repec.org/a/spr/ jqecon/v17y2019i1d10.1007_s40953-019-00159-x.html.

Part IV: The art

Chapter 16: Evolutionary change for society, revolutionary change for government

1. Ajay Shah, 'Bureaucrats are not stakeholders', *The Economic Times*, 4 June 2013, http://www. mayin.org/ajayshah/MEDIA/2013/bureaucrats_stakeholders.html.

Chapter 17: Cross the river by feeling the stones

1. A six-part-long battle against corruption is sketched in: Vijay Kelkar and Ajay Shah, 'Six battlegrounds for the war on corruption', *Mint*, 21 November 2016, http://www.mayin.org/ajayshah/ MEDIA/2016/six_battlegrounds.html.

2. As an example, in 2018, the US SEC undertook the 'Tick Size Pilot Program', https://www.sec.gov/ticksizepilot.

3. Purva Chitnis, 'Penalty, Jail And More: How Mumbai Will Enforce The Plastic Ban', *Bloomberg Quint*, June 2018, https://www.bloombergquint.com/business/penalty-jail-and-more-how-mumbai-will-enforce-the-plastic-ban.

4. Samuel R. Gross et al., 'Rate of false conviction of criminal defendants who are sentenced to death', *National Academy of Sciences, Vol.* 111, No. 20, March 2014, https://www.pnas.org/content/early/2014/04/23/1306417111.

Chapter 18: Adapting from the international experience?

1. Suyash Rai, 'A Pragmatic Approach to Data Protection', *The Leap Blog*, February 2018, https://blog.theleapjournal.org/2018/02/a-pragmatic-approach-to-data-protection.html; Anirudh Burman, 'Privacy, Aadhaar, Data Protection: Statist liberalism and the danger to liberty', *The Leap Blog*,

September 2018, https://blog.theleapjournal.org/2018/09/privacy-aadhaar-data-protection-statist.html.

2. For surveillance by the Indian state, see Rishab Bailey et al., *'Use of personal data by intelligence and law enforcement agencies'*, technical report (NIPFP, August 2018), https://macrofinance.nipfp.org.in/releases/BBPR2018-Use-of-personal-data.html.

3. This is an economists' adaptation of the concepts of Clifford Geertz, *The Interpretation of Cultures* (New York: Basic Books, 1973), https://books.google.co.in/books?id=pl2NDgAAQBAJ.

Chapter 19: Test match, not IPL

1. See Uwe Hoering, 'What it takes to clean a river', *Down To Earth*, June 2015, https://www.downtoearth.org.in/coverage/climate-change/what-it-takes-to-clean-a-river-19098; FE Online, 'Germany to help India clean Ganga, says "took 30 years, 45 bn euros to clean Rhine"', *Financial Express*, 30 August 2018, https://www.financialexpress.com/india-news/germany-to-help-india-clean-ganga-says-took-30-years-45-bn-euros-to-clean-rhine/1297562/; Nikhil Ghanekar, 'Clean Ganga Mission: Lessons we can learn from Europe's Rhine river cleaning', *DNA India*, 18 April 2016, https://www.dnaindia.com/india/report-clean-ganga-mission-lessons-we-can-learn-from-europe-s-rhine-river-cleaning-2203178.

2. For an example of a project plan to build a new regulator, see Ravi Narain, *'Building the Insolvency and Bankruptcy Board of India'*, technical report (Ministry of Company Affairs, 2016), https://web.archive.org/web/20170922121138/http://www.ibbi.gov.in/Wg-01%20Report.pdf.

3. Mobis Philipose, 'Will the real SEBI please stand up?', *Mint*, 31 July 2019, https://www.livemint.com/opinion/columns/will-the-real-sebi-please-stand-up-1564594293741.html; Jayanth R. Varma, 'A petty money dispute holds market to ransom', *Prof. Jayanth R. Varma's Financial Markets Blog*, July 2019, http://faculty.iima.ac.in/~jrvarma/blog/index.cgi/Y2019-20/petty-money-dispute.discuss.

Chapter 20: What is hard and what is easy

1. Lant Pritchett and Michael Woolcock, 'Solutions when *the* solution is the problem: Arraying the disarray in development', *World Development, Vol.* 32, No. 2, pp. 191–212, 2004, offers a two-dimensional scheme based on the intensity of transaction and the intensity of discretion.

2. This section builds on Ajay Shah, 'Monetary policy is easy; Financial regulation is hard', *Financial Express*, 29 July 2010, http://www.mayin.org/ajayshah/MEDIA/2010/finance_vs_MP.html.

3. Ajay Shah, 'Improving governance using large IT systems', in *Documenting Reforms: Case Studies from India*, ed. S. Narayan (New Delhi: Macmillan

India, 2006), pp. 122–148, http://www.mayin.org/ajayshah/PDFDOCS/
Shah2006_big_it_systems.pdf.

4. The best survey of the field is Nandan Nilekani and Viral Shah, *Rebooting India: Realising a Billion Aspirations* (Penguin Allen Lane, 2016).

5. A detailed proposal for 'Indian Courts and Tribunals Service' (ICTS) is worked out in Pratik Datta et al., '*How to Modernise the Working of Courts and Tribunals in India*', technical report 258 (NIPFP, March 2019), https://macrofinance.nipfp. org.in/ releases/icts_concept_note-2019.html.

6. Ajay Shah, 'Sequencing in the construction of State capacity: Walk before you can run', *The Leap Blog,* August 2016, https://blog.theleapjournal. org/2016/08/sequencing-in-construction-of-state.html.

Chapter 22: Criticism and conflict have great value

1. Maria Popova, 'The Power Paradox: The Surprising and Sobering Science of How We Gain and Lose Influence', *Brain Pickings*, September 2016, https:// www.brainpickings.org/2016/09/28/power-paradox-dachter-keltner/.

2. C. Rajagopalachari, '*Why Swatantra?',* technical report (Swatantra Party, April 1973), https://www.livemint.com/Sundayapp/Xl vTGlfJcdJu9mQGZcksTI/ C-Rajagopalachari-Why-Swatantra. html.

3. Ajay Shah, 'The undersupply of criticism', *The Leap Blog*, May 2010, https:// blog.theleapjournal.org/2010/05/undersupply-of-criticism.html.

4. Chris Buckley, 'A Chinese Law Professor Criticized Xi. Now He's Been Suspended.', *New York Times*, 26 March 2019, https://www.nytimes. com/2019/03/26/world/asia/chinese-law-professor-xi.html.

Chapter 23: Coming out right, always, is too high a bar

1. See Oset Babur, 'Talking about Failure Is Crucial for Growth, Here's How to Do It Right', *New York Times*, 17 August 2018, https://www.nytimes. com/2018/08/17/smarter-living/talking-about-failure-is-crucial-for-growth-heres-how-to-do-it-right.html.

Chapter 24: A country is not a company

1. See Paul Krugman, 'A Country Is Not a Company', *Harvard Business Review*, January 1996; Steven Horwitz, 'Countries Are Not Companies', *Fee.org*, January 2017, https://fee.org/artic les/countries-are-not-companies/.

Chapter 25: System thinking

1. For the New Pension System, see Ajay Shah, 'Indian pension reform: A sustainable and scalable approach', in *Managing Globalization: Lessons from*

China and India, ed. David A. Kelly, Ramkishen S. Rajan and Gillian H.L. Goh (Singapore: World Scientific, 2006), http://www.mayin.org/ajayshah/ PDFDOCS/Shah2005_sustainable_pension_reform.pdf; Surendra Dave, 'India's pension reforms: A case study in complex institutional change', in *Documenting Reforms: Case Studies from India*, ed. S. Narayan (New Delhi: Macmillan India, 2006), pp. 149–170, http://www.mayin. org/ajayshah/A/ Dave2006_saga.pdf.

2. This treatment builds on Ajay Shah, 'Forced unbundling for greater competition', *Business Standard*, 27 June 2016, http://www.mayin.org/ ajayshah/MEDIA/2016/unbundling.html.

Part V: The public policy process

Chapter 27: Policymaking is siege-style assault

1. Peter Brinsden, 'Thirty years of IVF: The legacy of Patrick Steptoe and Robert Edwards', *Human Fertility, Vol.* 12, January 2009, https://www.researchgate. net/publication/38112869_Thirty_years_of_IVF_The_legacy_of_Patrick_ Steptoe_and_Robert_Edwards.
2. Ajay Shah, 'Lessons from the Indian currency defence of 2013', *The Leap Blog*, June 2015, https://blog.theleapjournal.org/2015/06/lessons-from-indian- currency-defence-of.html.
3. Vadilal Dagli, *'Report of the Committee on Controls and Subsidies'*, technical report (Ministry of Finance, 1979).

Chapter 28: Choosing from pillars of intervention

1. The shift from a transactional approach to a long-term relationship, in PPP, is at the essence of Vijay Kelkar, *'Report of the committee on revisiting and revitalising the public private partnership model of infrastructure'*, technical report (Department of Economic Affairs, Ministry of Finance, November 2015), https://www.pppinindia.gov.in/infrastructureindia/documents/10184/0/ kelkar+Pdf/0d6ffb64-4501-42ba-a083-ca3ce99cf999.
2. The best exposition of the need for digital identity and the policy possibilities that flow from it are Nandan Nilekani, *Imagining India: Ideas for the New Century* (New York: Penguin Allen Lane, 2010); Nandan Nilekani and Viral Shah, *Rebooting India: Realising a Billion Aspirations* (Penguin Allen Lane, 2016).

Chapter 29: Walk before you can run

1. Vijay Kelkar and E.A.S. Sarma, 'Development of energy resources', in *India: Development Policy Imperatives*, ed. Vijay Kelkar and V.V. Bhanoji Rao (Tata McGraw-Hill Publishing, 1996), pp. 336–419.

2. Ajay Shah, 'Sequencing issues in building jurisprudence: the problems of large bankruptcy cases', *The Leap Blog,* July 2018, https://blog.theleapjournal. org/2018/07/sequencing- issues- in- building.html.
3. This idea, and the phrase 'organizational rout' is from Matt Andrews, Lant Pritchett and Michael Woolcock, *Building State Capacity* (Oxford: Oxford University Press, 2017).
4. From Matt Andrews, Lant Pritchett and Michael Woolcock, *Building State Capacity* (Oxford, 2017).
5. Vagda Galhotra, 'Why We Need to Repeal More Criminal Laws', *The Wire*, September 2018, documents some of this problem, https://thewire.in/law/ why-we-need-to-repeal-more-criminal-laws.

Chapter 30: Low state capacity changes policy design

1. Sveriges Riksbank, '*Annual Report for Sveridges Riksbank 2018*', technical report (March 2019), https://www.riksbank.se/en-gb/press-and-published/ publications/annual-report/.
2. There were three Kelkar committees in tax policy: on direct taxes, on indirect taxes and on the FRBM implementation (which designed the GST). The key idea animating all the three reports was this agenda, of simplification.
3. Prasanth Regy, 'RBI's proposal for a Public Credit Registry', *The Leap Blog*, August 2017, https://blog.theleapjournal.org/2017/08/rbis-proposal-for-public-credit-registry.html.

Chapter 31: Rolling up your sleeves to build state capacity

1. Daniel Enemark et al., 'Effect of holding office on the behavior of politicians', 2016, shows that persons who have formerly held office are more likely to engage in reciprocity. https://www.pnas.org/content/113/48/ 13690.
2. This report is by Vijay Kelkar, '*Ministry of Finance for the 21ˢᵗ Century*' (Ministry of Finance, 2004).
3. The terminology of exit, voice and loyalty is from Albert O. Hirschman, *Exit, Voice, Loyalty* (Cambridge: Harvard University Press, 1970).
4. Cellular *Operators Association of India and Ors vs Telecom Regulatory Authority of India and Ors*, AIR 2016 SC 2336, 2016.
5. The Ministry of Corporate Affairs (MCA) Working Group on establishing IBBI had such a philosophy. See Ravi Narain, '*Building the Insolvency and Bankruptcy Board of India*', technical report (Ministry of Corporate Affairs, 2016), https://web.archive.org/web/20170922121138/http://www.ibbi.gov. in/Wg-01%20Report.pdf.

Chapter 32: Dealing with constraints in information

1. As an example, concerns about GDP data are summarized in Rajeswari Sengupta, 'The great Indian GDP measurement controversy', *The Leap Blog*, September 2016, https://blog.theleapjournal.org/2016/09/the-great-indian-gdp-measurement.html.

2. The ban on microfinance in Andhra Pradesh is studied in Renuka Sane and Susan Thomas, 'The Real Cost of Credit Constraints: Evidence from Micro-finance', *The B.E. Journal of Economic Analysis & Policy*, Vol. 16, No. 1 (January 2016), pp. 151–183.

Part VI: Applying these ideas: some examples

Chapter 34: Building the perfect GST in a low-capacity state

1. The material of this chapter is based on three government reports: Vijay Kelkar, '*Report of the task force on implementation of the FRBM Act, 2003*', technical report (Ministry of Finance, July 2004), https://dea.gov.in/sites/default/files/FRBM_report.pdf; Arbind Modi, '*Report of the task force on GST*', technical report (Thirteenth Finance Commission, December 2009), http://www. prsindia.org/sites/default/files/bill_files/Report_of_Task_Force-_GST.pdf; and Vijay Kelkar, '*Thirteenth Finance Commission*', technical report (Government of India, December 2009), http://www.prsindia.org/uploads/media/13financecommissionfullreport.pdf.

Chapter 35: Health policy

1. Lawrence K. Altman, 'India Declared Free of Smallpox', *The New York Times*, 3 July 1975, https://www.nytimes.com/1975/07/03/archives/india-declared-free-of-smallpox-2-countries-left.html.

2. 'The Great Stink' was an event in central London in July and August 1858, which led to the beginning of modern sanitation in London. 'The Great Smog of 1952' was a severe air-pollution event in London in December 1952, which set off the policy response that led up to the Clean Air Act in 1956.

3. David D. Parrish et al., 'Air quality progress in North American megacities: A review', *Atmospheric Environment, Vol.* 45, No. 39, pp. 7015–25 (December 2011). The authors examine air quality in Los Angeles, which was once among the worst in the world. They say, '*It is fair to say that this mega-city has gone from being one of the most polluted in the world 50 years ago to presently one of the least polluted cities of its size.*' http://gahp.net/wp-content/uploads/2017/10/Air-Quality-Progress-in-North-American-Megacities-A-Review-1.pdf.

4. See the special issue of *Health Systems & Reform* on *financing common goods for health*, September 2019, https://www.who.int/health_financing/topics/ financing-common-goods-for-health/en/.

5. Joseph William Bhore, '*Health Survey and Development Committee report*', technical report (Government of India, 1946).

6. Jeffrey Hammer, Yamini Aiyar and Salimah Samji, 'Understanding Government Failure in Public Health Services', *Economic and Political Weekly, Vol.* 42, No. 40 (October 2007), pp. 4049–57, https://www.jstor.org/stable/40276648.

7. The journey from colonial public health to government-funded health insurance is described in Ila Patnaik, Shubho Roy and Ajay Shah, '*The Rise of Government-Funded Health Insurance in India*', technical report 231 (NIPFP, May 2018).

8. For an analysis of the difficulties in health insurance, see Shefali Malhotra et al., '*Fair play in Indian health insurance*', technical report (NIPFP, May 2018), https://macrofinance.nipfp.org.in/releases/MPSS-Fair_play_in_Indian_ health_insurance.html.

9. National Health Service, 'GPs per 1000 patients', *NHS*, 2015, https://www. nhs.uk/Scorecard/Pages/IndicatorFacts.aspx?MetricId=100063.

Chapter 36: Financial economic policy

1. Money can be viewed as a public good that facilitates transactions. This function can be equally achieved by US dollars or cryptocurrencies; the creation of the Indian rupee is not essential.

It is the second dimension of money—reducing business cycle volatility— where the Indian state adds value.

There is also a third element to money creation: seigniorage income. The central bank earns income on the asset side of its balance sheet, which is paid out to the treasury as a dividend. This income accrues to the Indian government when Indian rupees are used, while this is not the case when the Indian economy transacts through US dollars or cryptocurrencies.

2. B.N. Srikrishna, '*Report of the Financial Sector Legislative Reforms Commission*', *Vol.* 1 (Ministry of Finance, March 2013), https://dea.gov.in/sites/default/ files/fslrc_report_vol1_1.pdf.

3. For an example of the problems of consumer protection in Indian finance, see Monika Halan, Renuka Sane and Susan Thomas, 'The case of the missing billions: Estimating losses to customers due to mis-sold life insurance policies', *Journal of Economic Policy Reform, Vol.* 17, No. 4, 2014, pp. 285–302, http:// ifrogs.org/releases/HalanSaneThomas2013_missellingLifeInsurance.html.

4. Ajay Shah, 'Designing the monetary policy committee', *The Leap Blog,* January 2014, https://blog.theleapjournal.org/2014/01/designing-monetary-policy- committee.html.

5. See Ajay Shah, 'Monetary policy is easy; Financial regulation is hard', *Financial Express*, 29 July 2010, http://www.mayin.org/ajayshah/MEDIA/2010/finance_vs_MP.html.

6. The *Monetary Policy Framework Agreement* was signed on 20 February 2015, and established year-on-year CPI inflation of 4 per cent as the objective of the RBI. In 2016, this was placed into the RBI Act.

7. Shubho Roy et al., 'Building State capacity for regulation in India', in *Regulation in India: Design, Capacity, Performance*, ed. Devesh Kapur and Madhav Khosla (Oxford: Hart Publishing, 2019), https://macrofinance.nipfp.org.in/releases/RSSS_building-state-capacity.html.

8. The basic structure doctrine laid down by the Supreme Court in the landmark case of *Kesavananda Bharati vs State of Kerala, Supreme Court of India*, [1973] 2 Supp. SCR 1, provides that the Constitution has certain basic features, which cannot be amended by the Parliament. The separation of powers between the legislature, the executive and the judiciary has been held by courts as one of the elements of this basic structure. Also see Mathew, J., in *Indira Nehru Gandhi vs Raj Narain, Supreme Court of India,* [1976] 2 SCR 347.

9. For a treatment of this period, see Ajay Shah and Susan Thomas, 'Securities Markets', in *India Development Report 1997*, ed. Kirit S. Parikh (Oxford: Oxford University Press, February 1997), pp. 167–192; Ajay Shah and Susan Thomas, 'David and Goliath: Displacing a primary market', *Journal of Global Financial Markets, Vol.* 1, No. 1, 2000, pp. 14–21, http://www.mayin.org/ajayshah/PDFDOCS/ShahThomas2000_jgfm.pdf; John Echeverri-Gent, 'Financial globalization and India's equity market reforms', *India Review, Vol.* 3, No. 4, 2004, pp. 306–32, https://www.tandfonline.com/doi/ abs/10.1080/1473648 0490895598?journalCode=find20; Susan Thomas, 'How the financial sector in India was reformed', in *Documenting Reforms: Case Studies from India*, ed. S. Narayan (New Delhi: Macmillan India, 2006), pp. 171–210, http://www.igidr.ac.in/faculty/susant/PDFDOCS/Thomas2005_financialsector reforms.pdf.

10. The five reports are U.K. Sinha, '*Working Group on Foreign Investment*', Committee Report (Department of Economic Affairs, Ministry of Finance, 2010), https://www.finmin.nic.in/sites/default/files/WGFI.pdf; Dhirendra Swarup, '*Financial Well Being: Report of the Committee on Investor Awarness and Protection*', technical report (Ministry of Finance, Government of India, 2010), http://bit.ly/2K1JLzk; Jahangir Aziz, '*Report of the Internal Working Group on Debt Management in India*', technical report (Ministry of Finance, 2008), https://www.finmin.nic.in/sites/default/files/Report_Internal_Working_Group_on_Debt_ Management.pdf; Percy Mistry, '*Making Mumbai an International Financial Centre*', Committee Report (Sage Publishing and Ministry of Finance, Government of India, 2007), https://dea.gov.in/sites/default/files/mifcreport.pdf; and Raghuram Rajan, '*Committee for Financial Sector Reforms*',

Committee Report (Planning Commission, Government of India, 2008), http://planningcommission.nic.in/reports/genrep/rep_fr/cfsr_all.pdf.

11. FSLRC, '*Indian Financial Code*', Version 1.1 (Ministry of Finance, July 2015), https://goo.gl/hdAQoW; Ila Patnaik and Ajay Shah, '*Reforming India's financial system*', technical report (Carnegie Endowment for International Peace, January 2014), https://carnegieendowment.org/files/reform_indian_financial_system. pdf.

12. Ajay Shah, 'FSLRC: The cast of 146', *The Leap Blog*, April 2013, https://blog. theleapjournal.org/2013/04/fslrccast- of-146.html.

Chapter 37: Dealing with macroeconomic and financial crises

1. This is the essence of the idea of the 'Taylor Principle'. John B. Taylor, *Monetary Policy Rules* (Chicago: University of Chicago Press, June 2001).

2. For a look at the things that broke down in India after the Lehman failure, see Ajay Shah, 'Recessions uncover what auditors do not', *The Leap Blog,* February 2016, https://blog.theleapjournal.org/2016/02/recessions-uncoverwhat-auditors-do-not.html.

3. For an example, see Liz Moyer, 'Maurice Greenberg Loses Bid for Damages From A.I.G. Bailout', *New York Times*, 9 May 2017, https://www.nytimes. com/2017/05/09/business/dealbook/aig-bailout-maurice-greenberg.html.

4. Eamon Javers, 'Inside Obama's bank CEOs meeting', *Politico*, 3 April 2009, https://www.politico.com/story/2009/04/inside-   obamas-bank-ceos-meeting-020871.

5. This calls for a refinement of the notion that transaction-intensive problems are harder in the public policy process. Part of why crises are a difficult problem is that they only occur occasionally.

6. As an example, a close examination of late 2008 is in Ila Patnaik and Ajay Shah, 'Why India choked when Lehman broke', *India Policy Forum, Vol.* 6, No. 1, 2009–10, pp. 39–73, https://www.nipfp.org.in/media/medialibrary/2013/04/wp_2010_63.pdf.

7. Ajay Shah, 'The strategy and the tactics', *Business Standard*, 3 June 2019, http://www.mayin.org/ajayshah/MEDIA/2019/strategy_tactics.html.

8. A first draft of history of the 2008 crisis is P. Vaidyanathan Iyer, 'How They Saved the India Story', *The Indian Express*, 27 September 2010, which shows this combination of intellectual capacity and team coherence that runs across administrative boundaries, http://archive.indianexpress.com/news/how-they-saved-the-india-story/683133/0.

9. Andrew Filardo et al., '*The international financial crisis: Timeline, impact and policy responses in Asia and the Pacific*', technical report 52 (Bank for International Settlements, July 2010), https://www.bis.org/publ/bppdf/bispap52c.pdf.

10. Fiscal policy in the macroeconomic crisis of 2012 is addressed in Vijay Kelkar, 'Roadmap for fiscal consolidation', technical report (Department of Economic Affairs, Ministry of Finance, September 2012), https://www.finmin.nic.in/sites/default/files/Kelkar_Committee_Report.pdf.

11. As an example of the difficulties associated with exchange rate policy when faced with a downturn, see Ajay Shah, 'Lessons from the Indian currency defence of 2013', The Leap Blog, June 2015, https://blog.theleapjournal.org/2015/06/lessons-from-indian-currency-defence-of.html.

12. Peter Thal Larsen, James Mackintosh and Jennifer Hughes, 'FSA bans short-selling of banks', Financial Times, 19 September 2008, https://www.ft.com/content/16102460-85a0-11dd-a1ac-0000779fd18c.

13. Vijay Kelkar, 'Roadmap for fiscal consolidation', technical report (Department of Economic Affairs, Ministry of Finance, September 2012), https://www.finmin.nic.in/sites/default/files/Kelkar_Committee_Report.pdf.

Part VII: Parting words

Chapter 38: Do no harm

1. James C. Scott, Seeing Like a State: How Certain Schemes to Improve the Human Condition Have Failed (New Haven: Yale University Press, 1998), is a remarkably influential book.

2. Robert K. Merton, 'The Unanticipated Consequences of Purposive Social Action', American Sociological Review, Vol. 1, No. 6, 1936, pp. 894–904, http://www.jstor.org/stable/2084615.

3. Jayana Bedi et al., 'Disruption on Demand', in 'Doing Business in Delhi: A Study of Initiated and Uninitiated Regulatory Reforms', ed. Bhuvana Anand, Alston D'Souza and Ritika Shah (Centre for Civil Society, 2018), https://ccs.in/research/doing-business-delhi-study-initiated-and-uninitiated-regulatory-reforms.

4. Suyash Rai et al., 'The Economics of Releasing the V-band and E-band Spectrum in India', technical report (NIPFP, April 2018), https://macrofinance.nipfp.org.in/releases/DMSS2018-Spectrum.html.

Chapter 39: Prioritize institution building over just GDP growth

1. Matt Andrews, Lant Pritchett and Michael Woolcock, Building State Capacity (Oxford: Oxford University Press, 2017).

2. Daniel Kaufmann and Aart Kraay, 'Growth without Governance', Economia, Vol. 3, No. 1, 2002, is a remarkable result which finds that institutions help growth, but growth harms institutions, https://EconPapers.repec.org/RePEc:col:000425:008687.

Chapter 40: Conclusion

1.   Latecomers in development have often played this two-part strategy: of a state that first addresses missing markets by supplanting the private market system, and then retreating to a regulatory role as the private sector finds its feet. For the Japanese story of this transition, see Andrea Boltho, *Japan: An Economic Survey, 1953–1973* (London: Oxford University Press, 1975).

2.   One of the early articles which clearly saw the problems of the Mark 1 strategy is Arun Shourie, 'Controls and the Current Situation: Why Not Let the Hounds Run?', *Economic and Political Weekly*, Vol. 8, Nos. 31-33, August 1973, pp. 1467–88, https://www.jstor.org/stable/4362927.

3.   A big picture of the evolution from Mark 1 to Mark 2 is in Arvind Virmani, '*The dynamics of competition: Phasing of domestic and external liberalization in India*', technical report 4/2006 (Planning Commission, April 2006), http:// planningcommission.gov.in/ reports/wrkpapers/wp_dc_pdel.pdf; Ashok V. Desai, '*The Economics and Politics of Transition to an Open Market Economy: India*', technical report 155 (OECD Publishing, October 1999), https://ideas.repec. org/p/oec/devaaa/155-en.html.

4.   The investments data is from the CMIE Capex database, and the labour data is from the CMIE household survey database.

5.   Joshua Felman and R. Nagaraj were among the first people who saw the difficulties of the 2003-08 boom. For an example, see R. Nagaraj, 'India's Dream Run, 2003-08: Understanding the Boom and Its Aftermath', *Economic and Political Weekly*, Vol. 48, No. 20, May 2013, pp. 39–51, https://www.jstor. org/stable/23527367.

Index